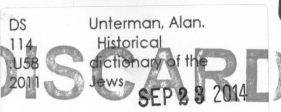

HISTORICAL DICTIONARIES OF PEOPLES AND CULTURES
JON WORONOFF, SERIES EDITOR
Edited by Jon Woronoff

1. *Kurds*, by Michael M. Gunter, 2004. *Out of print. See No. 8.*
2. *Inuit*, by Pamela R. Stern, 2004.
3. *Druzes*, by Samy Swayd, 2006.
4. *Southeast Asian Massif*, by Jean Michaud, 2006.
5. *Berbers (Imazighen)*, by Hsain Ilahiane, 2006.
6. *Tamils*, by Vijaya Ramaswamy, 2007.
7. *Gypsies*, 2nd ed., by Donald Kenrick, 2007.
8. *Kurds*, 2nd ed., by Michael M. Gunter, 2011.
9. *Jews*, by Alan Unterman, 2011.

Historical Dictionary of the Jews

Alan Unterman

*Historical Dictionaries
of Peoples and Cultures, No. 9*

The Scarecrow Press, Inc.
Lanham • Toronto • Plymouth, UK
2011

Published by Scarecrow Press, Inc.
A wholly owned subsidiary of The Rowman & Littlefield Publishing Group, Inc.
4501 Forbes Boulevard, Suite 200, Lanham, Maryland 20706
http://www.scarecrowpress.com

Estover Road, Plymouth PL6 7PY, United Kingdom

British Library Cataloguing in Publication Information Available

Library of Congress Cataloging-in-Publication Data

Unterman, Alan.
  Historical dictionary of the Jews / Alan Unterman.
    p. cm. -- (Historical dictionaries of peoples and cultures ; 9)
  Includes bibliographical references.
  ISBN 978-0-8108-5525-0 (cloth : alk. paper) -- ISBN 978-0-8108-7508-1
(ebook)
  1. Jews--History--Chronology--Dictionaries. 2. Acronyms--Dictionaries. 3.
Abbreviations--Dictionaries. I. Title.
  DS114.U58 2010
  909'.04924003--dc22

For Sandra, Yossi, and Michael,
with thanks for their encouragement.

Contents

Editor's Foreword

The Jews are certainly not one of the larger groups of people numerically, not even among those covered in this series of Historical Dictionaries of Peoples and Cultures, but they are undoubtedly among the most influential, in every sense of the term. There may be 15 million Jews, depending on definitions and sources, and this is not even two tenths of a percent of world population, but in any listing of "famous persons," there will be considerable multiples who are Jews. The Jews trace their origins far back in history, more accurately, although sometimes just approximately, to the early tribes of Judah and Moses. They have fought many of their neighbors and have been driven out of the "promised land" by some, including the ancient Egyptians and Persians. They were a minority in the land ruled by the British Empire and largely populated by Arabs, with whom they still contend. They spread across much of the Western world, but also parts of Africa and Asia, over the centuries until they were crushed by the Holocaust or found refuge in the United States and the new State of Israel, where the largest Jewish community lives today. And yet, through it all, they have survived and also produced countless exceptional artists, writers, musicians, scientists, businessmen, political leaders, and others.

So this *Historical Dictionary of the Jews* assumes quite another dimension from the other books in the series. Its historical scope is exceptional, including some four millennia, from the foundations of ancient Israel, through the early Christian era, the expulsion from Spain, the Holocaust, the creation of the modern State of Israel, and its present activities. Its geographic scope is no less impressive, tracing the Jewish Diaspora around the world, referring to communities in the Arab world, Europe, and the Americas, as well as the Jews in Israel today. And it does mention many of the famous Jews, especially those related to its various struggles, as including those in other fields would take us too far. Of course, there are also dictionary entries on the religion, its basic principles, various facets of its structure, assorted practices, and traditions. This is more than enough to fill the dictionary section. The chronology, while only highlighting the most important events, stretches over millennia and not just centuries. Finally, the introduction has to put this all into context. This book is obviously just a start, a broad and solid foundation, but there is so much more to know that the bibliography is actually one of the most important sections, with extensive lists of further reading on many different topics.

This volume was written by Alan Unterman, whose career has been sufficiently varied that he could approach the topic from several different angles. He was educated at two British universities, Birmingham and Oxford, as well as in Delhi, and he has worked as part-time lecturer of comparative religion at Manchester University. At the same time, he was the minister of an Orthodox synagogue in the south of Manchester. He was also educated at Talmudic academies (*yeshivot*) in Great Britain and Israel, where he now lives. Over the years, he has contributed to two reference works on religion in general and written a number of books specifically on Judaism, namely *The Wisdom of the Jewish Mystics, Judaism and Art, Jews: Their Religious Beliefs and Practices*, and *Dictionary of Jewish Lore and Legend*. Thanks to this background, Dr. Unterman has produced a very informative volume that should serve as a good starting point for a greater understanding of Judaism and Jews.

Jon Woronoff
Series Editor

Preface

This historical dictionary of the Jews deals with the main events and personalities of the Jewish people, from ancient times until the present, and includes elements of political, social, intellectual, and religious history. It is particularly the latter category that I believe is important in understanding how the Jews survived as a people without a land for the past 2,000 years until the rebirth of the State of Israel in 1948.

The history of the Jewish people is integrally related to their religion. Indeed it is Judaism that has defined Jewish ethnicity and Jewish identity down the ages. The followers of the Jewish religion are referred to differently in different periods. In the Biblical period, they were known as Hebrews (ivriim, "those who pass over"), a term that may refer to their status as nomads or to people who originally came from across the river (possibly the Euphrates). They were later also called Israelites, descendents of the Biblical Patriarch Jacob, who was given the name Israel (taken in the Bible to mean "who has struggled with God") after wrestling alone with an angelic figure. Jacob's sons are regarded as the founding fathers of the 12 tribes of Israel.

A working knowledge of these social and religious factors provides an understanding of the history of Jews and the themes that have characterized this history. Jews have both an ethnic and a religious identity. Their ethnicity is based on claimed biological descent from the Biblical Patriarch Abraham and has manifested itself in national aspirations associated with the Land of Israel as a distinct people possessing a common destiny. Their religious identity has been shaped by a shared series of interpretations of Biblical and post-Biblical ideas and practices.

The religion of the Hebrews, Israelites, and Jews itself went through various phases, from temple-based sacrificial offerings in the Holy Land both before and after the Babylonian captivity to a full-fledged Rabbinic tradition that maintained them in the centuries of Diaspora life after the Jerusalem temple was destroyed by the Romans in 70 CE.

The unifying factors behind the self image shared down the generations were provided by the Hebrew Bible in a series of laws, stories, and images that created a Jewish cultural milieu.

For much of their history, Jews were living as a minority in exile mostly among dominant host communities of Christians and Muslims. They were often persecuted and subject to anti-Semitism, both because their separate ethnic identity led to xenophobia and because of their religion, which was in conflict with many of the beliefs and practices of their hosts. These persecutions have profoundly affected Jewish consciousness, creating a sense of divinely appointed victimhood, as depicted in the passage of the Suffering Servant of God in Isaiah, chapter 53, about whom the nations will eventually say that

> He was despised and rejected by men, . . . and we hid our faces from him; he was despised, and we esteemed him not. Surely he has borne our sicknesses, and carried our sorrows; yet we esteemed him stricken, struck by God, and afflicted. But he was wounded because of our transgressions, he was bruised because of our iniquities; . . . the Lord has laid on him the iniquity of us all. . . . He was brought like a lamb to the slaughter . . . although he had done no violence, and there was no deceit in his mouth.

Jews regard themselves as a "light unto the Gentiles" (Isaiah 49:6), acting in this role according to God's mysterious ways. They thus fulfil God's promise to the Patriarch Abraham "through you and your seed shall all the families of the earth be blessed" (Genesis 28:14). One way we may understand this is by comparing the role of the People of Israel to that of a canary in a mine. Miners would take a canary with them because canaries are more sensitive than humans to any gases that might be escaping in the mine. If the canary was affected or died, the miners would know that they too were in danger and had to leave the mine immediately. Thus with the Jews also; when they are persecuted, this should act as a warning sign to others.

Jews were buoyed up by the belief in a future messianic redemption, indeed the greater the suffering, the brighter this hope in redemption burned. They believed that prior to the Messianic age, great wars and suffering would come upon the world and especially upon the Jews. Massacres and anti-Semitic persecutions and finally the Nazi genocide during the Holocaust have all been interpreted as events preceding the Messianic period, as the darkness before a new dawn. This hope has helped Jews to survive.

Their belief in their role as the Chosen People of God added to the antagonism toward them but also enabled them to withstand the worst of persecutions. Even the Zionist secularists in the late 19th century and early 20th century were inspired by a quasi-messianic belief in utopia that found its expression in the kibbutz movement. Religious Zionists took this inspiration further, interpreting the Holocaust as the birth pangs of the Messiah and the foundation of the State of Israel as the beginning of Redemption.

Many individuals of Jewish origin have played an important role in the history of the modern world in the post-Enlightenment period. Thinkers and political theorists like Karl Marx (1818–83); psychiatrists like Sigmund Freud (1856–1939), the founder of psychoanalysis; and scientists like Albert Einstein (1879–1955) have all helped shape our thinking. Their contribution as Jews specifically to Jewish life, however, was not of great significance. A number of commentators have tried to find a Jewish dimension behind the ideas of Marx, such as a Messianic element in Marxism, but this has not won universal acceptance. Freud himself wrote a small book, *Moses and Monotheism*, but it was at best a footnote to his major work on the human psyche. Einstein, as one of the most eminent scientists, was asked if he would accept the presidency of the State of Israel, which he declined.

It is true that Jews have taken great pride in the achievements of such eminent thinkers, as well as in the achievements of the many Jewish Nobel prize winners, yet I have not included them in this book, preferring to restrict myself to those individuals and movements more integrally involved with the Jewish people and their history.

Acronyms and Abbreviations

ACJ	American Council for Judaism
ADL	Anti-Defamation League
AIDS	Acquired Immune Deficiency Syndrome
AIU	Alliance Israélite Universelle
BCE	Before the Common Era (i.e., B.C.)
Besht	Baal Shem Tov
Betar	Berit Trumpeldor
Bund	Algemeiner Yiddisher Arbeter Bund
CE	Common Era (i.e., A.D.)
ch.	chapter
DNA	deoxyribonucleic acid
Gestapo	Geheime Staats-Polizei
Ha-Ari	Ha-Elo-hi Rabbi Isaac
HIV	Human Immunodeficiency Virus
HUC	Hebrew Union College
IDF	Israel Defense Force
Irgun	Irgun Tzevai Leumi
JDC	American Jewish Joint Distribution Committee
JDL	Jewish Defense League
JNF	Jewish National Fund
Joint	American Jewish Joint Distribution Committee
JTS	Jewish Theological Seminary
Lechi	Lochamei Cherut Yisrael
Machal	Mitnaddevei Chutz La-Aretz
Mizrachi	Mercaz Ruchani
Mossad	Ha-Mossad Le-Modiin Ule-tafkidim Meyuchadim
Nazi	Nationalsozialistische Deutsche Arbeiterpartei
Palmach	Peluggot Machaz
PLO	Palestine Liberation Organization
Shin Bet	Sherut Ha-Bitachon

SS	Schutzstaffeln
Stern Gang	Lochamei Cherut Yisrael
Tenakh	Torah (Pentateuch) Neviim (Prophets) Ketuvim (Hagiographa)
UNRWA	United Nations Relief and Works Agency
WZO	World Zionist Organization
ZOB	Żydowska Organizacja Bojowa

Chronology

c. 2000–1700 The age of Biblical Patriarchs and Matriarchs.

c. 1700–1300 The Israelites in Egypt.

c. 1300 Moses leads the exodus of the Israelites from slavery in Egypt. The revelation of the Ten Commandments. The Israelites wander in the desert for 40 years.

c. 1260 The Israelites enter Canaan under Joshua.

1000–c. 920 Reigns of Kings David and Solomon.

920 Split between northern Kingdom of Israel and southern Kingdom of Judah after Solomon's death.

722 The Kingdom of Israel is conquered by the Assyrians, and the Ten Lost Tribes are taken into captivity.

586 The Kingdom of Judah is conquered by the Babylonians, the temple is destroyed, and the Judeans are taken into captivity.

539 Jews return to Jerusalem by permission of the Persian king Cyrus after the Persians conquer Babylonia and start to rebuild the Second Temple.

167–65 The Hasmoneans, under Judah Maccabee, lead a revolt in Palestine against the Seleucids.

164 Judah Maccabee rededicates the Jerusalem Temple, an event celebrated in the Chanukah festival.

157 The Hasmonean dynasty is established in Judea.

63 The Romans conquer Palestine.

37   Herod reigns as king of the Jews under Roman patronage.

CE

1st century   Jewish religion in Palestine comprises Essenes, Sadducees, and Pharisees.

67–70   A major Jewish revolt takes place against Rome, at the end of which the Romans destroy the Second Temple. The Sanhedrin moves out of Jerusalem to Yavneh.

70–100   Josephus writes his history of the Jews.

73   Masada, the last stronghold of the Jewish revolt, falls to the Romans.

132–35   Bar Kokhba leads a new revolt against Rome. After he is defeated, the Roman emperor Hadrian forbids Jews to enter Jerusalem and renames Judea "Syria Palaestina."

210   The Mishnah, the first official text of Rabbinic Judaism, is edited by Judah the Nasi.

400   The Jerusalem Talmud is edited.

500   The Babylonian Talmud is edited.

7th century   The rise of Islam. The Covenant of Omar offers limited rights to non-Muslims.

615   The earliest reference to a specific Jewish oath, in Italy.

8th century   The Khazars (a Turkic people from Central Asia) convert to Judaism. Karaite Jews reject the Talmud.

9th century   The appearance of Eldad Ha-Dani, a mysterious figure claiming to be from the Ten Lost Tribes.

871   A marriage contract of this year is the earliest dated document in the Cairo Genizah.

1096   The beginning of the Crusades. Thousands of Jews are killed by crusaders in Europe and the Middle East.

12th century   David Alroy leads a messianic movement in Kurdistan. Benjamin of Tudela records his extensive travels.

1135–1204 The life of Moses Maimonides, a leading Sephardi halakhist and philosopher who composed the Mishneh Torah code as well as the *Guide for the Perplexed.*

1144 A Blood Libel occurs at Norwich.

1148 The beginning of fanatical Almohad rule in Spain and the forced conversion of non-Muslims.

1189 The Third Crusade begins.

1190 The Jews of York commit suicide in Clifford's Tower.

1240 A disputation is held in Paris.

1242 The Talmud is burned in Paris by the Inquisition.

1255 A Blood Libel occurs at Lincoln.

1263 A disputation is held in Barcelona.

1286 The Zohar is disseminated by Moses de Leon.

1290 The Jews of England are expelled by Edward I.

1348 Jews are blamed for the spread of the Black Death and are massacred.

1391 Many Spanish Jews are forcibly converted to Christianity.

1394 The Jews of France are expelled by Charles VI.

1478 The Spanish Inquisition is begun by Ferdinand and Isabella.

1483 Tomas de Torquemada is appointed inquisitor general.

1492 All nonconverted Jews are expelled from Spain.

1516 The first ghetto is established in Venice.

1523 The adventurer David Reuveni sets out on a mission to the pope in Rome.

1532 Solomon Molcho is burned at the stake in Mantua.

1543 Joseph Joselmann of Rosheim obtains a ban on the anti-Jewish writings of Martin Luther.

1553 The Talmud is burned in Rome.

1565 Joseph Caro's code, the Shulchan Arukh, is published.

1568 The White Jews build a synagogue in Cochin.

1569 Moses Isserles publishes glosses to the Shulchan Arukh.

1570 Isaac Luria propounds a new Kabbalistic system.

1587 Saul Wahl becomes the legendary king of Poland for a day.

1648 Bogdan Chmielnicki massacres Ukrainian Jews.

1655 Manasseh ben Israel submits a petition to Oliver Cromwell.

1656 Oliver Cromwell readmits Jews to England.

1665 Nathan of Gaza proclaims Shabbetai Tzvi as the Messiah.

1666 Shabbetai Tzvi converts to Islam.

1683 The Doenmeh sect begins.

18th century The Enlightenment begins.

1727 Catherine I expels Jews from Russia.

1733 Joseph Oppenheimer becomes state counselor to the duke of Württemberg.

1736 Haidamak bands attack Jews in the Ukraine. The Baal Shem Tov begins to preach Chasidic teachings.

1759 The followers of Jacob Frank convert to Roman Catholicism.

1772 Elijah of Vilna condemns Chasidism.

1791 France grants citizenship rights to Jews. Russia restricts Jews to the Pale of Settlement.

1806–7 Napoleon Bonaparte calls together an Assembly of Jewish Notables and a French Sanhedrin.

1808 The Consistoire is founded by Napoleon.

1818 A reform temple is opened in Hamburg.

1827 The Jews of Russia are conscripted to serve as Cantonists.

1837 Moses Montefiore is the first Jew to receive a knighthood.

1839 The Jews of Meshed are forcibly converted to Islam.

1840 Jews are attacked during the Damascus Blood Libel.

1843 Bnai B'rith is founded.

1848 German Jews begin to be granted civil rights.

1858 The Mortara Affair takes place in Italy. Lionel de Rothschild enters the British parliament.

1860 Alliance Israélite Universelle is founded in Paris.

1868 Benjamin Disraeli becomes the first British prime minister of Jewish origin. Joseph Halévy is sent as an emissary to the Falashas of Ethiopia.

1870 Mikveh Israel, the first Jewish agricultural school, is founded in Palestine. Jews are emancipated in Italy.

1871 Jews are emancipated throughout Germany.

1875 Hebrew Union College is founded in Cincinnati.

1876 The Austrittsgesetz law is passed.

1878 The Congress of Berlin takes place.

1879 The term *anti-Semitism* is coined to refer to anti-Jewish prejudice.

1880 A mass emigration of Jews from Russia begins. Over the next 30 years, more than two million Jews emigrate.

1881 Eliezer ben Yehudah begins the revival of Hebrew in Palestine.

1887 The Jewish Theological Seminary is founded in New York.

1894 The Dreyfus Affair begins in France. Action Française is founded.

1896 The Cairo genizah is discovered. Theodor Herzl publishes *Der Judenstaat*.

1897 The Bund is formed in Russia. The First Zionist Congress takes place in Basel, and the World Zionist Organization comes into being. The Isaac Elhanan Theological Seminary is founded in New York.

1898 Herzl meets the German Kaiser Wilhelm II in Palestine.

1901 The Jewish National Fund is founded. The Conservative Rabbinical Assembly is founded in New York. Herzl meets the Ottoman sultan.

1902 Herzl publishes *Altneuland*. The Mizrachi Organization is founded.

1903 A pogrom takes place in Kishinev, in which 49 Jews are killed. *The Protocols of the Elders of Zion* is published in St Petersburg.

1904 Theodor Herzl dies.

1906 Alfred Dreyfus is pardoned.

1909 Tel Aviv, the first Jewish city in Palestine, is founded. Deganiah, the first kibbutz, is founded.

1912 An anti-Zionist Conference of Agudat Israel is held in Kattowitz.

1913 The Anti-Defamation League is founded by Bnai B'rith. The United Synagogue of America is founded by Conservative Judaism.

1914 The American Jewish Joint Distribution is founded.

1915 Yeshiva College is founded in New York.

1917 The Balfour Declaration is issued by the British government. The Beis Yaakov educational network is founded in Poland.

1918 General E. H. Allenby enters Jerusalem.

1920 Henry Ford prints *The Protocols of the Elders of Zion*. Great Britain is granted the League of Nations mandate for Palestine.

1922 Transjordan is separated from Palestine by the British.

1923 Betar is founded. The Bnai B'rith Hillel Foundation begins.

1925 The Hebrew University of Jerusalem is established. The Revisionist Zionist Movement is founded. Adolph Hitler publishes *Mein Kampf*.

1928 The Jewish autonomous region of Birobidzhan is established.

1929 Arabs massacre Jews in Hebron. The Jewish Agency is founded.

1931 The Irgun Tzevai Leumi is founded.

1933 Hitler becomes chancellor of Germany. The Ha-Tikvah is adopted as the Zionist anthem. Revisionists are accused of murdering Chaim Arlosoroff.

1934 Hitler, as Führer, receives 85 percent of German votes.

1935 The Nuremberg Race Laws against Jews are passed.

1938 German Jewish men and women have to add *Israel* and *Sarah* respectively to their names. At the Evian Conference, no countries wish to accept Jewish refugees. Ernst von Rath is shot by Herschel Grynszpan. Kristallnacht takes place when German synagogues are burned down.

1939 The British government issues a White Paper on Palestine limiting Jewish immigration. The Nazis invade Poland.

1940 The Auschwitz Camp is set up. The Stern Gang is founded in Palestine.

1941 Jews are massacred at Babi Yar in the Ukraine. The Palmach is founded.

1942 The Wannsee Conference plans the Final Solution of the Jews. Zyklon B gas is used for the first time at Auschwitz-Birkenau. The American Council for Judaism is founded. The Biltmore Program is composed in a New York hotel.

1943 The Bergen-Belsen Camp is established. The Warsaw Ghetto uprising takes place. The Danish underground rescues Danish Jews by transporting them to Sweden by sea.

1944 San Nicandro villagers convert to Judaism. Raoul Wallenberg, a Swedish diplomat, rescues many Hungarian Jews by issuing them protective diplomatic papers. Oskar Schindler saves his Jewish slave laborers from Plaszow concentration camp. Anne Frank dies in Bergen-Belsen concentration camp.

1945 Auschwitz is liberated by Soviet forces. Buchenwald is liberated by American forces. Bergen-Belsen is liberated by British forces.

1946 Poles massacre returning Jewish refugees in Kielce.

1947 The United Nations votes to divide Mandate Palestine into Jewish and Arab states. The Dead Sea Scrolls are discovered by a Bedouin shepherd.

1948 David Ben Gurion declares an independent State of Israel, which is accepted by the United Nations. Five Arab armies invade the new state. Ben Gurion orders the sinking of the *Altalena*. The Arab refugee problem begins.

1949 Chaim Weizmann is elected the first president of Israel.

1950 Operation Magic Carpet brings Yemenite Jews to Israel. The Law of Return is passed by the Knesset.

1951 The Conference on Jewish Material Claims against Germany is founded.

1956 Israel launches the Sinai Campaign against Egypt.

1957 Rudolf Kasztner is assassinated.

1960 Adolph Eichmann is kidnapped from Argentina by Israeli agents.

1961 Yevgeni Yevtushenko publishes *Babi Yar*.

1962 After a trial in Israel, Eichmann is hanged.

1964 The Roman Catholic Church, in Vatican II, issues a document freeing Jews from guilt over the crucifixion of Jesus.

1965 Eli Cohen is publicly hanged as a spy in Damascus. The Memorial Foundation for Jewish Culture is established.

1967 Israel fights the Six-Day War.

1968 The Polish state expels most of the remaining Jews from Poland. The Jewish Defense League is founded.

1969 Golda Meir becomes prime minister of Israel.

1972 The first woman rabbi is ordained at Hebrew Union College.

1973 The Yom Kippur War is fought.

1975 The United Nations passes a resolution that "Zionism is racism."

1976 Entebbe hostages are rescued by Israel.

1977 Menachem Begin becomes Israeli prime minister. Anwar Sadat, the president of Egypt, visits Jerusalem.

1978 Israel and Egypt sign the Camp David Peace Accords.

1979 The Nobel Peace Prize is awarded jointly to Menachem Begin and Anwar Sadat.

1981 Anwar Sadat is assassinated in Egypt.

1982 Israel invades Lebanon to prevent attacks by the Palestine Liberation Organization.

1983 Patrilineal descent as a criterion of Jewish identity is officially accepted by American Reform Judaism. Women enter the Jewish Theological Seminary rabbinical school.

1984 The mass aliyah of Falasha Jews from Ethiopia takes place.

1991 The Madrid Peace Conference opens.

1993 The PLO and Israel sign the Oslo Accords.

1994 The death occurs of the Lubavitcher Rebbe, believed by many of his followers to be the Messiah. Jordan and Israel sign a peace treaty. The Nobel Peace Prize is awarded to Yitzchak Rabin, Shimon Peres, and Yasser Arafat. Palestinians are massacred in Hebron by Baruch Goldstein.

1995 Yitzchak Rabin, Israeli prime minister, is assassinated.

2000 Israel withdraws all its troops from the south of Lebanon.

2001 Ariel Sharon, head of the Kadimah Party, is elected prime minister of Israel.

2005 Israel withdraws all Jewish settlers from the Gaza Strip. Ariel Sharon falls into a coma.

2006 Israel attacks Hizbullah forces in Lebanon. The Iranian government holds a Holocaust denial conference in Teheran.

2008 Israel attacks Gaza in Operation Cast Lead to prevent shelling of Israeli towns and villages.

2009 Benjamin Netanyahu, leader of the right-wing Likkud Party, becomes prime minister of Israel for the second time.

Introduction

Jews have regarded their history as the story of God's guidance of a unique people who were not subject simply to the vicissitudes of historical forces. Despite this theological perspective on Jewish history as "salvation history," it is obvious that various forces have shaped the history of the Jews, just as these have shaped the history of other peoples.

One distinctive feature of the history of the Jews is their relationship with their homeland, the Holy Land of Israel, from which they have been expelled on a number of occasions and to which they have returned after shorter and longer periods of exile. This experience of exile and return gave Jews an exceptional perspective on themselves and on the inhabitants of the host countries in which they lived often for hundreds of years. They endeavored to preserve their identity as a Semitic people of Middle Eastern origin, remembering their religion while adapting to the dramatically different situations of their hosts.

In modern times, two central events have shaped Jewish history in a dramatic way. The first was the Nazi Holocaust, which was seen by many Jews as the culmination of anti-Semitism and ended their hopes of emancipation and equality with the Christians of Europe. The second was the return of Jews to independent existence in their historic homeland. The rebirth of a Jewish state in the Land of Israel brought Jews into ongoing conflict with the Arab and Muslim world. These events have increased the sense that Jews have of themselves from Biblical times as a "people that dwells alone" (Numbers 23:9).

In the course of their long exiles, Jews have been influenced by many of the movements and events taking place around them, particularly in Europe. Secularization after the Enlightenment led to the rise of secular Jewish nationalism in the Bund and Zionist Movements, as well as attempts to modernize Jewish religion by reforming its practice and beliefs in Reform Judaism and Conservative Judaism. The State of Israel, by providing a whole new focus for national and religious identity, has changed the orientation of Jewish life both in the Holy Land and in the Diaspora.

BIBLICAL ORIGINS

It is usual for Jews to trace themselves back to the Biblical Patriarch Abraham the Hebrew and his wife, the Matriarch Sarah. According to Biblical chronology, they lived more than 3,000 years ago in the Middle East and received a call from God to migrate eastward from their original home of Ur in Mesopotamia, modern-day Iraq, to the Land of Israel, then known as Canaan. Abraham and Sarah were the first persons to spread the belief in one God, which eventually became the monotheistic faith of Judaism.

Abraham is regarded as a prophet inspired by God, and the Biblical stories about him and his family have been told and retold by Jews down the ages. Like so many characters from the sacred history of the Jewish religion, Abraham and Sarah are not seen merely as antiquated figures from the distant past. They are regarded as near contemporaries of each generation, and lessons are drawn from their experiences for Jewish life in the here and now.

THE PROMISED LAND

Of special importance in the story of Abraham is the promise made to him by God that he and his seed would inherit the Holy Land, later called Palestine by the Romans. This land became particularly significant for Jewish history because it was always regarded as the Jewish homeland whether inhabited by Jews or not.

Indeed, during the lifetime of Joseph, the great grandson of Abraham, his family left the Holy Land for Egypt to escape a famine and was subsequently enslaved there. It was several hundred years later that Moses, the greatest of the Hebrew prophets, led the Israelites, descendents of Abraham, through the desert after their miraculous exodus from slavery in Egypt to the borders of the Promised Land.

Although Moses was not allowed by God to take his people across the river Jordan, the land was settled by the Israelite tribes under Joshua, successor of Moses, after fierce battles with the native peoples living there. The 12 tribes settled in different areas of the land and were ruled over by prophets, judges, priests, and then kings. It was the establishment of kingly rule that united the somewhat fractious tribes. King David made Jerusalem his capital in a territory that had not belonged to any of the tribes. There, his son, King Solomon, built the First Temple, the central sanctuary of Jewish religion, making it not only the political capital but also the religious center for all the tribes.

After the reign of Solomon, the Israelite tribes split into two groups in the 10th century BCE. The 10 northern tribes formed the breakaway kingdom of Israel, with its capital in Samaria, modern-day Nablus, while the remaining two tribes formed the southern kingdom of Judah, ruled by kings of the Davidic line, with its capital in Jerusalem.

ASSYRIAN AND BABYLONIAN EXILES

The 10 tribes disappeared from history after the kingdom of Israel was conquered by the Assyrians in 722 BCE. Assyrian policy was to take the leaders and some of the inhabitants of conquered peoples into exile, and this was the fate of many of the inhabitants of Israel. The whereabouts of these Israel exiles is unknown, and according to legend, they have continued a hidden existence.

Though they most probably either assimilated into Assyrian society or rejoined their brethren in the southern kingdom of Judah, their story has given rise to the belief in Jewish folklore about the Ten Lost Tribes. They are thought to continue a semi-independent existence as Jews beyond the mythical river Sambatyon, and they will be reunited with their brethren when the Messiah comes.

Various characters in the Middle Ages, like Eldad Ha-Dani (9th century) and David Reuveni (15th–16th centuries), either claimed to come from one of these tribes or to have personal acquaintance with them. Different exotic Jewish groups, like the Falashas (the black Jews of Ethiopia), the Khazars (who in fact were Turkic converts to Judaism), the Chinese Jews of Kaifeng, the Bene Israel (the brown Jews of India), and the Krimchak Jews of the Crimea, were all mistakenly identified as remnants of the Ten Lost Tribes. Today, there are people who claim that their nation was indeed originally one of these lost tribes; perhaps the best known of these claimants are the British Israelites.

Many of the inhabitants of Judah (yehudah) were exiled by the Babylonians in 586 BCE, when they conquered the southern kingdom and destroyed the Jerusalem Temple. The Judeans (yehudim), from whom the name Jew (yehudi) is derived, only returned from Babylonian captivity several generations later under Ezra and Nehemiah and rebuilt the Temple in Jerusalem after the Persians conquered the Babylonian empire.

THE HASMONEAN PERIOD

During the time of the Second Temple, the religion practiced by the Jewish inhabitants of the Land of Israel was focused on the Temple as the center of worship and was guided by the Sanhedrin, a council of elders, as the supreme religious authority. Although the land was under foreign rule, severe problems only arose when the Seleucid Greek rulers of Palestine, as part of their policy of uniting their empire, wished to introduce Greek religion in place of Hebrew religion throughout the Holy Land. This led to a revolt by a priestly clan, the Hasmoneans (also known as the Maccabees), whose military leader, Judah Maccabee, helped them wage a successful guerilla war against the Seleucids until they regained religious freedom and a measure of political independence. Under their rule as high priests and kings, Judaism was once again the official religion of the land.

This situation continued even under Roman rule of Palestine, when Herod (d. 4 BCE), a favorite of Rome, ruled Judea. It changed dramatically after a major revolt against Rome was crushed and the Second Temple destroyed in 70 CE. We have accounts of this revolt from the 1st-century Jewish historian Josephus Flavius in his *The Jewish War*, admittedly written to show the positive side of Roman rule, as he had transferred his allegiance to the cause of Rome.

POST-TEMPLE JUDAISM

After the destruction of the Temple in Jerusalem, a crucial period of religious reconstruction took place within Palestinian Judaism. The Temple, its sacrifices, and its priestly establishment, characteristic of Biblical religion, gave way to Rabbinic religion. Henceforth, priests were replaced by sages; the Jerusalem Temple—now destroyed—was replaced by the synagogue and the home; and sacrifice was replaced by prayer, ritual, and Torah study. This enabled ordinary Jews, guided not by priests but by rabbis, to become more deeply involved in everyday religious life.

Of the various groups within Palestinian Judaism in the 1st century, it was the Pharisees, with their emphasis on the centrality of Torah, who survived best and whose legacy shaped Rabbinic Judaism. Of the others, the Sadducees were a more temple-based sect, mainly of priests, whose religion was completely undermined by the loss of the temple. Essene groups, some of whose writings are among the library of the Dead Sea Scrolls at Qumran that were secreted away in a makeshift genizah in nearby caves, were very strict in their purity regulations involving frequent bathing in a mikveh. Their rejection of everyday life did not appeal to the masses. The early Christians gradually moved away from Jewish practice to form a new religion in which sacrifice and atonement were connected to the death and resurrection of Jesus. Samaritans had their own temple in Samaria and were less affected by the destruction of the Jerusalem temple but remained sectarian and were too conservative in their interpretation of the religion to influence the wider Jewish community.

The Jewish survivors of the revolt against Rome were traumatized by the destruction of the Second Temple, but the change in religious orientation enabled Judaism to survive in exile. When the First Temple was destroyed by the Babylonians in 586 BCE, many Jewish exiles had been taken into captivity in Babylon and went through a similar trauma. There, they had created a new type of sacred space for the expression of Jewish religion, the synagogue. It was known literally as a "house of assembly" and was originally used as a place for the exiles to gather together. By the end of the 1st century CE, synagogues had evolved into religious centers for prayer and the study of holy texts and came to serve as alternative sanctuaries to the temple.

A number of priestly laws and rituals were introduced into the synagogue and Jewish home as common practices in memory of the Temple. Though people expected the Temple to be rebuilt speedily, the delay meant religious activities in the home and the synagogue became the central part of Judaism for all Jews. The Jewish dietary laws were expanded, and the festivals of the Jewish ritual year were given a more distinctive character in terms of the religious calendar. Sacred time replaced sacred space. The three pilgrimage festivals Passover, Pentecost, and Tabernacles were now associated more with historical events of the past; the New Year Festival and the Day of Atonement became periods of repentance; fast days like the 17th of Tammuz and the 9th of Av remembered the destruction of the Second Temple as well as the first; Purim was celebrated as the time when Haman, the old enemy of Israel, was defeated, and newer enemies would be overcome as well. Above all, there was a focus on the Sabbath in the home and in the synagogue.

RABBINIC LITERATURE

As part of this new religious direction, Jewish scholars in Palestine in the first few centuries of the common era produced their own religious literature, interpreting the Bible text to fit the new situation. Although the spoken language in Palestine was Aramaic, the sages, under the leadership of Judah the Nasi, published collections of the Oral Torah that they edited in a terse 2nd-century CE Hebrew text known as the Mishnah.

Other types of Rabbinic literature also emerged in support of the new type of Judaism, such as Bible commentary known as midrash, a term meaning the "seeking out" of the meaning of a text, and the two Talmuds, which were extended commentaries on the Mishnah. Earliest collections of midrash dealt solely with halakhah, that is, legal and ritual aspects of religion. Later collections, like the Talmuds themselves, were much broader in nature, also dealing with aggadah, that is, nonlegal material of theology, ethics, and narratives. The Midrashic collections and eventually the Palestinian Talmud, edited around 400 CE, thus became important vehicles for the expression of new developments within Judaism and for polemics against heretical beliefs.

Life in Palestine deteriorated following the Bar Kokhba revolt against Rome (132–35 CE), which was crushed with great bloodshed after some initial success by the rebels. Later Jews would associate the period of the Omer, between Passover and Pentecost, with mourning for this revolt, only celebrating the 33rd day of the Omer, Lag B'Omer, as a special festive day. The centers of Jewish life moved away from the Holy Land to the Diaspora to the Aramaic-speaking Jews of Babylonia. There, a Babylonian edition of the Talmud was edited around 500 CE. Like the Palestinian Talmud, this was a collection of teachings of the Oral Torah based around the Mishnah text but was much larger and more wide ranging than the Palestinian version.

THE BABYLONIAN TALMUD AND DIASPORA JUDAISM

There was already a substantial Jewish presence in the Greek-speaking cities of Egypt and the European areas of the Roman Empire. Jews lived in Italy, Spain, and southern Europe. They were a minority living first among Christian host communities and then among Muslim ones, and they flourished in Spain particularly after its conquest by the Muslims. What enabled them to survive was the portable form of Rabbinic Judaism substantially developed by the Babylonian Talmud. This divorced Jewish religion from its attachment to the rituals of the Holy Land and enabled Jews to practice a Torah-centered religion wherever they were while spiritually still attached to the Land of Israel. They were sustained by a belief in the Messianic Age and the Resurrection.

The Babylonian Talmud imposed its vision of Judaism on Jewish communities as they spread throughout the Diaspora, eventually becoming the most authoritative expression of Rabbinic Judaism. As a religion of home and synagogue, Rabbinic Judaism could be practiced in any land where a community of Jews was settled, for God Himself was experienced as a universal deity not localized in one Middle Eastern country. Post-destruction Judaism thus developed in new ways and created a novel religious identity.

THE KARAITES

The Talmud's role was not without opposition, however, and various groups, mostly sectarian, did not accept its authority. The most powerful of these groups opposing the Talmud was the Karaite Movement, founded in 8th-century Babylonia by Anan ben David, who came from one of the leading families there and was an unsuccessful candidate for the position of exilarch. Anan and the Karaites advocated a return to a more literal understanding of the Bible and explicitly rejected the traditions of the Talmud. We know how widely Karaism spread from medieval travelers' reports, such as those of Benjamin of Tudela (12th century), and from finds in the Cairo Genizah. Though the Karaites posed a serious challenge throughout the Middle Ages to the Rabbanites, as supporters of the Talmud were known, eventually the schism was contained, and today Karaites are only a small minority of the Jewish people with little influence on the Rabbanite majority.

It was not until the 19th century that another powerful movement arose that queried the Talmudic interpretation of Judaism. This was Reform Judaism, which, like Karaite Judaism, was also regarded as a heretical sect by Orthodox Jews because it rejected Talmudic authority while subscribing to the Bible as Scripture.

ASHKENAZIM AND SEPHARDIM

Diaspora Jews found themselves divided between Christian and Muslim host cultures, which were often at war with each other, particularly during the Crusades. Jews living in Muslim lands came to be known as Sephardim, and those living in Christian Europe were known as Ashkenazim. "Sepharad" was the Hebrew name for Spain, from where many of the Sephardim originated and sought refuge in Islamic countries after being expelled by Christian rulers. "Ashkenaz" was the Hebrew name for Germany, from where most of the Ashkenazim spread to Central and Eastern Europe. While Ashkenazim spoke Yiddish, a Jewish dialect of German, among themselves, many Sephardim spoke Ladino, a Judeo–Spanish dialect, or varieties of Judeo–Arabic. On the whole, Jews in Muslim lands were officially protected by the Covenant of Omar, and only in isolated cases, such as in the Iranian town of Meshed, were they forcibly converted to Islam.

Sephardi Jews reached their greatest development in Muslim Spain, where Jews were stimulated to think theologically by their contact with Islam, having come into contact with Greek philosophy via Arabic translations. By contrast, Ashkenazi Jews in Christian Europe had little intellectual contact with Christianity, or with philosophy, and concentrated on the development of rituals and liturgy.

THE CODIFICATION OF HALAKHAH

At the center of Jewish life during the Middle Ages, for both Ashkenazim and Sephardim, was halakhah, Jewish law that emerged out of the discussions of the Talmud. Attempts were made to codify this, the most important early codification being that of the Spanish sage Moses Maimonides (1136–1204). He set out the halakhah found in Rabbinic literature in a systematic manner in his code, the Mishneh Torah, even including laws affecting the Temple and the renewal of kingship, which were merely applicable in the Messianic era. He only omitted elements that he regarded as superstitious because his approach to Judaism was based on Aristotelian philosophy.

Maimonides' code was most influential among Sephardi Jews, who followed the traditions of Spanish and Portuguese Jewish culture. The Christian persecutions in Spain in 1391 led to the forced conversion of a large number of Jewish communities. Many of these forced converts, known as Marranos, lived a double life, outwardly Catholic Christians but secretly remaining Jews who practiced their religion as best they could. The existence of Jewish communities in Spain who had avoided conversion enabled the Marranos to continue with their faith by providing knowledge of Jewish practice and facilities for Jewish life.

Once the whole of Spain was reconquered from the Muslims by the Christian rulers Ferdinand and Isabella in 1492, the Inquisition, under the leadership of Tomas de Torquemada, insisted that nonconverted Jews should be prohibited from living in the Iberian Peninsula. Thus the Jewish community was expelled from Spain in 1492 and from Portugal in 1499. A large body of Sephardi refugees spread throughout North Africa, the Ottoman Empire, and East Asia, mostly settling in Muslim lands. Those Conversos, who continued to live a double life, secretly maintaining Jewish practices as Marranos, risked being caught by the Roman Catholic Inquisition, tortured, sentenced at an auto de fe to a cruel death at the stake, and having all their possessions confiscated. Even the New Christians who remained in Spain and avoided the Inquisition were not readily accepted by their Christian hosts, and some managed to escape to Spanish colonies or join the Sephardi Diaspora.

Maimonides' code was less authoritative among Ashkenazi Jews living in Christian Europe, who had different customs and a different approach to halakhah than the Sephardim. Though his Mishneh Torah did not win universal acceptance, all later codes referred back to it with great respect. A variety of smaller codes were produced after Maimonides, but it took another 400 years before a code was produced that gained universal acceptance among most sections of Jewry. This code is known as the Shulchan Arukh and was written in 1565 by Joseph Caro (1488–1575), who, like Maimonides, was a Sephardi Jew. Its acceptance by Ashkenazim came through the additions that were made to Caro's code by Moses Isserles (1525–72), an Ashkenazi rabbi who added the Ashkenazi traditions of Germany and Poland.

One of the factors that aided the acceptance of the Shulchan Arukh, in its combined Sephardi and Ashkenazi form, was its appearance at a time when printing made books available in a cheaper and more widespread form to Jewish communities. Previously texts were handwritten and copied manually, which limited their number and made them too expensive for poor Jews to buy. They had to rely on the library of their local synagogue or study center, bet hamidrash, if they wished to study them.

Soon after its composition, the Shulchan Arukh was printed and widely distributed. It, together with the commentaries on it, became the halakhic textual authority in most Jewish communities. It created uniformity of Jewish practice, which has remained until today among Orthodox Jews in the celebration of the festivals, the Jewish dietary laws, marriage and divorce, and the liturgy, despite some variations between Ashkenazim and Sephardim.

JEWS IN CHRISTIAN LANDS

In Christian countries, Jews suffered significantly more than they did in Muslim ones. Muslims regarded Jews as second-class citizens, dhimmis, who in theory at least were protected so that they were not subject to mob violence continuously and only faced forced conversion infrequently. Under Christian rule, by contrast, the existence of Jews was often insecure. Both clergy and lay Christians found the presence of Jewish neighbors disturbing and suspected that they refused to become Christians because they were disciples of the devil. During the Black Death, they were accused of poisoning the wells and at various times also of Host Desecration. They were attacked for supposedly killing Christian children for their blood, an accusation known as the Blood Libel. Even as late as the 19th century, the accusation leveled against Jews by Christians in Damascus, known as the Damascus Blood Libel, led to the founding of the Alliance Israélite Universelle.

Ashkenazi Jews were often separated from their Christian hosts and forced to live in ghettos, where they created their own Jewish subculture with yeshivah academies for studying sacred texts. Despite their enforced isolation, they were required to attend disputations, such as the great Disputation of Barcelona, intended to prove the truth of Christianity. Despised as Christ killers, they faced anti-Semitic persecution and at different times were expelled from almost all European countries, giving rise to the legend of the Wandering Jew. From their experiences of pogroms, a whole literature of martyrdom emerged.

The fact that their economic life was often restricted to the practice of usury increased the animosity toward them, and they were made to swear an insulting oath, Oath More Judaico. In the Ashkenazi folk memory, Christianity came to be regarded as a cruel and intolerant religion, with beliefs about the divinity of Jesus that Jews regarded as idolatrous.

Nonetheless, some influential Jews were able to attain positions of power with local dukes and lords as court Jews and, while working for their masters, endeavored to improve the position of the local Jewish community. Among them were Joseph Joselmann (1478–1554) of Rosheim, Joseph Oppenheimer (1698–1738) of Württemberg, Saul Wahl (1541–1617) of Brest-Litovsk, and later on the Rothschild and Sassoon families in Great Britain. Though Jews had a measure of self-government in Poland and Lithuania in the Councils of the Lands, the overall situation did not change until the 18th-century Enlightenment, when European Jews in Western and Central Europe emerged from the ghettos into European culture.

JEWISH MYSTICISM

At the end of the 13th century, a work of Jewish mysticism appeared in Spain that helped to spread Kabbalistic ideas among a wide readership. This work, known as the Zohar, was produced by a group of mystics led by Moses de Leon (d. 1305). It was a unique work that profoundly affected the outlook of traditional Jews. According to Jewish mystical teachings, new Kabbalistic ideas are believed to come from heaven through the agency of the prophet Elijah, who never died but ascended alive into heaven (2 Kings, ch. 2). He is sent from there by God with messages to humans and secret teachings for the mystics.

In the view of the Zohar, the secret teachings of Kabbalah are the real meaning of Scripture, and the true essence of Judaism is contained in its mysticism. Ordinary Jews misunderstand the Torah as merely containing stories and laws, whereas it should be read as a symbolic code that depicts the interplay between the male and female aspects of God and takes the powers of evil seriously.

Evil is a world of antimatter, called the Sitra Achra ("Other Side"), which itself was a product of divine emanation but subsequently became an independent force. The sinful actions of humans give strength to the Sitra Achra, which, as it were, takes control of the female aspects of God, causing chaos. In the Messianic, era the power of the Sitra Achra will be broken, and the light of holiness will shine. The Zohar set up an alternative source of authority to Rabbinic halakhah as outlined in the Talmud. It introduced the belief in reincarnation, interpreting it as a punishment for the soul and an opportunity to make restitution for sexual sins committed in past lives.

When Sephardi Jews were expelled from Spain, they were deeply affected by the pain and anguish of the expulsion. They brought their mystically oriented Judaism to North Africa and the Orient, and their catastrophic exile generated Messianic beliefs associated with David Reuveni (15th–16th centuries) and Solomon Molcho (1500–32). It also generated a whole new mystical movement, Lurianic Kabbalah, which was initiated by Isaac Luria (1534–72). This was based on the Zohar, but it put the experience of exile at the heart of its outlook. God had exiled Himself by an act of contraction, tzimtzum, to make room for the creation of the world. Exile was thus a part of the divine experience in creating the world and not merely a human experience.

MESSIANISM

There were strong Messianic elements in Luria's teaching that man's task is to help bring about the Messianic age by performing religious acts of rectification, tikkun. This led to two major Messianic movements in the 17th and early 18th centuries, the Shabbatean and Frankist Movements, both under the influence of Lurianic Kabbalah. There had been many such developments before, particularly in 1st-century Palestine. They were found throughout the Middle Ages, even in distant reaches of the Diaspora, thus David Alroy led a Messianic movement in Kurdistan in the 12th century. None of them affected Jewish life as strongly as the Shabbatean Movement, which took place in the Ottoman Empire and centered around a Messianic pretender, Shabbetai Tzvi (1626–76), and his leading follower, Nathan of Gaza (1643–80).

Messianic fervor swept through many Jewish communities, and the upheaval it caused disturbed the Turkish authorities. The Turkish sultan offered Shabbetai Tzvi the alternatives of conversion to Islam or execution. When he chose the former, the movement came to a traumatic climax. Some followers who continued to support the Messiah maintained that breaking of the law, in this case conversion to another faith, was a necessary part of the Messianic redemption. A small number, known as Doenmeh, actually followed Shabbetai Tzvi's lead and outwardly converted to Islam while preserving their Kabbalistic faith. The remaining Jewish followers of Shabbetai Tzvi were confronted by forceful opposition from the rest of Jewry.

Shabbateanism strongly influenced another, smaller, Messianic movement that met a somewhat similar fate. This was led by Jacob Frank (1726–91), who claimed to be the Messiah and was regarded by many of his followers as a divine incarnation. Frank and his adherents, whose practice of Judaism involved strong antinomian elements, including orgies, converted to Catholicism in Poland to escape persecution by their fellow Jews.

THE CHASIDIC MOVEMENT

The Shabbatean and Frankist movements were essentially sectarian, but they did generate a mystical movement, Chasidism, which remained within Rabbinic Orthodoxy. It was instigated by Israel ben Eliezer (1700–60), known as the Baal Shem Tov ("Master of the Good Name"), a Kabbalistic wonder worker who could effect miraculous healing and who engaged in magical activities through the use of the divine name.

The Baal Shem Tov gathered together a group of disciples, drawn by his spiritual teachings, who were later known as Chasidim. He emphasized the importance of ecstatic fervor in prayer rather than the intellectual study of Torah, which was the common ideal of his rabbinic contemporaries, and also the spiritual practice of cleaving to God in all activities of life, both ritual and everyday. This enabled ordinary people to feel that they were serving God and rectifying the world according to the doctrine of Lurianic Kabbalah.

The Chasidic Movement followed on the Chmielnicki and Haidamacks Pogroms in 17th- and 18th-century Ukraine, which left Jewish communities poverty stricken as they tried to aid those Jews who fled the massacres. Chasidism, with its positive approach to serving God with joy, even by simple people, spread widely throughout Eastern and Central Europe. Each Chasidic subgroup was headed by a great-souled leader, tzaddik, who was regarded as inspired by the Holy Spirit.

The early opposition to Chasidism was extreme. Its opponents, known as members of the Mitnaggedic Movement, were led by Elijah of Vilna (1720–97), who saw Chasidism as merely a variation on the Shabbatean and Frankist heresies. The Mitnaggedim excommunicated the Chasidim by putting them in Cherem, a social and religious ban. A generation later, the opposition was more muted, and Chaim of Volozhin, the main disciple of Elijah of Vilna, took a much more tolerant view of the Chasidim. The Mitnaggedim themselves eventually started their own movement of spiritual renewal, the Musar Movement founded by Rabbi Israel Salanter (1810–83). As time went on and Chasidism did not evolve into extreme sectarianism, it was accepted as part of the Orthodox establishment despite the changes that Chasidim made to certain rituals and their encouragement of singing, dancing, and the drinking of alcohol.

THE ENLIGHTENMENT

While Chasidism was transforming Jewish life in Eastern Europe and the Russian Pale of Settlement, Jews in Western and Central Europe were emerging from a medieval outlook into modernity. The Jews were readmitted to Protestant England under Oliver Cromwell (1599–1658) in the mid-17th century after a petition presented by Manasseh ben Israel, having been expelled two and a half centuries previously. Before the modernizing influence of the Enlightenment, Jews in most European countries lived in physical and mental ghettos, speaking Yiddish, a coarse German–Jewish dialect, and cut off from their wider Christian environment. It was only the more liberal Enlightenment form of Protestant Christianity that made general society more accepting of Jews. It thus allowed people like Moses Mendelssohn (1729–86), the spiritual leader of the modernizing trend among German Jewry, to gain intellectual and social access to European culture.

Mendelssohn was mostly self-taught in European languages, and in order to encourage his coreligionists to cease speaking Yiddish, he translated the Bible into German, written in Hebrew characters. Mendelssohn himself won recognition from leading non-Jewish intellectuals for his philosophical writings in German.

Although he remained an Orthodox Jew throughout his life, there was considerable opposition by traditionalists to his efforts to modernize Judaism and to him personally. They blamed him for the secularization of German Jewry and for Jews abandoning the traditional style of religion. Though he did not intend it, his efforts at modernization led to greater assimilation and to many of the wealthier and better-educated Jews becoming Christians. It was also an indirect cause of the emergence of Reform Judaism in Germany, Austria, and France, which sought to update Judaism in line with the Enlightenment.

Another major factor in this process of modernization was the desire of Napoleon Bonaparte (1769–1821) in France to move toward full Jewish emancipation. He called together an Assembly of Jewish Notables in 1806 and also a Sanhedrin of leading Jewish thinkers in 1807 to resolve some of the problems involved. Napoleon was responsible for the setting up of the Consistoire, the umbrella body of French Jewry. The efforts of Mendelssohn and Napoleon had the effect that, by the middle of the 19th century, many Jews spoke, dressed, and behaved just like their Christian neighbors.

REFORM AND CONSERVATIVE JUDAISM

It was Reform Judaism that prevented these largely assimilated Jews from completely rejecting Judaism by founding synagogues that resembled churches in their decorum and services. A minority of more radical Reform rabbis even believed that prayer services should be totally in the vernacular, with no Hebrew, and proposed that the Sabbath day should be changed to Sunday. Reform Judaism brought the Jewish religion closer to Christianity, and as a consequence, it allowed those who wished to stay Jews to relate to their places of worship, much in the same way that Christians did to theirs.

The attractiveness of Reform Judaism was most strongly felt in Central and Western Europe and particularly in North America. It spread throughout the United States and led to the foundation there of a major institute for the training of Reform rabbis, the Hebrew Union College. A more traditional version of Reform Judaism, known as Conservative Judaism, led in its early days by Solomon Schechter (1847–1915), also became a powerful influence on the religious scene of the United States. It too set up a highly regarded institute for training Conservative rabbis, the Jewish Theological Seminary. Both Reform and Conservative Judaism gave greater place to women in public religious life than did Orthodox Judaism, where their accepted role was in the home as wives and mothers.

ENLIGHTENMENT AND ORTHODOXY

The Orthodox reaction to the Enlightenment and to Reform Judaism was very antagonistic. Eastern European Jews suffered greatly under the Czarist regime, which at one time forcibly conscripted Jewish youth as Cantonists, and later on, they fared even worse under Soviet Communism with the heavy hand of the Yevsektsiya. Yet many of their rabbinic leaders did not welcome the Enlightenment. One common response was the rejection of modernity and change in all its forms, with the emphasis on preserving the traditional life of the shtetl. Mendelssohn, Napoleon, and Reform Judaism were viewed as destructive of Jewish life lived according to the Shulchan Arukh and were not welcomed as harbingers of a new age. By introducing a policy of emancipation for Jews, they were thought of as inevitably encouraging the weakening of religious practice and of Jewish identity.

Less extreme traditionalists did accept aspects of the Enlightenment but believed that one could partake in European culture while remaining Orthodox, so they dissociated themselves completely from Reform Judaism. In Germany, Rabbi Samson Raphael Hirsch (1808–88), the spiritual leader of a small community in Frankfurt, began a movement known as Neo-Orthodoxy precisely to combine modernity with Orthodoxy, but he refused to alter any laws, customs, or beliefs. He did befriend some modernists, like the historian Heinrich Graetz (1817–91), but refused to adjust tradition to fit their ideas.

ZIONIST BEGINNINGS

Because anti-Semitism was deeply ingrained in Christian countries, Gentiles were unwilling to accept Jews fully into civil society, so the Enlightenment disappointed many Jews in Europe. With the rise of nationalism as new nation states were formed out of the old European empires, even emancipated Jews were regarded as aliens. It is true that Great Britain elected Benjamin Disraeli (1804–81), a Christian of Jewish origin, to Parliament in 1837, and he eventually became prime minister, but no professing Jew was allowed to take his seat in Parliament until 1858, when one of the Rothschilds did. Jews were still surrounded by numerus clausus restrictions in many areas.

The Mortara Case of the 1850s brought home the difficulties Jews confronted with the Catholic Church in Europe, and even the efforts of Sir Moses Montefiore, the president of the Board of Deputies of British Jews, had no effect. As a result of continued anti-Semitism and restrictions on the acceptance of Jews as full citizens in post-Enlightenment society, Jewish nationalism began to reassert itself in the late 19th century.

It was Theodor Herzl (1860–1904) who brought together Jewish national groups in a movement that eventually came to be known as Zionism. Herzl convened the first Zionist Congress in Basel in 1897, which was attended by Jewish socialist, secularist, religious, and even Messianic Zionists. There, they set out the Basel Program for Zionism. He also wrote a novel, Altneuland, putting forward his ideas of how a Jewish state could function.

Herzl became a Zionist because of his experience of anti-Semitism, particularly when he worked as a journalist covering the Dreyfus Affair in Paris. Alfred Dreyfus (1859–1935), a Jewish captain in the French army, was found guilty on flimsy evidence of spying for Germany. The fate of Dreyfus and the anti-Semitism of the mobs in the streets of Paris helped convince Herzl that Jewish emancipation would never make Jews acceptable to a culture permeated by anti-Jewish prejudice. They needed their own homeland.

Herzl was a political Zionist, believing that a Jewish homeland would come about through negotiations with the world powers. The East European Zionist supporters of Chibbat Tzion wanted mass emigration, aliyah, to Palestine, the Holy Land, as a prerequisite to establishing a Jewish state there. Other Zionists, like Asher Ginsburg (1856–1927), who wrote under the pen name of Achad Ha-Am, saw the future Jewish homeland as a spiritual center but not necessarily as a place for all Jews to live. He had considerable influence on the philosopher Martin Buber (1878–1965).

In its early days, Zionism was a minority interest. Some leading figures, like British Chief Rabbi Joseph Hertz (1872–1946), supported the Zionist cause, which was invigorated by the Balfour Declaration of 1917, but many religious leaders were indifferent or hostile. Religious Zionists formed themselves into the Mizrachi Movement within the wider framework of the World Zionist Organization.

Many Orthodox Jews regarded Zionism as a purely secular movement that had nothing to do with God's plan to return the people of Israel to Zion in the Messianic Era. They formed themselves into several movements, the most important of which was Agudat Israel. Assimilated Jews and most Reform Jews agreed, but for a different reason because they saw Zionism as negating their identity as Jewish citizens loyal to their host countries. In the United States, the American Council for Judaism represented those Reform Jews who even after the Holocaust still retained this position. Some secular left-wing Jews in the Bund were ideologically opposed to separate nationalism and supported a multicultural existence where Jewish life, based on Yiddish, would continue in the Diaspora.

THE HOLOCAUST

The anti-Semitism implicit in the post-Enlightenment world, found in the Kishinev Pogroms, came to a head with the racist policies of the Nazis and their allies, like the Rumanian Iron Guard, during World War II, initially with the Nuremberg Laws and then with the Final Solution of the Jews. The Nazis used every opportunity to increase their persecution of the Jews; the assassination of a German official by a young Jew, Herschel Grynszpan, led to the destruction of Kristallnacht.

The genocide that took place during the Holocaust and Adolph Hitler's policy of making Europe free of Jews, Judenrein, was for many Jews (and especially for those who survived camps like Auschwitz, Bergen–Belsen, and Buchenwald) the end of the dream of emancipation and equality. Their experience of the Gestapo, of incarceration in ghettos, of concentration camps, and of kapos were ones of unforgettable cruelty. Some, like Anne Frank (1929–45), were in hiding for years, and though they survived with the help of non-Jews, this convinced them that there was no place for them in Gentile society. This feeling of alienation and victimization was reinforced by the Kielce Pogrom in Poland after the war.

Texts like the Protocols of the Elders of Zion had prepared the ground for a generalized anti-Semitism among the ordinary population of Europe. This inherent prejudice ushered in Bnai B'rith's Anti-Defamation League, and it also eventually led to the founding of a militant group in the United States, the Jewish Defense League. During the Holocaust, some Jews did try to negotiate with the Nazis. Rudolf Kasztner (1906–57) and Joel Brand (1906–64) tried to save Hungarian Jews by making contact with Adolph Eichmann but with limited success.

The Holocaust reinforced the original message of Zionist nationalism because it was Jewish ethnic identity as much as religion that was the focus of Nazi persecution. Most Jewish victims of the Nazi genocide simply could not believe that they were facing extermination. The killing of men, women, and children, like that which took place in Babi Yar, Ukraine, or the mass gassing of inmates in the death camps were of an inconceivable magnitude. There was some resistance among Jewish partisans and in the uprisings against the Nazis, the largest of which was the Warsaw Ghetto Uprising.

THE STATE OF ISRAEL

It was the Holocaust that made possible Herzl's vision of the return to Zion and galvanized Zionist leaders into formulating the Biltmore Program for a Jewish state in Palestine. It influenced those nations that voted in the United Nations for the creation of the Jewish State of Israel and also changed the minds of many Jews who were skeptical about Zionism. The Soviet Union had tried its own version of a Jewish national homeland by setting up Birobidzhan, but it won little support from Jews.

There was considerable resentment on the part of Palestinian Arabs toward Zionist pioneers coming to Palestine. They instigated continual attacks on them, led by Haj Amin Husseini. During the British Mandate in Palestine, Jewish groups were formed to protect the Jewish community from these Arab attacks. The Jewish Agency helped set up the Haganah, a Jewish military force, with an active unit, the Palmach. This was strengthened after World War II by soldiers of the Jewish Brigade, who had returned to civilian life in Palestine. Some Zionist leaders, like Chaim Weizmann (1874–1952), believed in full cooperation with the British.

While the Holocaust had its heroes, liked the Polish Jewish doctor Janusz Korczak (1878–1942), who chose to die with the children of his orphanage rather than escape, the Zionist settlers in Palestine produced their own national heroes, like Joseph Trumpeldor (1880–1920), who was killed while protecting a Jewish settlement, or Hannah Szenes (1921–44), who parachuted from Palestine into occupied Europe. Apart from the Haganah, there were other right-wing forces associated with the Revisionist Zionist Movement that were inspired by Vladimir Jabotinsky (1889–1940). Some of these, like the Irgun Tzevai Leumi led by Menachem Begin (1913–92) or the Stern Gang, believed in struggle

against the British as well as defense against the Arabs. Their member-
ship drew on young men and women of Betar, the youth movement of
Revisionism, who had been active in Berichah, smuggling refugees into
Palestine. Infighting among the Jewish military groups led David Ben
Gurion (1886–1973) to order the sinking of an arms ship, the Altalena,
off the Tel Aviv coast in a lull during the War of Independence.

Some of the fighters in these self-defense groups and in the nascent
Israeli army were survivors of the concentration camps and ex-partisans
who had come to Palestine after the war. The new state introduced a
Holocaust Remembrance Day on the anniversary of the Warsaw Ghetto
Uprising in recognition of what Jews had been through in the Holocaust, as well as Israel Independence Day celebrating the founding of
the Jewish State. The Jewish National Fund, which had been set up to
acquire land in Israel, continued its work after the state was founded,
and the American Jewish Joint Distribution, which was founded in 1914
to help Jews, contributed to the needs of immigrants to the state.

Israel has many social and political divisions, between Ashkenazim
and Sephardim, between religious and secular, and between left-wing
and right-wing ideologies. The first Ashkenazi chief rabbi Abraham
Isaac Kook (1865–1935) tried to heal some of these divisions, but the
political ones proved irreconcilable. The Socialist Zionists produced
many of the early leaders of the state, including Yigal Allon, Golda
Meir, Shimon Peres, Yitzchak Rabin, and Yigal Yadin.

The rebirth of a Jewish state after 2,000 years seemed a semimiracu-
lous event to people, showing that God was still active in the world.
The survival of the State of Israel against the attack by the armies of
five Arab states in the 1948 War of Independence and its victory in the
Six-Day War, which brought the holy city of Jerusalem under Jewish
control, reinforced this view. It has inspired a new Messianic consciousness among Jews, who see the Holocaust and the return of Jews to Zion
as precursors of the coming of the Messiah.

Jewish life has flourished in Israel. The national language, Hebrew,
having become a merely literary language, regained a new vigor. It was
an uphill struggle to get Jews coming from every continent and speaking a variety of languages, some as obscure as the Tat language of the
Mountain Jews of the Caucasus, to start speaking Hebrew. The revival
of Hebrew was initially undertaken by Eliezer ben Yehudah (1858–
1922) and has been supported by the Brit Ivrit Olamit and monitored
by the Academy of the Hebrew Language.

The connection between the State of Israel and the Holocaust is a profound one and is manifest in the Holocaust Center Yad Vashem. Many of the older Ashkenazi settlers were refugees from Europe or survivors of the Nazi camps. Since 1948, Sephardi Jews escaping persecution in Arab lands have been brought to Israel , and this is also the case with Jews from isolated communities, like the Falashas from Ethiopia or the Bene Israel from India. There has also been a mass aliyah of people with Jewish family ties from the former Soviet Union, many of whom would not be considered Jewish according to the halakhah. They have come because, according to Israel's Law of Return passed by the Knesset, not only Jews but their relatives have the right to Israeli citizenship. The background to this law is that anti-Semites, particularly those of the Nazi era, defined Jews by race rather than strictly by halakhic norms. Some of these Russian "Jews" have become proselytes to Judaism, while many others remain non-Jewish Israelis.

Israel is a fully fledged independent Jewish state with its own army, the Israel Defense Force; its own national anthem, the Ha-Tikvah, and its own flag bearing the Magen David. It has a number of internationally known universities, the oldest of which is the Hebrew University of Jerusalem, founded in 1925. It has engaged in a number of major wars with its Arab neighbors, such as the Sinai Campaign and the Six-Day War; it has its heroes, like the one-eyed general Moshe Dayan (1915–81) or the spy Eli Cohen (1924–65), and has undertaken daring enterprises like the raid on Entebbe. The capture and trial of Adolph Eichmann was ordered by Ben Gurion to help raise awareness of a younger generation of Israelis about the horrors of the Holocaust. Eichmann was described by Hannah Arendt (1906–75) as an example of the "banality of evil."

Its secular leadership has even turned festivals like Chanukah into national rather than purely religious celebrations, while by contrast religious Zionists celebrate Israel Independence Day as a semireligious occasion. The internal critics of Israel are either right-wing religious groups like the Neturei Karta, who refuse to recognize a pre-Messianic Jewish state, or left-wing groups who feel that Israel had not dealt fairly with the plight of Arab Refugees. The Israeli leadership, helped by the Conference on Jewish Material Claims against Germany, has also been criticized for taking money from Germany in compensation for losses during the Holocaust.

After the Six-Day War of 1967, many of the holy places of Judaism were in Israeli hands, such as the Wailing Wall and the Temple Mount in Jerusalem and the cave of the Patriarchs in Hebron. It would be extremely difficult for Israel to return the holy places in Jerusalem to Palestinian control under any peace agreement, and this has made peace negotiations between Israelis and Palestinians very problematical.

WORLD JEWRY TODAY

Outside of the approximately 6 million Jews in Israel, the main center of Jewish life today is the United States, with almost the same number of Jews and with many of the main social, cultural, and religious institutions of Jewish life. The next biggest Jewish population center is France, where the population of more than half a million is the result of the influx of Jewish refugees from the Arab countries of North Africa. Canada has nearly 400,000 Jews, and the United Kingdom and the Russian Federation both have more than a quarter of a million Jews. Given the size of the Jewish population there and the importance of the United States in world affairs, the influence of the American Jewish lobby is a major factor in support for Israel, although other sections of U.S. society, particularly evangelical Christian groups, also promote pro-Israel policies.

Jews in all the countries of the Diaspora depend upon the religious and political leadership of Israel and the United States. The main difference between Israel and the large demographic concentrations of Jews in the Diaspora is that the populations of Jews in the United States, France, Canada, Great Britain, and the Russian Federation are shrinking fast through assimilation and intermarriage. In Israel, though, there is a large secular population and much less intermarriage because the Jewish population there is a substantial majority. Pessimistic estimates of the future of Jewish life in the Diaspora are that, in the next 40 or 50 years, only communities of strictly Orthodox Jews will be left as viable entities in countries outside Israel. This is because without the ideological and practical bonds of religious life, there is little to preserve Jewish identity in tolerant and multicultural societies.

Unlike their more secular coreligionists, strictly Orthodox Jews have large families, live in tight-knit communities with shared values, and sharply differentiate themselves from surrounding Gentile societies. By contrast, more secularized Jews live in open societies sharing much of the local culture. They have small families, and their ties to their coreligionists are much weaker. Many of the more committed Jews, even those not specifically religious in practice, have made aliyah to Israel, where they feel their identity is strengthened.

Pessimistic forecasts of the virtual disappearance of Diaspora Jewry may not be entirely accurate because they do not take into account other factors at play. One of these is the influence the very existence of a Jewish state has on Jews outside Israel as a focus of their identity, as a homeland to visit if not to live in, and as a source of ethnic pride. Anti-Israel attitudes, even in the most liberal of Western democracies, and the resurgence of anti-Semitism often inspired by Islamic extremism have raised fears among Jews that the Holocaust was merely a terrifying eruption of a deep, ongoing hatred. The Holocaust, the State of Israel, and anti-Jewish prejudice in their different ways have contributed to strengthening Diaspora Jewish life.

The Dictionary

– A –

AARON (BIBLICAL FIGURE). *See* TABERNACLES (HEBREW SUKKOT).

ABDULLAH, KING OF JORDAN. *See* MEIR, GOLDA.

ABRAHAM. Biblical figure and first **Patriarch** of the People of **Israel**. According to the biblical account, Abraham was called by God at age 75 to migrate with his family to the land of Canaan, which was promised to his descendants (Genesis 12:1–5). Abraham is regarded by Jews as the first monotheist and founder of the Jewish faith, and all **proselytes** to Judaism are regarded as children of Abraham and his wife **Sarah**. The details of Abraham's life, and of his son Isaac and grandson **Jacob**, have served as religious models for Jews down the ages who trace their claims to the **Holy Land** of Israel, in Roman times known as **Palestine**, to the divine promise of Canaan to Abraham.

ABULAFIA, ABRAHAM (SPANISH MYSTIC). *See* SAMBATYON.

ABYSSINIA. *See* ETHIOPIA.

ACADEMY OF THE HEBREW LANGUAGE (HEBREW VAAD HA-LASHON HA-IVRIT). A language institution whose purpose is to preserve and safeguard spoken and written **Hebrew** as the language of the State of **Israel**. Its work deals with promoting Hebrew equivalents of foreign words, their pronunciations, and their spellings in official and educational contexts. Popular Hebrew, by contrast,

1

often uses loan words of non-Semitic origin. This is because the language spoken by the Israeli in the street is usually influenced by films and television rather than by the views of the academy. *See also* BEN YEHUDAH, ELIEZER (1852–1922); BRIT IVRIT OLAMIT (HEBREW, "WORLD HEBREW COVENANT").

ACHAD HA-AM (HEBREW, "ONE OF THE PEOPLE"). Pseudonym of Asher Hirsch Ginsberg (1856–1927). Ginsberg was a Russian-born **Zionist** thinker who rejected the Jewish religious faith of his childhood. He believed in a rational approach to all issues and advocated cultural, rather than political, Zionism as a solution to the problems of **Diaspora** Jewish life.

As a leader of the **Chibbat Tzion** movement, Ginsberg disagreed with the diplomatic efforts of **Theodor Herzl** to found a Jewish state, which he regarded as impractical, and instead thought that Zionists should concentrate on fostering Jewish cultural awareness and pride in their national identity. For Ginsberg, Jewish life in the **Land of Israel** should act as a "spiritual center" for the Diaspora and a bulwark against **assimilation**. He was a highly controversial thinker opposed by many in the mainstream of the Zionist Movement.

ACTION FRANÇAISE. A French **anti-Semitic** movement formed after the **Dreyfus Case** and operational from the mid-1890s until World War II. Action Française regarded Jews as detrimental to the national identity of France, specifically Catholic France. Together with other alien groups, such as Freemasons and Protestants, they were accused of undermining national life. The anti-Semitism of Action Française was thus, for its members, an expression of French self-preservation.

ADAM (BIBLICAL FIGURE). *See* HEBRON.

ADAR (MONTH). *See* CALENDAR; JEWISH RITUAL YEAR; PURIM.

***AGAINST APION* (BOOK).** *See* JOSEPHUS FLAVIUS (1ST CENTURY CE).

AGGADAH (HOMILETICAL MATERIAL). *See* TALMUD.

AGUDAT ISRAEL (ALSO KNOWN AS AGUDAH). An **Orthodox Jewish** political movement that is anti-**Zionist** and seeks to preserve all aspects of traditional Judaism. Agudat Israel began among European **Ashkenazi** Jews who were perturbed by the inroads made by **Enlightenment, assimilation, Reform Judaism**, and especially the decision of the 10th Zionist Congress for Zionism to become involved in the cultural life of Jews. At a conference in 1912 at Kattowitz, the nascent Agudah Movement expressed its opposition to Zionism and, at least on the part of the East European delegates, an opposition to modernity. Both secular and religious Zionists were regarded by Agudah as rebelling against God, who only in the age of the **Messiah** would recreate a Jewish state in the **Holy Land**.

After the **Holocaust**, when many of the population centers of Agudat Israel were destroyed, the movement mellowed, and it has participated as a junior partner in **Israeli** governments, specifically to safeguard financial aid to Orthodox Jews. Agudah politicians had first to get permission from the Council of Sages, the supreme authority of the Agudah, for such participation with Zionism. *See also* NETUREI KARTA (ARAMAIC, "GUARDIANS OF THE CITY"); WOMEN IN JUDAISM.

AHASUERUS (LEGENDARY FIGURE). *See* WANDERING JEW.

AHASUERUS, KING. *See* PURIM.

AIDS. *See* FALASHAS (ALSO KNOWN AS BETA ISRAEL).

AKIVA, RABBI. *See* BAR KOKHBA (d, 135 CE).

ALGEMEINER YIDDISHER ARBETER BUND. *See* BUND (SHORT FORM OF ALGEMEINER YIDDISHER ARBETER BUND).

ALIYAH (HEBREW, "GOING UP," PLURAL ALIYOT). A term used for the migration of Jews from the **Diaspora** to the **Land of Israel**, as well as for ascent in a religious context, such as the "going up" to read from the **Torah** scroll in the **synagogue**. The origin of this term is in the biblical description of the "ascent" of the Israelites to the **Holy Land** after the **Exodus** from Egypt and of the return of the exiled Judeans from **Babylon**. The idea of "going up" to the Holy Land comes from the hilly nature of parts of **Palestine**, particularly of the area around **Jerusalem**.

Throughout the ages, Jews have made the effort to migrate to the Land of Israel and live there or at least to make a **pilgrimage** to the Holy Land, despite a multiplicity of obstacles. From the late 19th century, there were mass migrations of Jews escaping from **anti-Semitism** in Eastern Europe and inspired by **Zionist** aspirations. These mass aliyot continued throughout the 20th century, including Jewish refugees from Nazi-occupied Europe before and after the **Holocaust** and those from Arab countries.

The British Mandate in Palestine restricted immigration of Jews to Palestine because of Arab opposition, culminating in the 1939 White Paper to this effect, which was bitterly opposed by the Jewish community in Palestine. Illegal aliyot, mostly of refugees from Nazi-occupied Europe, continued. After the independence of the State of **Israel** in May 1948, a policy of the ingathering of Jewish **exiles** became a prime task of the new government. Jews from all over the Diaspora were encouraged to make aliyah.

ALIYAH LE-REGEL (HEBREW, "ASCENT BY FOOT"). *See* PILGRIMAGE (HEBREW ALIYAH LE-REGEL, "ASCENT BY FOOT").

ALLIANCE ISRAÉLITE UNIVERSELLE (AIU). An international Jewish organization founded in 1860 whose purpose is to help Jews suffering because of **anti-Semitism** and their religion. The background to this organization includes the **Damascus Blood Libel** accusations and persecution of 1840 and the **Mortara Case** of 1858. A number of French Jews were convinced that Jews needed a self-help organization and brought together leading figures from other European countries to create the AIU.

The idea was to develop international solutions to problems affecting Jews and, though based in Paris with a majority of French committee members, the AIU became the first international Jewish organization in modern times. Its aims were mainly philanthropic and diplomatic, but in the eyes of anti-Semites, it represented a world Jewish conspiracy that was later expressed in the anti-Jewish tract the **Protocols of the Elders of Zion**.

The AIU was responsible for setting up the first Jewish agricultural school in **Palestine**, Mikveh Israel ("Hope of Israel"), in 1870 with the support of **Baron Edmund James de Rothschild**. Rothschild, who was inspired to act by **pogroms** in Russia, became the main supporter of Jewish settlements in the **Land of Israel** and was known by the Hebrew name Ha-Nadiv ("the Benefactor"). Like the founders of the AIU, he believed that French Jews should play a leading role in helping less-fortunate Jews in other countries, an attitude that was resented as patronizing by some of the East European pioneers in the **Holy Land**.

When **Theodor Herzl** greeted the German Kaiser Wilhelm II in 1898, he did so at the gate of the Mikveh Israel school. There was a certain irony in this choice of location because, as the principal advocate of political **Zionism**, Herzl did not approve of the quiet settlement policy advocated by the AIU, Rothschild, and the practical Zionists.

Education of **Sephardi** children was one of the main activities of the AIU, particularly in North Africa and in other Arab countries, and some of these continued to function even after the foundation of the State of **Israel**. With the rise of antagonism to Zionism, however, AIU schools closed down their networks in Syria, Iraq, and Egypt. AIU educational activities continued in France, where many Jews from Arab lands settled, and in other European countries with a network of schools and colleges. In Israel, the absorption of disadvantaged **Falasha** immigrants from **Ethiopia** and the many Russian Jews who made **aliyah** from the former Soviet Union has been the focus of AIU activities in recent times.

ALLON, YIGAL (1918–80). Israeli politician and general. Allon served in the **Haganah** during the Arab riots of the 1930s and 1940s and commanded the **Palmach** in World War II. He masterminded the defeat of the Egyptian army in the Negev in the Israeli **War of Independence**. Allon was deputy prime minister of **Israel** from 1969 until 1977 and put forward the Allon Plan for Israel's borders after the victory of the **Six-Day War**. This plan called for a minimum of Jewish security settlements along parts of Israel's new borders with her Arab neighbors but was unacceptable to the Arab states concerned, who wanted a full Israeli withdrawal from their lands.

ALMOHADS (ISLAMIC SECT). *See* CONVERSOS; MAIMO-
NIDES, MOSES (1135–1204); MARTYRDOM (HEBREW KID-
DUSH HASHEM, "SANCTIFICATION OF (GOD'S) NAME");
SEPHARDIM.

ALROY **(NOVEL).** *See* DISRAELI, BENJAMIN (1804–81).

ALROY, DAVID (12TH CENTURY). Mystic and messianic pretender
who appeared in Kurdistan when the massacres of the First **Crusade** encouraged Jews to believe that these were the birth pangs of the **Messiah**.
Alroy planned an uprising among Persian Jews after being expelled from
Kurdistan, involving those Jews who believed that the age of redemption
had arrived. He was murdered, however, before the armed messianic
revolt that he was planning could come to fruition, although some of his
followers continued to believe in him after his death.

ALTALENA. Ship loaded with arms brought to the newly founded
State of **Israel** in 1948 by the **Irgun Tzvai Leumi**, a right-wing underground militant group. Although the Irgun and the official Israeli
forces of the **Haganah** were fighting on the same side, the extreme
militancy of the Irgun led to condemnation of them by the Haganah.
The Israeli provisional government demanded that the *Altalena* and
all its arms be handed over, but the Irgun wanted some of the arms
for itself. This standoff ended when, on **David Ben Gurion**'s orders,
the Haganah blew up the ship off the shores of Tel Aviv on June 20,
1948, killing a number of Irgun fighters and destroying much-needed
military supplies but ultimately guaranteeing that the State of Israel
would have only one united army.

ALTER (YIDDISH, "Old Man") OF NOVARDOK. *See* MUSAR
MOVEMENT.

ALTNEULAND **(NOVEL). Zionist** novel published by **Theodor
Herzl** in 1902 in which he imaginatively foretold the future new
society of Jews in their own land. Although Herzl's **assimilationist**
vision was far from the realities of Jewish culture and religion and
had no use for the **Hebrew** language—the sacred tongue—his novel
nevertheless made a powerful impression on the early Zionist Movement. Herzl's watchword was "If you will it, it is not a fable."

AMALEK. *See* PURIM.

AMEN. *See* SYNAGOGUE (HEBREW BET KNESSET).

AMERICAN COUNCIL FOR JUDAISM (ACJ). Anti-**Zionist** movement in the United States. The ACJ, founded in 1942, claims that Jews are not a national group but merely members of a religion. Its founders were **Reform** rabbis who were universalistic in outlook and opposed both the Zionist influence on American Jewish life and moves to establish a Jewish state in the **Land of Israel**. The approach of the ACJ is generally pro-**Palestinian**. It continues to maintains the early Reform antagonism to Zionism, though most contemporary Reform communities have long since rejected this and identify with Zionism and the Jewish state. *See also* NETUREI KARTA (ARAMAIC, "GUARDIANS OF THE CITY").

AMERICAN JEWISH JOINT DISTRIBUTION (JDC, OR THE JOINT). A relief organization founded in 1914 for the benefit of Jews suffering in wartime. It brought together the "joint" efforts of different social and religious groups involved in raising funds for Jews. World War I saw aid from the Joint for Jews in **Palestine** and Eastern Europe, while the massive destruction of Jewish communities during the **Holocaust** in Nazi-controlled Europe led to major aid efforts following the defeat of the Axis powers. In the early days of the State of **Israel**, the Joint played an important part in funding the transfer of impoverished immigrants to the new state, particularly those from Arab countries. It continues to fund social work training centers in Israel to help disabled Jews.

AMIR, YIGAL. *See* RABIN, YITZCHAK (1922–95).

ANAN BEN DAVID (8TH CENTURY). Founder of the **Karaite** sect. As a relative of the **exilarch**—the leader of **Babylonian** Jewry—Anan was extremely annoyed to be passed over when the position of exilarch became vacant. He rejected the **Talmudic** interpretation of the **Bible**, and suspicions about his attitude to the Talmud may have been why his brother was preferred to him for the highest office. According to other reports, his rejection as exilarch became the catalyst for his rebellion against the Babylonian religious establishment.

Whatever the reason for Anan's rebellion, he gathered around himself a small number of other Jews who were equally rebellious against the official Rabbanite position. After his death, his ideas were continued by the Karaite Movement, into which his followers merged.

ANGELS. *See* ISRAEL; JACOB; MARTYRDOM (HEBREW KIDDUSH HASHEM, "SANCTIFICATION OF (GOD'S) NAME"); SABBATH (HEBREW SHABBAT); SARAH; TEMPLE (HEBREW BET HA-MIKDASH).

ANIELEWICZ, MORDECAI. *See* WARSAW GHETTO UPRISING.

ANTI-DEFAMATION LEAGUE (ADL). An organization run by **Bnai B'rith** whose aim is to identify elements of **anti-Semitism** and to work for the end of discrimination against Jews. The ADL began in 1913 in New York and has since spread beyond the United States to Europe and **Israel** in order to monitor anti-Jewish discrimination worldwide. In the period before and after World War II, the ADL employed a professional staff of researchers to monitor any defamatory depiction of Jews in the media and to encourage legislation outlawing racism, unfair treatment of Jews, and anti-Jewish injustice.

The ADL also has a series of publications about discrimination and extremism, as well as a major educational program about the **Holocaust**. It has branched out to tackle racism, hatred, and bigotry in all its forms, whether involving Jews or other minority groups.

Among the achievements of the ADL was the case against Henry Ford, who bought a newspaper, *The Dearborn Independent*, and used it to publish extreme anti-Semitic articles about the problems caused to the world by an international Jewish conspiracy, even publishing the **Protocols of the Elders of Zion** in the 1920s. Eventually Ford closed down his paper in 1929. Various Fascist groups in the United States were exposed by the ADL in the 1930s and 1940s, and it took up the fight against the application of **numerus clausus** by Ivy League universities restricting Jewish entry. It has also not been afraid to tackle anti-Semitic extremism among sections of the African American community. After the foundation of the State of Israel, the ADL monitored and exposed anti-Semitic material published in Arab states and in the western world under the guise of anti-**Zionism**.

ANTIOCHUS EPIPHANES, KING. *See* JUDAH MACCABEE (2ND CENTURY BCE).

***ANTIQUITIES OF THE JEWS* (BOOK).** *See* JOSEPHUS FLAVIUS (1ST CENTURY CE).

ANTI-SEMITISM. Generally used term for anti-Jewish attitudes and hostile activities. Its first use was in Germany in the 1870s, as Jews were regarded racially as Semites, descendants of the biblical character Shem. Since then, it has been widely used, and frequently abused, to refer to a whole range of bigoted ideas and prejudicial acts.

Anti-Semitism has been described as the oldest prejudice, but in different ages it has manifested itself in many different forms. In the early Christian period, antagonism toward Jews was based on a form of theological prejudice associated with the differences between Christianity and Judaism. This was strengthened in the Middle Ages by economic resentment of Jews who were moneylenders at a time when **usury** was forbidden to Christians. There were even elements of racist or ethnic anti-Semitism in discrimination against **New Christian** Jewish converts to Christianity.

At the basis of the religious bias was the belief that Jews had rejected Jesus and crucified him; therefore they were cursed, so their treatment was an expression of Christian teaching. Christian anti-Semitism often led to expulsions and massacres, particularly during the **Crusades**, and accusations of **blood libel** and **host desecration**. These attitudes, involving the demonization of Jews, remained within Christian consciousness throughout the centuries, although in modern times, the purely theological antagonism was often in the background.

With the **Enlightenment**, anti-Semitism did not die out, and it was still found in a virulent form in many European countries, often leading to **pogroms**. Realization of its hold on modernity generated a Jewish reaction in the emergence of political **Zionism**. Although Nazi anti-Semitism, culminating in the **Final Solution** of the Jewish problem by the mass murder of Jews in the **Holocaust**, was the most extreme form of government-sponsored anti-Jewish behavior, it was only possible because of what had gone before. Anti-Semitism was less prevalent in Muslim countries, though the anti-**Israel** propaganda of some Arab states has openly used anti-Semitic elements like the **Protocols of the Elders of Zion**, and some, at least, of the anti-Israel and anti-Zionist attitudes of individuals in the West seem to be a mask for anti-Semitism. *See also* ACTION FRANÇAISE; ALLIANCE ISRAÉLITE UNIVERSELLE (AIU); ANTI-DEFAMATION LEAGUE (ADL); BABI YAR; BLACK DEATH; BRITISH ISRAELITES; CHMIELNICKI MASSACRES; CRUSADES; DAMASCUS BLOOD LIBEL; DREYFUS CASE; GHETTO; HAIDAMACKS; HAMAN; INQUISITION; IRON GUARD; JEWISH DEFENSE LEAGUE (JDL); JUDENREIN (GERMAN, "FREE OF JEWS"); KIELCE POGROM; KISHINEV POGROMS; KRISTALLNACHT (GERMAN, "NIGHT OF BROKEN GLASS"); MARTYRDOM (HEBREW KIDDUSH HASHEM, "SANCTIFICATION OF (GOD'S) NAME"); NUMERUS CLAUSUS (LATIN, "CLOSED NUMBER"); NUREMBERG LAWS; OATH MORE JUDAICO; TORQUEMADA, TOMAS DE (1420–98); WANDERING JEW; YAD VASHEM; YEVSEKTSIYA.

ANTONINUS (ROMAN EMPEROR). *See* JUDAH THE NASI.

ARAB REFUGEES. The establishment of the State of **Israel** in post-Mandate **Palestine** in 1948, and the subsequent **War of Independence** when the new state was attacked by its Arab neighbors, led to the Arab refugee problem. Palestinian Arabs left their homes, either driven out by advancing Israeli forces or encouraged to leave temporarily by Arab media. After the ceasefire, most of them were not able to return, although Arab governments promised them that they would go back one day. The situation was exacerbated by the **Six-Day War** of 1967, when Israel conquered the West Bank and Gaza. Many Palestinian refugees have been living in refugee camps in the Arab world supported by United Nations Relief and Works Agency (UNRWA), and their desire to return to their homes in Israel, with their descendants, is a major obstacle to any peace agreement between Israel and the Palestinians. *See also* HUSSEINI, HAJ AMIN (1893–1974).

ARAFAT, YASSER. *See* PERES, SHIMON (1923–); RABIN, YITZCHAK (1922–95).

ARAMAIC. A northwest Semitic language related to **Hebrew**. Some sections of the **Bible** are in ancient Aramaic, particularly the Books of Ezra and Daniel. Aramaic was spoken throughout the Middle East in different dialects in the first few centuries of the Common Era and was the language of the Jews of **Palestine** at the time of Jesus. The Palestinian and Babylonian **Talmuds** were both written in Aramaic, the former in a Western dialect and the latter in an Eastern one, and the main text of the **Kabbalah**, the **Zohar**, is written in a purely literary Aramaic.

Paradoxically, Kabbalists in the Middle Ages thought of Hebrew as the holy tongue through which God created the world and of Aramaic as the language of the demonic powers, the sitra achra, which seek to undermine holiness. In the first few centuries of the Common Era, Hebrew was a literary language, the **Mishnah** being mostly written in a postbiblical Hebrew in the late 2nd century. The Hebrew of the Bible was not understood by ordinary Jews, and the Scriptural text was translated into Aramaic when it was read in **synagogue**, these translations being known as targum. The best-known Aramaic translation of the Pentateuch is Targum Onkelos, which achieved the status of a quasi-holy text, and in Rabbinic literature, Aramaic is simply referred to as targum. Because of the central role that the Babylonian Talmud played in Jewish religious life, Aramaic had considerable influence on such Jewish dialects as **Yiddish**, and in Modern Hebrew, words of Aramaic origin have been adapted to contemporary use.

ARENDT, HANNAH (1906–75). Political thinker. Arendt left Germany after the Nazis came to power and eventually escaped to the United States. She is rumored to have had an affair with Martin Heidegger, a leading German philosopher and one-time supporter of Nazism. Arendt became a major cultural critic of western society and its lack of real freedom. As a journalist covering the trial of **Adolph Eichmann** in **Jerusalem**, she produced a book, *Eichmann in Jerusalem* (1963), claiming that Eichmann was an example of the "banality of evil."

ARK OF THE COVENANT. *See* DAVID; ETHIOPIA; JERUSALEM; TEMPLE (HEBREW BET HA-MIKDASH); TEN COMMANDMENTS (OR DECALOGUE).

ARLOSOROFF, CHAIM. *See* REVISIONIST ZIONISTS.

ARROW CROSS (FASCIST GROUP). *See* KASZTNER, RUDOLF (1906–57).

ASERET HA-DIBROT. *See* TEN COMMANDMENTS (OR DECA-LOGUE).

ASHKENAZIM (SINGULAR ASHKENAZI). A term describing **Jews** of Christian Europe. The word *Ashkenaz* was used in the Middle Ages to refer to Germany, the home of Ashkenazi Jewish culture. Because of the political divide between Christian and Muslim lands, Ashkenazi Jews developed differently from their **Sephardi** coreligionists, originally from the Iberian Peninsula, who mostly lived under Muslim rule. Ashkenazim developed their own common language, **Yiddish**, a series of Jewish dialects of German, which they took with them as they migrated or were expelled to Eastern Europe, particularly to Poland. Ashkenazi Judaism generally shunned philosophical speculation and concentrated on the **halakhic** aspects of Jewish life and of **Torah** study, preserving its own customs, which were different from Sephardi ones.

The first Jews who returned to Great Britain in the 17th century, under **Oliver Cromwell**, were Sephardim, as were the early settlers in the United States. They were better educated, more highly cultured, and wealthier than most of the Ashkenazi migrants who began to flood westward from Central Europe and from the **Pale of Settlement** in the 19th century. The Sephardim initially regarded their Ashkenazi coreligionists as uncouth and strongly discouraged intermarriage with them. Gradually, however, German and Austrian Ashkenazim, like the **Rothschild family**, attained high social status and positions of power rivaling those of **Sir Moses Montefiore** and the **Sassoon family**, and together they became members of a mixed Sephardi/Ashkenazi aristocracy. The mass migration of Ashkenazi Jews from Poland and Russia changed the demographic makeup of the United States and Western Europe, with the Sephardim coming to represent only a small portion of the Jewish population.

Most of the early **Zionist** pioneers who made **aliyah** to **Palestine** at the end of the 19th century and the beginning of the 20th century were Ashkenazi Jews from Eastern Europe. They were secular in lifestyle and Marxist in ideology, founding **kibbutzim** and other quasi-utopian settlements. The majority of Jews already living in the **Land** of Israel, known as the old *yishuv*, by contrast, were very traditional Sephardim whom the **Enlightenment** had barely touched. Cultural clashes between the two were inevitable.

The secular Ashkenazi pioneers looked down on religious Jews, who seemed to be living with all the superstitions of the past, and they particularly could not identify with the **Orthodox** Sephardim whose general cultural ethos was Islamic. The Sephardi Jews of the old yishuv in turn bitterly resented the elitism, arrogance, and immodest behavior of the newcomers, who, in their eyes, were desecrating the **Holy Land**.

The divisions between the two communities still exist today, but they are less acute than they were in the past because Jews in Israel have been united by the struggle for survival in the face of Palestinian and Arab aggression. Relations were also improved by the aliyah of many religious Ashkenazim, who had much in common both with the older Sephardi community and also with newer Sephardi immigrants who arrived in the State of **Israel** as refugees from Arab lands and the Orient. Other uniting factors have been shared service in the **Israel Defense Forces**, which brings Jews from different backgrounds together in the same military units, and by intermarriage between Ashkenazim and Sephardim. Right-wing political parties in the **Knesset**, even those led by Ashkenazi politicians, have appealed to Sephardi voters more than the socialist parties did. In fact, the victory of the Likkud Party in 1977, which brought **Menachem Begin** to power as prime minister, was mainly due to the support he gained from Sephardi voters. *See also* KOSHER ("FIT FOOD," HEBREW KASHER, KASHRUT).

ASSEMBLY OF JEWISH NOTABLES. *See* NAPOLEON BONAPARTE (1769–1821).

ASSIMILATION. Jews as a minority have faced the problem of loss of identity in the face of the majority host culture in which they lived. Although the process of assimilation was at work in the Jewish **Diaspora** throughout the ages, it only became a serious problem for Jewish existence following the **Enlightenment** of the 18th and 19th centuries in Europe. The Enlightenment created a more open society, allowing Jews to move outside their cultural and religious **ghettos**. It also liberalized Christianity, making the transition from Judaism to a less-demanding Christian faith easier for Jews.

The pressure on Jews outside the ghetto to assimilate as they strove for **emancipation** as citizens of European society was very powerful. It was the wealthier Jews who assimilated first because they were better educated and spoke the vernacular language. Christianity, particularly Protestantism, seemed more civilized to them than the Judaism they were leaving behind. The Nazi persecution of the Jews in the 1930s and 1940s was deeply felt by the many assimilated Jews caught up in the **Holocaust**. For traditional Jews, the tragedy was a continuation of centuries of hostility, persecution, and **anti-Semitism**, although on a much larger scale. For assimilated Jews, who felt part of their host societies in Europe, it was an incomprehensible catastrophe. The Holocaust and the foundation of the State of **Israel** in 1948 have added a powerful ethnic and national dimension to Jewish identity that has held the drive to assimilation in check.

ASSYRIANS. *See* BRITISH ISRAELITES; DIASPORA; HOLY LAND; ISRAEL; SAMARITANS; SAMBATYON; TEN LOST TRIBES.

AUSCHWITZ. A Nazi concentration camp near the Polish town of Oswiecim, known in German as Auschwitz. The Auschwitz complex of camps is the most infamous of all concentration camps and has come to symbolize the **Holocaust** itself. It began in 1940 as a small camp but was soon extended to incorporate a number of large camps, including Birkenau, and slave labor camps. The extermination of Jews began early in 1942 at Birkenau with the gassing of inmates using Zyklon B in line with the Nazi policy of the "**Final Solution** of the Jewish problem." More than a million Jews were murdered, plus Russian prisoners and gypsies, in gas chambers disguised as shower rooms, and their bodies were burned in crematoria. At the end of the war, the gas chambers were destroyed to hide the evidence of atrocities, and the surviving inmates were led on a forced march to Germany, during which many of them died. The camp was liberated by Soviet forces at the beginning of 1945. *See also* ANTI-SEMITISM; BERGEN-BELSEN; BUCHENWALD; EICHMANN, ADOLPH (1906–62); GESTAPO (GEHEIME STAATS-POLIZEI); HITLER, ADOLPH (1889–1945); KAPO.

AUSTRITTSGESETZ (LAW PERMITTING SEPARATION). *See* NEO-ORTHODOXY.

AUTO-DA-FÉ ("ACT OF FAITH"). Portuguese name for the sentence of the Catholic **Inquisition** on backsliders, most of whom had been forcibly converted to Christianity, in Spain and Portugal. The guilty were handed over to the secular authorities for punishment, which in serious cases entailed burning at the stake. These ceremonies of sentence, accompanied by sermons, lasted for nearly four centuries from the late 15th century to the 19th century. It is calculated that several hundred thousand Jews, Muslims, and dissident Christians were punished by the Inquisition and secular authorities mostly for Judaizing or religious practices not approved of by the Catholic Church. *See also* CONVERSOS; MARRANO; NEW CHRISTIANS.

AV (MONTH). *See* CALENDAR; JEWISH RITUAL YEAR.

AVENUE OF THE RIGHTEOUS GENTILES. *See* YAD VASHEM.

– B –

BAAL KERIAH (TORAH READER). *See* SYNAGOGUE (HEBREW BET KNESSET).

BAAL SHEM TOV, ISRAEL BEN ELIEZER (1700–60). Israel ben Eliezer, the charismatic founder of the **Chasidic Movement** in the Ukraine and Poland, was known as the Baal Shem Tov, or the Besht for short, a title meaning "Master of the Good Name."

According to legend, the Besht did not receive a formal Rabbinic education but was instructed in the Jewish mystical teachings of the **Zohar** and the **Kabbalah** of **Isaac Luria**. At the age of 30, he began his mission as a faith healer and gathered together a number of gifted disciples through his teachings about the importance of ecstasy and joy in Jewish religious life. His ideas, and those of his followers, were severely criticized by the Rabbinic establishment in Eastern Europe, who suspected Chasidism of continuing the heresy of **Shabbetai Tzvi**.

The Chasidic reorganization of community life around the figure of the **Tzaddik**, the great-souled mystical leader, appealed to scholars and the semiliterate Jewish masses alike. In the century after the death of the Besht, many of the Jewish communities in Eastern

Europe were affiliated to one or another of the subgroups within Chasidism, which were a major factor in resisting the modernization of Jewish life brought about by the **Enlightenment**.

BABI YAR. A ravine near the Ukrainian city of Kiev in which the Nazi SS and their Ukrainian allies massacred nearly 35,000 Jews within the space of two days at the end of September 1941. Although there were many such mass killings during the **Holocaust**, and the shooting of Jews and gypsies continued at the ravine for several years, this particular massacre has taken on an iconic quality. This was partly because of the size of the massacre and partly through the poem *Babi Yar* (1961) by the **Gentile** Russian poet Yevgeni Yevtushenko, later set to music by the composer Dmitri Shostakovich. Yevtushenko criticized the **anti-Semitism** of the Soviet government, which erected a memorial to all those Soviet citizens killed at Babi Yar but refused to acknowledge that the victims were mainly Jews. *See also* FINAL SOLUTION.

BABYLONIA. An ancient country and civilization situated between the Tigris and the Euphrates Rivers, corresponding approximately to the modern state of Iraq. When the Babylonians captured the southern kingdom of **Judah** and destroyed **Jerusalem** and its **Temple** in 586 BCE, they took many of the leading citizens into captivity in Babylon. The term *Jew* (Hebrew yehudi) derives from the name given to these Judean exiles from Judah (Hebrew yehudah).

The religion of the Judeans, originally centered on Temple ritual, underwent a metamorphosis during their captivity. When Babylonia was eventually occupied by the Persians, the Jews were allowed by the Persian king Cyrus to return and rebuild their Temple. By then, the embryonic institution of the **synagogue**, with several of its basic rituals, had already been formed. Some Jews remained in the Babylonian **Diaspora**, and after the destruction of the Second Temple by the Romans in 70 CE, it once again became the main center of Jewish life. The most important text of Rabbinic Judaism, the Babylonian **Talmud**, was composed there.

BALFOUR, LORD ARTHUR JAMES. *See* BALFOUR DECLARATION; HEBREW UNIVERSITY OF JERUSALEM; WEIZMANN, CHAIM (1874–1952); ZIONISM.

BALFOUR DECLARATION. A letter from British Foreign Secretary Arthur James Balfour to Lord Lionel Walter Rothschild (*see* ROTH-SCHILD FAMILY), dated 2 November 1917 and declaring British sympathy with **Zionist** aspirations has come to be known as the Balfour Declaration. It stated that the British government viewed with favor the establishment of a national home for the Jewish people in **Palestine**, with certain reservations to safeguard the Arab population of Palestine and the position of the Jews in the **Diaspora**. The British government hoped by issuing the Balfour Declaration to enlist the sympathy of U.S. Jewry to the British cause and thus to encourage American participation in World War I. There was also considerable pressure from Zionist activists, like **Chaim Weizmann**, on government members to favor Zionist aspirations.

BARCELONA, DISPUTATION OF. A forced **disputation** where Jews had to defend their religion against Christian criticism that took place at Barcelona in 1263 in the presence of the King of Aragon. The Christian side was represented by Dominicans and Franciscans and the Jewish side by Rabbi Moses ben Nachman, known as Nachmanides. The main topic of the disputation was whether Jewish texts proved that Jesus was indeed the **Messiah**, and thus Christianity had superseded Judaism. Jewish reports of the disputation relate that Nachmanides was able to show the spuriousness of the Christian claims, while the Catholic version of the disputation naturally depicts him as defeated by the Christian arguments. *See also* ANTI-SEMITISM; CONVERSOS.

BAR ILAN UNIVERSITY. *See* YESHIVAH (HEBREW, "PLACE OF SITTING," PLURAL YESHIVOT).

BAR KOKHBA (d. 135 CE). The leader of a major revolt against Roman rule in **Palestine** that began in 132 CE and lasted until 135 CE, when the last stronghold at **Betar** fell to Roman legions. Bar Kokhba means "son of a star" in **Aramaic**, the spoken language of that time, and it was a quasi-**messianic** title given by his followers to their leader, Simeon bar Koseba. The revolt, occurring only some 60 years after the Jewish war against Rome that led to the destruction of the **Temple** in **Jerusalem**, was put down with much bloodshed. It was sparked by the harshness of Roman rule and Roman disregard for

Jewish religious sensitivities. The fact that Bar Kokhba was able to resist the Romans for three years, unite the Jews of Palestine behind him, and win over Rabbi Akiva, one of the leading rabbis of the time, to his messianic claims testifies to his strong and charismatic leadership. Various letters and coins of the period of the revolt have been found by **Yigal Yadin** and other archaeologists in the Judean desert.

BAR MITZVAH/BAT MITZVAH ("COMING OF AGE"). At the onset of adulthood, a Jewish boy is known as a bar mitzvah (Aramaic and Hebrew, literally "son of the commandment"), and a Jewish girl is known as a bat mitzvah (Hebrew, literally "daughter of the commandment"). Boys are considered adult after their 13th **Hebrew** birthday and girls after their 12th Hebrew birthday, reckoned according to the Jewish **calendar**. In both cases, these ages are an approximation to the onset of puberty, which was originally dependent on the growth of pubic hairs. From bar and bat mitzvah on, boys and girls have to keep all the commandments laid down for them by the **halakhah**, and boys can be counted in the **minyan** to make up a quorum for public prayer.

A rite of passage accompanies a child becoming bar mitzvah, and this involves the bar mitzvah boy being called up to make a blessing on the scroll of the **Torah** for the first time. He will usually chant all or some of the weekly Torah reading from the Pentateuch or sing the haftarah section from the Prophets. In many **Orthodox** families, there is no public ceremony marking the bat mitzvah of a girl, but Modern Orthodox, **Conservative**, and **Reform** communities have all created ceremonies to mark that occasion. In many cases, such bat mitzvah ceremonies either involve the girl giving a talk about a religious topic, or they mirror the bar mitzvah of a boy in all its details. It is customary for the parents to celebrate this coming of age of their child with a party, either simply a kiddush on the **Sabbath** after the ceremony or with a more elaborate dinner for family and friends on a weekday. *See also* WAILING WALL (HEBREW KOTEL HA-MAARAVI, "WESTERN WALL"); WOMEN IN JUDAISM.

BASEL PROGRAM. At the First **Zionist Congress**, convened by **Theodor Herzl** in Basel in 1897, the aims and objectives of the **Zionist** Movement were decided on. They were formulated as the establishment of a home for Jews in **Palestine**, promotion of the means for Jews to settle there as laborers, encouragement of the feeling of national identity among Jews, and political negotiation with governments to obtain their consent for such a Jewish home. *See also* BILTMORE PROGRAM; WORLD ZIONIST ORGANIZATION (WZO).

BATH SHEBA. *See* DAVID; SOLOMON (10TH CENTURY BCE).

BAT MITZVAH (GIRL'S COMING OF AGE). *See* BAR MITZVAH/ BAT MITZVAH ("COMING OF AGE"); WOMEN IN JUDAISM.

BATORY, KING STEFAN. *See* WAHL, SAUL (1541–1617).

BEACONSFIELD, EARL OF. *See* DISRAELI, BENJAMIN (1804– 81).

BEDOUIN ARABS. *See* DEAD SEA SCROLLS; ISRAEL; ISRAEL DEFENSE FORCE (IDF).

BEGIN, MENACHEM (1913–92). Prime minister of **Israel** and one-time terrorist leader. Begin became a commander of the **Irgun** a year after his arrival in Mandate **Palestine** in 1942 and as a wanted man had to go into hiding, disguised as a **Chasidic** Jew, to avoid arrest by the British authorities. After the foundation of the State of Israel in 1948, Begin became a member of the **Knesset**, the Israeli parliament. When the party he led, the Likkud, emerged from the 1977 elections as the largest party, he was appointed prime minister. It was Begin, the right-wing nationalist, who signed the Camp David agreement with Egypt in 1978, for which he was jointly awarded the Nobel Peace Prize. *See also* ASHKENAZIM (SINGULAR ASHKENAZI); JABOTINSKY, VLADIMIR (1889–1940).

BEIS YAAKOV (EDUCATION NETWORK). *See* YESHIVAH (HEBREW, "PLACE OF SITTING," PLURAL YESHIVOT); WOMEN IN JUDAISM.

BENE ISRAEL. An Indian Jewish community originally living in Mumbai (Bombay) and the surrounding area. Their origins are unknown, but because trading links existed between the **Holy Land** and

India from biblical times, they could be the descendants of Jewish merchants who established trading posts on the coast of Maharashtra. According to Bene Israel legend, the community came about after seven families of Jews from **Palestine** were shipwrecked off the Indian coast in the early centuries CE.

In appearance, the Bene Israel are similar to other Indians, indicating that some native Indians, over the centuries, converted to Judaism, married Jews, and joined the community. They are divided into two groups, or castes: the Gora group, or white Bene Israel, and the Kala, or black Bene Israel. In the past, they kept caste restrictions similar to those found in Hindu society, not intermarrying with one another, not eating together, and with the Gora regarding themselves as of higher caste than the Kala. These restrictions are rarely kept anymore.

The Bene Israel lived an isolated life as Jews, cut off from other Jews for a long time, and retained only residual elements of their faith. It was Jews from Cochin who discovered their Bene Israel coreligionists and taught them Hebrew and Jewish traditions. When **Sephardi** Jews from Baghdad moved to Bombay in the 19th century, they further raised the standards of **halakhic** practice of the Bene Israel, although the Baghdadis tended to look down on the native Jews.

Under British rule in India, many Bene Israel had successful careers in the army and the civil service. After Indian independence in 1947, the majority of the community made **aliyah** to **Israel**, where, after some controversy, they have been officially recognized as Jews. Emigration to Israel and European countries has left only a remnant of the community of Bene Israel still in India.

BEN GURION, DAVID (1886–1973). Socialist **Zionist** leader in the struggle for Israeli independence, founding father of the State of **Israel**, and its first prime minister. Ben Gurion was head of the **Jewish Agency** before the founding of the state in 1948. He had been reluctantly willing to accept the partition of **Palestine** between a Jewish and an Arab state and took a leading role in declaring independence after British troops withdrew. When Israel's Arab neighbors attacked the fledgling state, he assumed the responsibility of uniting the new Israeli army in the **War of Independence**.

Ben Gurion was instrumental in the sinking of the *Altalena* arms ship belonging to the **Irgun** and the elimination of the Irgun as a separate fighting force. He believed in the rejection of the **Diaspora** and its values, was a strong advocate of **Hebrew** as the only language for Jews, encouraged **aliyah**, and persuaded Israelis to adopt new Hebraized names (he was born Gruen) and a new Israel identity. When he left office in 1953, he started **kibbutz** Sdeh Boker in the Negev in order to act as a pioneering role model for young people.

Ben Gurion was deeply involved in intellectual pursuits, not only with the **Bible** but also with ancient philosophy and Asian religions, practicing yoga daily. He took an active role in the 1956 **Sinai Campaign** as defense minister and controversially took aid money from Germany to help the Israeli economy. He encouraged the abduction of **Adolph Eichmann** from Argentina, and his subsequent trial in Israel, so that the younger generation of Israelis would understand something of the nature and horrors of the **Holocaust**.

BENJAMIN OF TUDELA (12TH CENTURY). Jewish traveler and author. In the record of his travels, lasting several years, there is a mass of valuable data, not only about the Jewish communities of the Mediterranean, the Middle East, and West Asia but also of general interest. Benjamin records details of Jewish scholarship and religious practice, of **Samaritan** and **Karaite** sects, and even of the rudiments of a little-known Jewish sect in Cyprus. Although the numbers he gives of Jewish inhabitants in different places may sometimes be inflated, he provides accurate information about Jewish communities and details of distances and locations. His descriptions of trade and economic conditions, both of Jews and of their surrounding societies, is of considerable historical value. His book of travels has been widely translated.

BEN YEHUDAH, ELIEZER (1858–1922). The father of the modern **Hebrew** language. A committed **Zionist**, Ben Yehudah emigrated from his native Lithuania to **Palestine** at the age of 23. He was convinced that the return of the Jewish people to their ancestral land must be accompanied by the revival of Hebrew so that Jews would have a spiritual center and a common culture. To implement this plan, he would speak to his wife and children only in Hebrew. He also taught in the **Jerusalem** school of the **Alliance Israélite Universelle** in Hebrew. Together with like-minded colleagues, he coined new Hebrew words and was one of the founding members of the Vaad Ha-Lashon Ha-Ivrit, which eventually became the **Academy**

of the Hebrew Language. His magnum opus was a dictionary of ancient and modern Hebrew, which was completed after his death in 17 volumes. *See also* BRIT IVRIT OLAMIT (HEBREW, "WORLD HEBREW COVENANT").

BERGEN-BELSEN. A concentration camp near Hanover established by the Nazis in 1943. It was originally meant as a transit camp for Jews and others who might be exchanged with the Allies. By the end of the war, however, there were around 60,000 inmates still remaining and so emaciated because of the terrible camp conditions that many of them died after liberation. Bergen-Belsen was liberated by the British army in April 1945. *See also* AUSCHWITZ; BUCHENWALD; FINAL SOLUTION; HOLOCAUST.

BERICHAH (HEBREW, "FLIGHT"). An organization active in 1944-48 that aided Jewish refugees from European countries to make **aliyah** to their eventual destination in **Palestine** as illegal immigrants. Most of the refugees were **Holocaust** survivors, and the people who helped them in the Berichah organization were either Jewish ex-**partisans** or members of **Zionist** organizations. The main points of departure for Palestine were Italian ports, and because the British Mandate authorities in Palestine wished to prevent illegal immigration, the British army tried to block access to that country. Polish **anti-Semitism** and attacks against Jews, such as the **Kielce Pogrom**, after World War II made their escape more urgent. Around a quarter of a million Jews escaped.

BERIT TRUMPELDOR. *See* BETAR (ACRONYM OF BERIT TRUMPELDOR).

BERNADOTTE, COUNT FOLKE. *See* WAR OF INDEPENDENCE (HEBREW MILCHEMET HA-ATZMAUT).

BERURIAH. *See* WOMEN IN JUDAISM.

BESHT. *See* BAAL SHEM TOV, ISRAEL BEN ELIEZER (1700–60).

BETA ISRAEL. *See* FALASHAS (ALSO KNOWN AS BETA ISRAEL).

BETAR (ACRONYM OF BERIT TRUMPELDOR). Right-wing **Zionist** youth movement that began in 1923 in Eastern Europe and was affiliated with the **Revisionist Zionist** tendency. Betar promoted the ideal of **aliyah** to the **Land of Israel** and the creation of a Jewish state there on both sides of the Jordan River. This ideology was based on the views of **Vladimir Jabotinsky** and the activism of **Joseph Trumpeldor,** who died in defense of Jewish settlements in the **Holy Land.** The name is reminiscent of Betar, the last bastion of the **Bar Kokhba** revolt against Rome that was destroyed in 135 CE after Bar Kokhba withdrew there from Jerusalem. The name thus appealed to nationalist sentiments.

Betar members were accused of fascist tendencies, and they sometimes came to blows with other Zionist youth. The first world conference of Betar was held in 1931, and as a militant movement, it encouraged self-defense courses for all its members. As well as assisting Jews to immigrate illegally to **Palestine,** its members were involved in the **ghetto** uprisings against the Nazis, particularly the **Warsaw Ghetto Uprising,** and some survived the **Holocaust** as **partisans.** In the postwar era, **Israel** became the main center of the Betar Movement, where it was best known for its sports centers and support for the somewhat controversial Betar **Jerusalem** Football Club.

BET HAMIDRASH. *See* SYNAGOGUE (HEBREW BET KNESSET); YESHIVAH (HEBREW, "PLACE OF SITTING," PLURAL YESHIVOT).

BETHLEHEM. *See* PILGRIMAGE (HEBREW ALIYAH LE-REGEL, "ASCENT BY FOOT").

BET KNESSET. *See* SYNAGOGUE (HEBREW BET KNESSET).

BET YOSEF (HALAKHIC WORK). *See* CARO, JOSEPH (1488–1575); SHULCHAN ARUKH (HEBREW, "LAID TABLE").

BIBLE. The Hebrew Bible, known by Christians as the Old Testament, is referred to by **Jew**s as the Tenakh. This title is an acronym of the three parts of the Bible: **Torah** ("Teaching," the Pentateuch, or Five Books of **Moses**), Neviim ("Prophets," a collection of books written under prophetic inspiration), and Ketuvim ("Writings" or

Hagiographa, sacred works, many of which belong to the category of Wisdom Literature). There are 24 books in the Tenakh, and they are all considered part of God's revelation, but the most sacred section is the Torah.

Many commentaries and super-commentaries have been written on the biblical text explaining its meaning and developing its insights so they apply to the different circumstances Jews found themselves in. Though the rabbis had great respect for the text itself, they often did not understand it merely in a literal way, and this led to the great schism with the **Karaites**, who rejected any nonliteral interpretation of the Bible. It was also the subject of **disputations** with Christians, who saw the Old Testament as referring, both directly and indirectly, to the life and death of Jesus, which was totally unacceptable to Judaism.

The medieval sage **Moses Maimonides** was asked whether it was permitted to teach the Bible to Christians and Muslims. He replied in a responsum that it was permitted to teach the Hebrew Scriptures to Christians because they accept the same biblical text as Jews but interpret it incorrectly. If they are taught its true meaning, they may come to accept the Jewish point of view. He prohibited teaching Scripture to Muslims, however, because the Koran contains very different versions of the Bible stories. Muslims might therefore become more antagonistic to Jews when confronted by a Jewish holy book that contradicts their central religious text. *See also* KOSHER ("FIT FOOD," HEBREW KASHER, KASHRUT); TEN COMMANDMENTS (OR DECALOGUE).

BIELSKI, TUVIA. *See* PARTISANS.

BILTMORE PROGRAM. A policy statement composed at a meeting at the Biltmore Hotel in New York in May 1942 declaring that **Palestine** should become a Jewish state administered by the **Jewish Agency**. The meeting was held in place of the **Zionist Congress**, which was prevented by war, and was arranged after **Chaim Weizmann** had successfully engaged in Zionist propaganda in the United States. The policy statement was proposed by **David Ben Gurion**, head of the Jewish Agency, and caused some opposition from those who either did not favor a Jewish State or preferred a gradual working out of Jewish claims to independence in Palestine with the British Mandate and the United Nations. The Biltmore program did, how-

ever, become official Zionist policy adopted by the Zionist General
Council. *See also* ZIONISM.

BIMAH (HEBREW, "PLATFORM"). *See* SYNAGOGUE (HE-
BREW BET KNESSET).

BIROBIDZHAN. An area in Soviet East Asia near the Chinese border
set aside for an independent Jewish region far from the centers of
Jewish life in European Russia. The original Birobidzhan was an
area of very poor quality in terms of its infrastructure, and its land
was infested with insects and lacked basic sanitation. The Russian
authorities needed to populate this far-off province of their empire,
and the purpose of an autonomous Jewish region was meant to ap-
pease Jewish opinion in the West as well as countermand the **Zionist**
aspirations of Jews. From 1928, Jews were encouraged to migrate
there, and the official languages, **Yiddish** as well as Russian, were
also taught to **Gentiles**. Yiddish newspapers, a Yiddish theater, and
a Jewish library were established, as were Jewish collective farms,
and Jews were in prominent leadership positions. The idea of Birobidzhan, however, was really stillborn, and the Jewish population
never came anywhere near a majority. Today, it is a small percentage,
perhaps less than 5 percent, of the population.

BLACK DEATH. A plague-like disease that killed almost half the
population of Europe in the late 14th century and was particularly
virulent in urban areas. The disease may have been Bubonic plague,
although modern scholars have suggested other possibilities. It was
a disease certainly unknown to its contemporaries, and people turned
to religion, suspecting it was punishment for sins.

They also looked for a scapegoat, and the one most ready to hand
was the **Jew** because of the deep-rooted **anti-Semitic** attitudes of
some Christians who saw the Jew as a devil worshipper. It was also
perhaps because Jews did not die at the same rate as Christians because they had strict religious rules of hygiene, such as ritual washing of the hands after the toilet and before eating and bathing in the
mikveh. Jews were accused of poisoning wells and were frequently
slaughtered. Pope Clement IV tried to stem the violence in 1348 by
declaring that Jews were not responsible for the Black Death, without
much effect on the killings and expulsions.

BLOOD LIBEL. The accusation that **Jews** need blood for their rituals, particularly for the baking of unleavened bread for the **Passover**, and that they murder Christians, specifically Christian children, to obtain this blood. Though there was no truth in this libel, as the Jewish **dietary laws** prohibit the consuming of any blood as non-**kosher**, it seems to have arisen from a general fear of the Jew as alien, possibly a follower of the devil, and not really human. These fears were strengthened by the belief that Jewish men also menstruated and needed blood as a cure.

From the 12th century, there were many cases of blood libel accusations. Indeed often when a child was found dead or murdered, Jews were accused, tortured until they confessed, and massacred. The first recorded case of blood libel involved an English Christian child, William of Norwich (1144), and there were recorded cases in a number of European countries thereafter. Sometimes the child, supposedly killed by Jews, was elevated to sainthood, such as Saint Hugh of Lincoln (1255). Blood libel accusations and beliefs continued up to modern times. They were repudiated by the Catholic Church only in 1965 and were used by Nazi propaganda to enhance **anti-Semitism**. *See also* DAMASCUS BLOOD LIBEL.

BNAI B'RITH (HEBREW, "SONS OF THE COVENANT"). A Jewish organization providing support to the Jewish and wider communities. Founded in 1843 in New York, Bnai B'rith modeled itself on Masonic organizations, and its aims were inspired by the **Enlightenment** to support the highest ideals of Judaism, to help the poor and sick, to promote knowledge, and to resist persecution. Bnai B'rith is open to all Jews of different religious persuasions, **Orthodox**, **Conservative**, **Reform**, or secular, although it never appealed to ultra-Orthodox Jews who did not share its Enlightenment outlook, tolerance, and acceptance of modernity. It is divided into lodges and has chapters in all Western countries, mostly in North America.

As well as sustaining Jewish and **Gentile** welfare programs, Bnai B'rith has also been supportive of the State of **Israel**. In 1923, it extended it activities to the spiritual and material care of Jewish students by establishing the Hillel Foundation, which has a variety of individuals and institutions on almost every major campus throughout the world where there are Jewish students. The Hillel Foundation promotes Jewish culture and religion, publishes material, and services **kosher** food needs. *See also* ANTI-DEFAMATION LEAGUE (ADL).

BOARD OF DEPUTIES OF BRITISH JEWS. An organization dating back to the 1760s that is the main representative of British Jewry. In 1835, it attained government recognition and devised a constitution representing all of the **synagogues** in Great Britain. Eventually, other non-synagogue organizations were encouraged to join. Given the central role that the British Empire played in world affairs, the Board of Deputies was able in the 19th century to exert influence on the British government for the benefit of persecuted Jews as well as fighting for Jewish **emancipation** in Britain. This was particularly true when **Sir Moses Montefiore** was president from 1838 to 1874.

The board guaranteed the right of synagogues to conduct their own weddings and tried to Anglicize Jewish immigrants from Eastern Europe who came to Britain in droves from the 1880s. Though these immigrants spoke **Yiddish**, their offspring were turned into English children by attending schools, despite some opposition from those who regarded Anglicization as akin to **assimilation**. Although the board is guided by the religious authorities, particularly by the British chief rabbinate, it has fallen out with the ultra-**Orthodox**, who refused to belong to an organization that recognized the **Reform** rabbinate as a possible source of religious authority.

BONAPARTE, NAPOLEON (1769–1821). *See* NAPOLEON BONAPARTE (1769–1821).

BOOK OF JEWISH THOUGHTS. *See* HERTZ, JOSEPH HERMAN (1872–1946).

BRAND, JOEL (1906–64). Hungarian **Zionist** leader involved in efforts to save Jews from the Nazis. Brand worked with **Rudolf Kasztner** in negotiating with the Nazi leadership, including **Adolph Eichmann**. The latter sent Brand on a mission to Turkey in 1944 to arrange the exchange of Hungarian Jews for trucks. Brand was unable to meet representatives of the **Jewish Agency** there and had to continue on to **Palestine**. He was arrested en route by the British as a suspected Nazi spy and after his release stayed in Palestine rather than returning to Hungary, for by then the process of mass murder of Hungarian Jews was well underway.

BRITISH ISRAELITES. The **Ten Lost Tribes**, who were taken into captivity in 722 BCE after the Assyrians conquered the northern kingdom of **Israel**, have led to many myths about their continued existence. One of them involves the theory that the British are descendants of one of these tribes. Those who subscribe to this theory are known as British Israelites. Some of them, influenced by **anti-Semitism**, have even denied that the Jews are really Israelites at all but rather the descendants of the **Khazars**. The background to British Israelite belief is the Protestant interest in the Hebrew **Bible**, the Christian Old Testament, and the conviction that the Stone of Scone, used in coronations, is the very stone on which the Patriarch **Jacob** slept when he dreamed of a ladder leading up to heaven. The name *British* is interpreted to be the two Hebrew words *berit ish* meaning "the covenant of man."

BRITISH MANDATE FOR PALESTINE. *See* ALIYAH (HEBREW, "GOING UP," PLURAL ALIYOT); BALFOUR DECLARATION; BERICHAH (HEBREW, "FLIGHT"); BILTMORE PROGRAM; HAGANAH (HEBREW, "DEFENSE"); HEBREW UNIVERSITY OF JERUSALEM; HUSSEINI, HAJ AMIN (1893–1974); JABOTIN-SKY, VLADIMIR (1889–1940); JEWISH AGENCY; PALESTINE; REVISIONIST ZIONISTS; WAILING WALL (HEBREW KOTEL HA-MAARAVI, "WESTERN WALL"); WAR OF INDEPENDENCE (HEBREW MILCHEMET HA-ATZMAUT); ZIONISM.

BRIT IVRIT OLAMIT (HEBREW, "WORLD HEBREW COVENANT"). An organization whose main aim is the promotion of the **Hebrew** language. The inspiration behind this organization was the early **Zionist Congresses** of 1903 and of 1907, where there was a strong pro-Hebrew movement opposed to the adoption of German as a Jewish national language. In order to foster Hebrew in different countries, local organizations were set up in European countries where a modern form of Hebrew would be spoken and taught. Originally, they were strongest in Eastern Europe, where classical Hebrew was an integral part of Jewish education, but most of these communities were destroyed in the **Holocaust**. Once the State of **Israel** was established, modern Hebrew, spoken in a modified **Sephardi** accent, became the national language, and this led to a great expansion of Hebrew in **Diaspora** communities. Acting together with the **Jewish Agency**, the Brit Ivrit Olamit has produced written and media materials for Hebrew education and for the revival of Hebrew, as opposed to **Yiddish**, as the main Jewish language in the Western world. *See also* ACADEMY OF THE HEBREW LANGUAGE (VAAD HA-LASHON HA-IVRIT); BEN YEHUDAH, ELIEZER (1858–1922).

BUBER, MARTIN (1878–1965). Zionist philosopher. After an academic career in Austria and Germany, Buber attended the Third **Zionist Congress** in 1899 representing the approach of the cultural **Zionists**. He remained a committed Zionist, but his version of Zionism involved consideration for **Palestinian** Arabs. Buber's considerable influence stemmed from his writings about **Chasidism** and his interpersonal philosophy expressed in his book *I and Thou*, first published in 1937. His approach to God and to the camaraderie and romance of the Chasidic movement, as well as his utopian views of genuine relationships between people, were all an expression of what he called **Hebrew** Humanism based on his philosophy of dialogue. Buber had considerable influence, particularly on the Christian world, but the movement he led, which advocated a State of **Israel** shared by Jews and Arabs, never won popular appeal. *See also* ARAB REFUGEES.

BUCHENWALD. A concentration camp in Germany that was liberated by American forces in April 1945. By that time, the prisoners had rebelled against their guards and taken over the camp. Most of its inmates during the eight years of Buchenwald's existence were Jews and Soviet prisoners of war, although for the last few years, it was also populated by common German criminals. The camp was used for slave labor and medical experiments, and many of the inmates, particularly the Russians, were put to death while the Jews were eventually deported to **Auschwitz**. *See also* BERGEN-BELSEN; FINAL SOLUTION; HOLOCAUST.

BUND (SHORT FORM OF ALGEMEINER YIDDISHER AR-BETER BUND). **Yiddish** socialist party that began in greater Russia at the end of the 19th century. The Bund opposed the **Zionist** ideology of settling Jews in the **Holy Land**. It regarded autonomous Jewish life in the **Diaspora** as the ideal, accompanied by Jewish culture, but it was very negative about Jewish religion. The Bund wanted to improve the condition of the Jewish working class while providing a cultural Marxist ideology for intellectuals. It sought the revival of Yiddish language and literature and for Jews to be fully **emancipated** but not **assimilated**. Bundists were active in resistance to Nazi persecution, participating in **ghetto** uprisings and with the **partisans**. *See also* WARSAW GHETTO UPRISING.

BURMA ROAD. *See* WAR OF INDEPENDENCE (HEBREW MILCHEMET HA-ATZMAUT).

– C –

CAIRO GENIZAH. A store room used for holy texts in the Ben Ezra **synagogue** of **Palestinian** Jews in old Cairo. Texts had been stored in the synagogue **genizah** since the 9th century, and in the 18th and early 19th century, some texts and fragments had been removed. The dry nature of the Egyptian climate helped to preserve many of the documents.

The bulk of the contents of the Cairo Genizah were removed to Cambridge by **Solomon Schechter** in 1896, after two Christian English ladies had shown him some pages from the genizah that they brought back from Cairo. Other fragments and documents went to major libraries and collections around the world. The genizah material is still being worked on more than 100 years after Schechter's discovery, and the Cairo Genizah material has revolutionized knowledge of linguistic, historical, liturgical, textual, religious, economic, and social elements of the Middle East. *See also* DEAD SEA SCROLLS.

CALENDAR. The Jewish year is essentially lunar, each month beginning with the new moon and lasting either 29 or 30 days, the new moon day being a minor holiday. Certain festivals of the ritual year, however, are solar, based on the agricultural seasons, so the lunar year has to be intercalated with 7 extra months every 19 years to bring the lunar and solar years back into agreement. The names of the months of the Jewish year were adapted from the **Babylonian**

months, which Jews borrowed during the Babylonian captivity. They are Tishri, Marcheshvan, Kislev, Tevet, Shevat, Adar (plus Second Adar in a leap year), Nisan, Iyyar, Sivan, Tammuz, Av, and Elul. Jewish communities in the **Diaspora** would keep an extra day for festivals, since information about the sighting of the new moon in the **Land of Israel** could not reach them in time.

Sometime after the 4th century CE, the calendar was fixed by the **Palestinian** rabbis based on calculation and not based merely on the sighting of the new moon, so that the solar dates of festival days were known in advance. Despite this, while **Reform Judaism** and **Conservative Judaism** have abolished these second festive days, **Orthodoxy** has continued to maintain them for Diaspora Jews. The symbolism of the moon retained its importance for Jews because **Israel** is compared to the moon, which continually renews itself, and in the future, **Messianic** Age will regain its former splendor. Every month, prayers are said a few days after the new moon day when the moon is clearly visible in the sky. These prayers are known as the Sanctification of the Moon, kiddush levanah, praising God for renewing the moon's cycle. *See also* BAR MITZVAH/BAT MITZVAH ("COMING OF AGE"); JEWISH RITUAL YEAR.

CAMP DAVID AGREEMENT. *See* BEGIN, MENACHEM (1913–92); DAYAN, MOSHE (1915–81).

CANAAN. *See* ABRAHAM; HOLY LAND; ISRAEL; JOSEPH; JUDAH (HEBREW YEHUDAH); LAND OF ISRAEL (HEBREW ERETZ YISRAEL); PROMISED LAND.

CANTONISTS. The government of Czarist Russia attempted to assimilate young Jews by conscripting them to the Russian army from an early age, making them serve for up to 25 years, and inculcating them with Christian teachings. The conscription began in 1827 and only came to an end in 1856 under Czar Nicholas II. The term *Cantonists* refers to the cantonment schools where the young children were incarcerated during their training for the army. Because the Jewish community was given a quota of children and teenagers who had to undertake military service, Jewish communities employed people to kidnap children to make up the quotas. These were known in **Yiddish** as chappers, "snatchers."

Some Jewish children managed to survive the harsh conditions and remained Jews despite the intense pressure to become Christians, amounting to forced baptism and the encouragement to abandon their Judaism. They were able to return to their families at the end of their 25 years military service, but few retained any remnants of Jewish identity and practice by then. It is estimated that between 30,000 and 70,000 Jewish boys served as Cantonists; and most never returned to their homes. *See also* CONVERSOS.

CARO, JOSEPH (1488–1575). Halakhic authority and mystic. Caro, who grew up in Ottoman Turkey, came from a family of Spanish exiles. He eventually settled in Safed, which was a center of **Kabbalah**. Caro is best known for his halakhic code, the **Shulchan Arukh** ("laid table"), which, together with the glosses of Moses Isserles, became the code followed in most Jewish communities, **Ashkenazi** and **Sephardi** alike. The Shulchan Arukh is a relatively short work summarizing Caro's conclusions in his more scholarly, and longer, work entitled *Bet Yosef.* Though there had been important codes before Caro, the fact that printing of **Hebrew** books was well established by the time his code was published made it more easily accessible to scholar and layman alike, so it became the standard code.

As a mystic, Caro was distinctive in that he kept a spiritual diary of the revelations of his daemon (maggid in Hebrew). This guiding spirit was the spirit of the **Mishnah**, and at least part of this diary was later published under the title *Maggid Mesharim.* His daemon often had to reassure Caro that the halakhic decisions he had taken in his code were the right ones, despite the fact that he sometimes contradicted the opinions of great **rabbis** who had preceded him. At one point, Caro asked his daemon whether he would have the merit to die as a **martyr** just like the revered **Solomon Molcho**, who was burned at the stake in 1532. The daemon told him he too would be a martyr, but this never transpired, and Caro died of natural causes at a ripe old age. *See also* MAIMONIDES, MOSES (1135–1204).

CATHOLIC ISRAEL. *See* SCHECHTER, SOLOMON (1847–1915).

CHAIM OF VOLOZHIN (1749–1821). Rabbi and leader of the **Mitnaggedic Movement.** Chaim was the main disciple of **Elijah of Vilna**, the most important opponent of **Chasidism**. Despite his master's attitude, Chaim took a more moderate position toward the Chasidic Movement, and rather than simply condemning it, he outlined a non-Chasidic ideology based on the **Kabbalah**. In his main work, the *Nefesh Hachaim*, he argued that the intellectual study of **Torah** was the highest goal of the religious life, touching the mind of God, as it were. The Chasidic emphasis on prayer and the inner spiritual life was played down by Chaim. In line with his emphasis on Torah study, he founded a **yeshivah** in Volozhin that became the model for all East European yeshivot.

CHALLAH (BREAD). *See* SABBATH (HEBREW SHABBAT).

CHAMBER OF HEWN STONE. *See* SANHEDRIN.

CHANUKAH. Minor festival of the Hebrew **calendar** usually falling in late December and commemorating the victory of the **Maccabees** in the 2nd century BCE. The Sages who instituted the festival did not want to celebrate a purely military event, even though the victory over the powerful armies of the Seleucid Greeks was regarded as miraculous, so they focused on the rededication of the **Temple** by the **Hasmonean** priests and the miracle story associated with the small container of undefiled olive oil that was found. According to this story, when the priests kindled this oil, which was barely sufficient for one day, it continued to burn for eight days. The Sages eventually instituted the ritual of kindling a flame for eight days in Jewish homes each evening accompanied by prayers and hymns.

In **Ashkenazi** communities, the custom is for every member of the household to light candles or oil lamps during Chanukah, one for the first night, two for the second, up to eight for the last night. In many **Sephardi** communities, only the master of the house lights candles, and the rest of the family join in the prayers and singing. It is also customary to eat special foods cooked in oil. Chanukah is a popular festival appealing both to Jewish national consciousness and to religious sensibilities.

Because it usually falls on, or close to, Christmas, Chanukah has taken on some of the secondary characteristics associated with the Christian festival, such as gifts to children. It is also a festival when Jews gamble with a four-sided spinning top, dreidl, and sometimes adults gamble at cards, much to the dismay of the **halakhic** authorities. Among some **assimilated** Jews in the United States, this spill-over from Christmas has even extended to having a Christmas-style tree for Chanukah, but this has been opposed by many Jewish religious leaders as simply imitating **Gentile** practices. *See also* JEWISH RITUAL YEAR; JUDAH MACCABEE (2ND CENTURY BCE).

CHAPPERS (YIDDISH, "SNATCHERS"). *See* CANTONISTS.

CHAREDIM (HEBREW, "ULTRA-ORTHODOX JEWS"). *See* HEAD COVERING; ORTHODOX JUDAISM.

CHARLES V, EMPEROR. *See* JOSELMANN, JOSEPH, OF ROSHEIM (1478–1554).

CHAROSET (RITUAL FOOD). *See* PASSOVER (HEBREW PESACH).

CHASIDIC MOVEMENT (ALSO HASIDIC). A movement founded by the followers of Israel ben Eliezer (1700–60), known as the **Baal Shem Tov** ("Master of the Good Name"). Israel was a **Kabbalist** who specialized in magical cures and faith healing. He taught a form of Judaism influenced by Jewish mysticism that enabled ordinary people to attach themselves to God. He also attracted scholars to his ranks who initiated the movement after his death.

The Chasidic Movement changed the face of East European Jewry. It created a new type of community led by a Chasidic **Tzaddik**, or Rebbe (a word akin to *rabbi*), who was usually a charismatic figure and who enabled Jews to resist the temptations of the **Enlightenment, assimilation**, and any subsequent abandonment of Judaism. Although many Chasidic communities and their leaders perished in the **Holocaust**, the movement has been revived since World War II, partly through the large families characteristic of Chasidim, who do not approve of birth control.

CHAVRUTA (ARAMAIC, "STUDY PARTNERS"). *See* YESHI-VAH (HEBREW, "PLACE OF SITTING," PLURAL YESHIVOT).

CHAZZAN (HEBREW, "CANTOR"). *See* SYNAGOGUE (HEBREW BET KNESSET); TALLIT (ARAMAIC, "PRAYER SHAWL").

CHEDER (HEBREW, "RELIGIOUS SCHOOL"). *See* YESHIVAH (HEBREW, "PLACE OF SITTING," PLURAL YESHIVOT).

CHEESE. *See* PENTECOST (HEBREW SHAVUOT).

CHEREM. A method of social control by excommunication. In premodern times, a cherem was one of the ultimate sanctions because the person subject to it could not benefit from the support of the community. This excommunication could be for a limited period, such as 30 days, or for an extended period. The degree of excommunication varied between total exclusion from the community to only partial exclusion from some communal activities. The person under a cherem was meant to regard himself as if in mourning and show contrition.

The sins for which a cherem could be applied varied from insulting or refusing to obey the religious authorities to causing a desecration of God's name. In extreme cases, the person excommunicated was treated as a **Gentile**, and his food was regarded as non-**kosher**. As far as the excommunicated individual was concerned, this was a living death. A cherem could be pronounced in a **synagogue** with the holy ark open or by someone holding a **Torah** scroll. The ram's horn, shofar, was blown and candles were lit and then blown out, accompanied by curses. *See also* ELIJAH OF VILNA (1720–97); FRANK, JACOB (1726–91); MITNAGGEDIC MOVEMENT (HEBREW, "OPPONENTS").

CHERUBIM. *See* TEMPLE (HEBREW BET HA-MIKDASH).

CHIBBAT TZION (HEBREW, "LOVE OF ZION"). A pre-**Zionist** mass movement centered in Eastern Europe in the 19th and early 20th centuries. The followers of the movement were known as Chovevei Tzion ("Lovers of Zion"). The purpose of the movement was to encourage Jews to return to the **Holy Land**. After the **pogroms** of the 1880s in Russia, groups of Chovevei Tzion made **aliyah**, that is they migrated to **Palestine** and founded agricultural settlements with the help of Baron Edmund de Rothschild (*see* ROTHSCHILD FAMILY). The father of the Zionist movement, **Theodor Herzl**, drew support for his political Zionism from the more practical Zionism of the Chibbat Tzion Movement. *See also* MIZRACHI (ABBREVIATION OF MERCAZ RUCHANI, "SPIRITUAL CENTER").

CHIEF RABBINATE, BRITAIN. *See* BOARD OF DEPUTIES OF BRITISH JEWS; HEBREW UNIVERSITY OF JERUSALEM; HERTZ, JOSEPH HERMAN (1872–1946); HIRSCH, SAMSON RAPHAEL (1808–88); JEWISH THEOLOGICAL SEMINARY (JTS).

CHIEF RABBINATE, FRANCE. *See* CONSISTOIRE.

CHIEF RABBINATE, ISRAEL. *See* FALASHAS (ALSO KNOWN AS BETA ISRAEL); HEBREW UNIVERSITY OF JERUSALEM; KOOK, ABRAHAM ISAAC (1865–1935); MIZRACHI (ABBREVIATION OF MERCAZ RUCHANI, "SPIRITUAL CENTER"); REVISIONIST ZIONISTS; YESHIVAH (HEBREW, "PLACE OF SITTING," PLURAL YESHIVOT).

CHILDREN OF ISRAEL. *See* ISRAEL; JACOB; PURIM; SAMBATYON.

CHILDREN OF MOSES. *See* SAMBATYON.

CHINA. *See* KAIFENG.

CHMIELNICKI, BOGDAN (1595–1657). *See* CHMIELNICKI MASSACRES.

CHMIELNICKI MASSACRES. The Cossack leader Bogdan Chmielnicki (1595–1657) led an uprising against the Polish rulers of the Ukraine in 1648. In the course of this revolt, the Cossacks massacred hundreds of Jewish communities with the purpose of eliminating the Jewish presence in the Ukraine. Many Jews worked as agents for the Polish nobility and were hated by the Ukrainian peasants even more than their Polish masters. Chmielnicki's **anti-Semitic** followers destroyed **synagogues** and desecrated holy scrolls during their **pogroms**.

For the Jews of Poland and the Ukraine, the memory of the slaughter led to a prolonged period of mourning, remembering the death of more than 100,000 Jews and the annihilation of Jewish communities. One of the consequences of the Chmielnicki Massacres was the welcome given by East European Jews to the claims of **Shabbetai Tzvi** to be the **Messiah** and to the rise of the **Chasidic Movement**. The victory of the Cossacks over the Poles led to the incorporation of the Ukraine in Russia. *See also* HAIDAMACKS.

CHOVEVEI TZION (HEBREW, "LOVERS OF ZION"). *See* CHIBBAT TZION (HEBREW, "LOVE OF ZION").

CHRISTIANITY. *See* ANTI-SEMITISM; ASSIMILATION; AUTO-DA-FÉ (ACT OF FAITH); BARCELONA, DISPUTATION OF; BLACK DEATH; BLOOD LIBEL; BRITISH ISRAELITES; BUBER, MARTIN (1878–1965); CANTONISTS; CHANUKAH; CONVERSOS; CRUSADES; DAY OF ATONEMENT (HEBREW YOM KIPPUR); DEAD SEA SCROLLS; DIASPORA; DISPUTATIONS; DISRAELI, BENJAMIN (1804–81); EMANCIPATION; ETHIOPIA; FALASHAS (ALSO KNOWN AS BETA ISRAEL); FRANK, JACOB (1726–91); GENTILE (HEBREW GOY, PLURAL GOYIM, "NATION" OR "PEOPLE"); GRAETZ, HEINRICH (1817–91); HOST DESECRATION; INQUISITION; ISRAEL; JERUSALEM; KHAZARS; KISHINEV POGROMS; KOSHER ("FIT FOOD," HEBREW KASHER, KASHRUT); MAIMONIDES, MOSES (1135–1204); MARTYRDOM (HEBREW KIDDUSH HASHEM, "SANCTIFICATION OF (GOD'S) NAME"); MENDELSSOHN, MOSES (1729–86); MESSIANIC MOVEMENTS; NEW CHRISTIANS; NUMERUS CLAUSUS (LATIN, "CLOSED NUMBER"); OATH MORE JUDAICO; OMAR, COVENANT OF; OPPENHEIMER, JOSEPH (1698–1738, KNOWN AS JEW SUESS); POGROM; REFORM JUDAISM; ROTHSCHILD FAMILY; SASSOON FAMILY; SEPHARDIM; SHTETL; TEN COMMANDMENTS (OR DECALOGUE); TORQUEMADA, TOMAS DE (1420–98); USURY; WANDERING JEW.

CHRISTMAS. *See* CHANUKAH.

CLEMENT IV, POPE. *See* BLACK DEATH.

CLEMENT VI, POPE. *See* MOLCHO, SOLOMON (1500–32).

CLIFFORD'S TOWER. *See* CRUSADES.

COHEN, ELI (1924–65). An Egyptian **Jew** who worked as a spy for Mossad, the **Israeli** intelligence service, and penetrated the Syrian government hierarchy. Cohen's father had migrated from Syria to Egypt, where Eli grew up, in 1914. After escaping from Egypt to Israel, he was trained as a spy. He entered Syria in 1962 in the guise of a rich Syrian Arab living in Argentina and joined the Baath Party. His high-level contacts with Syrian Baathists enabled him to report back to Israel about Syrian military preparations. He was taken on a tour of Syrian army emplacements on the Golan Heights and suggested that trees should be planted around them to provide shade for the soldiers stationed there. The Syrians responded to his suggestion, and during the **Six-Day War**, the Israeli air force knew exactly which sites to bomb. Eli Cohen was uncovered as a spy in January 1965, when his secret radio transmitter was located, and he was publicly hanged in Damascus later that year. *See also* ISRAEL DEFENSE FORCE (IDF).

CONCENTRATION CAMPS. *See* AUSCHWITZ; BERGEN-BELSEN; BUCHENWALD; GESTAPO (GEHEIME STAATS-POLIZEI); GHETTO; JUDENREIN (GERMAN, "FREE OF JEWS"); KAPO; KASZTNER, RUDOLF (1906–57); KIELCE POGROM; KORCZAK, JANUSZ (PSEUDONYM OF HENRYK GOLD-SZMIDT, 187–1942); KRISTALLNACHT (GERMAN, "NIGHT OF BROKEN GLASS"); WARSAW GHETTO UPRISING.

CONFERENCE ON JEWISH MATERIAL CLAIMS AGAINST GERMANY. A post-**Holocaust** organization that began in 1951. Its purpose was to coordinate the efforts to claim compensation for Jewish victims of Nazi oppression. The initiative to found the conference was taken by the **Israeli** government in the teeth of opposition from parliamentarians and individuals who believed that taking money from Germany was taking blood money and that forgiveness for the Holocaust could not be bought. Dr. Nahum Goldmann of the **Jewish Agency** was elected its first president. The conference eventually negotiated compensation for loss of life; injuries; professional disadvantage; and loss of valuables, property, and objects confiscated by the Nazis. In 1965, the Memorial Foundation for Jewish Culture was established to promote Jewish cultural life in memory of the Jews who were murdered in the Holocaust.

There has been serious criticism of the way the conference has spent the money it received. Though it engaged in a series of worthwhile projects to strengthen Jewish life, it paid its officials large salaries, and it is claimed that not enough help was extended to actual Holocaust survivors, many of whom were impoverished and in dire need.

CONFUCIANISM. *See* KAIFENG.

CONGRESS OF BERLIN. *See* DISRAELI, BENJAMIN (1804–81).

CONSERVATIVE JUDAISM. A modernist movement that began in the United States at the end of the 19th century. Conservatives sought to preserve large elements of Jewish tradition yet to modernize Jewish practice and thought. While **Reform Judaism**, particularly in America, reacted to the **Enlightenment** by radically updating Jewish practice, **synagogue** liturgy, and Jewish thought to make them acceptable to **emancipated** Jewish consciousness, Conservative Judaism purposely sought to follow the lead of the European Historical School, which favored change in line with the historical development of Judaism.

In 1887, the **Jewish Theological Seminary** was founded in New York to train **rabbis** in a traditional manner. Eventually the seminary became the main Conservative educational institution. **Solomon Schechter** was appointed head of the seminary in 1901 and reorganized the fledgling Conservative Movement into an intellectual and social power on the American scene. Graduates of the seminary and like-minded rabbis formed the Conservative Rabbinical Assembly of America, and Schechter organized the Conservative synagogues into the United Synagogue of America in 1913, modeled on the London United Synagogue. Unlike early Reform Judaism, Conservatism has adopted a positive attitude toward **Zionism** ever since Schechter published a pro-Zionist article in 1906.

Conservative Judaism has achieved considerable success among U.S. Jewry, suiting the desire of many Jews to be fully American and yet to keep some aspects of traditional Judaism. The two sides of the Conservative Judaism, its modernism and its traditionalism, have led to controversy both inside and outside the movement. Its modernism has meant that **Orthodox** Jewish leaders do not recognize the Conservative rabbinate, their conversions, or the divorces they issue. In 1983, the Jewish Theological Seminary allowed women into its rabbinical school, which led to controversy and split. Conservative traditionalism, on the other hand, has divided it from Reform. In

1985, Conservative leaders affirmed, against the Reform patrilineal definition of Jewish identity, the traditional definition of Jewish identity, which is matrilineal. *See also* BAR MITZVAH/BAT MITZVAH ("COMING OF AGE"); HEAD COVERING; KOSHER ("FIT FOOD," HEBREW KASHER, KASHRUT); TALLIT (ARAMAIC, "PRAYER SHAWL"); WOMEN IN JUDAISM.

CONSISTOIRE. French Jewish umbrella organization representing all Jewish communities since 1808. Its origins go back to the reforms of **Napoleon Bonaparte**, who sought to integrate the wider Jewish community into French society. It is centered in Paris, with more local consistoires in the regions being made up of chief **rabbis** and laymen. They are responsible for the maintenance of mainstream French Jewish life. In earlier times, all Jews had to register with the Consistoire, and each family had to pay toward its upkeep. The Consistoire is essentially a traditional organization and takes responsibility for the appointment of rabbis and the supervision of Jewish **dietary laws**. *See also* SANHEDRIN.

CONVERSOS. Jews who, having been forcibly converted to another religion, retained their secret lives as Jews. The Jews who were forcibly converted to Catholicism in Spain in 1391 and struggled to preserve their Jewish identity for several hundred years are known as **Marranos**. In modern times, however, most of these "**New Christians**" had **assimilated** too far and completely adopted a Catholic identity with only very residual Jewish elements.

For a long time, New Christians were not accepted by their new coreligionists and were persecuted by the **Inquisition** for real, or imagined, backsliding. They tended to marry among themselves to preserve their secret Judaism. It was only after the mass expulsion of Jews from Spain in 1492 to prevent them from influencing the conversos that the isolation of those conversos who did not escape from Spain led to a gradual but complete assimilation.

Apart from the New Christians, there were other groups of Jews who lived as conversos. Thus in 12th-century Spain, a fanatical Muslim sect, the Almohads, forcibly converted Jews in Spain and North Africa under the threat of conversion or death. Many Jews fled from them, including the family of **Moses Maimonides**, and those forcibly converted were only able to revert to open Jewish life after the defeat of the Almohads in 1212. There were also incidents of forced conversion to Shiite Islam in 18th- and 19th-century Persia in Isfahan and **Meshed**. In the latter case, the Meshedi Jews lived complete double lives, and even today when they are free to live as Jews, they tend to marry among themselves.

COUNCILS OF THE LANDS. Jews in Poland and Lithuania were allowed to govern their own internal affairs from the 16th to the late 18th centuries. The governing body was known as the Council of the Lands, more commonly the Council of the Four Lands. Respected rabbinical leaders met at the major fairs that were held twice a year and were also attended by leading merchants as well as communal heads. Matters of religion and society were thus determined for East European Jewry by their own central authority. *See also* CHEREM.

COURT JEWS. Due to the segregation of Jews from their Christian and Muslim hosts in the Middle Ages, individual Jews, usually wealthy merchants, used to represent the Jewish community to the local prince or lord and often acted as an adviser to him. These were known as Court Jews. They were able to negotiate Jewish rights of settlement in areas closed to Jews, as well as raise money for the prince and enter into trade agreements. Court life was full of intrigue, and because Court Jews were identified with the court itself, they were sometimes caught up in the opposition to the prince. In the struggles that followed the prince's demise, some Court Jews were executed on trumped-up charges. This happened to **Joseph Oppenheimer**, the Court Jew to the Duke of Württemberg and one of the best-known members of this class who was eventually executed. *See also* JOSEPH JOSELMANN, OF ROSHEIM (1478–1554); ROTHSCHILD FAMILY; SASSOON FAMILY; WAHL, SAUL (1541–1617).

COVENANT. *See* BNAI B'RITH (HEBREW, "SONS OF THE COVENANT"); BRITISH ISRAELITES; BRIT IVRIT OLAMIT (HEBREW, "WORLD HEBREW COVENANT"); GENTILE (HEBREW GOY, PLURAL GOYIM, "NATION" OR "PEOPLE"); JEW (HEBREW YEHUDI); MOSES; OMAR, COVENANT OF; PROMISED LAND.

CREMATION. *See* RESURRECTION.

CROMWELL, OLIVER (1599–1658). The Jews of England were expelled by an edict of King Edward I on July 18, 1290. From that time on, there were officially no Jews in England apart from a small number of **Marranos** who had come from Spain and Portugal and practiced Judaism in secret. This changed when Oliver Cromwell became Lord Protector of England in 1653. During his time as Lord Protector, he set in motion the readmission of Jews to the British Isles.

The initiative for resettlement was taken by **Manasseh ben Israel**, a leading **Sephardi** scholar based in the Netherlands, who argued in a "Humble Address" (1655) to Cromwell that before the **Messiah** could come, Jews should inhabit even the furthest isles, under which category England came. The petition was favorably received, but Jews were not immediately allowed to live in England, although those Marranos currently in England were allowed to open their own cemetery. Within a few years, however, they were informally allowed to return.

CRUSADES. Christian wars fought from the 11th to the 13th centuries to free the **Holy Land** from Muslim control. The European Crusader mobs en route to the Holy Land massacred Jewish communities in their path on the grounds that they, too, were infidels. **Anti-Semitic** sentiment was endemic because Jews were regarded as Christ killers, and for the Crusaders, the settled communities of the Rhineland were an easy and tempting target. **Ashkenazi** Jews have continued to commemorate these Crusader massacres and associated Jewish **martyrdom** with a period of mourning, the **Omer**, between the festivals of **Passover** and **Pentecost**. In some cases, Jews were given the choice of conversion to Christianity or death, most of them choosing the latter. The Jews of England suffered mostly in the Third Crusade (1189–92), when whole Jewish communities committed suicide rather than submit to the Christian mob. This was the fate of the Jews of York in 1190, who set themselves alight in Clifford's Tower where they had taken refuge. *See also* POGROM.

– D –

DAMASCUS BLOOD LIBEL. A modern version of the medieval **blood libel** accusation made in Damascus in 1840, when local Jews were accused of murdering a Capuchin monk and his servant, ostensibly to use their blood in **Passover** rituals. Given the strong anti-Jewish feelings both of the Catholic Church and of some Muslim groups, it was assumed that the Jews must be guilty, and after torture, a confession was achieved. A delegation of European Jews, including **Moses Montefiore**, traveled to the Middle East to intercede with Mohammed Ali, the pasha of Egypt, and eventually the sultan in Constantinople. The surviving Jewish defendants were released, and a firman was issued by the sultan in Constantinople to the effect that the blood libel had no foundation.

Despite this, there were **pogroms** against Jews throughout the Middle East, and the Damascus Catholics continued to treat the dead monk as someone martyred by Jews. Jews realized that they needed to organize against the strong undercurrents of **anti-Semitism** manifest in the Damascus Affair. This eventually led to the founding of the **Alliance Israélite Universelle**. In modern times, a number of Arab writers and politicians have used the Damascus Affair as an indictment of "bloodthirsty" Jews and, by association, the "bloodthirsty" State of **Israel**.

DANCE. *See* SYNAGOGUE (HEBREW BET KNESSET); TABERNACLES (HEBREW SUKKOT).

DANIEL, BOOK OF. *See* ARAMAIC; RESURRECTION.

DAVID. King of **Israel**, from the tribe of **Judah**, who was anointed by the prophet Samuel. According to the biblical account, David was descended from Ruth the Moabitess, a member of a non-Israelite tribe looked down upon by the Hebrew tribes. The young David was a talented musician who played to soothe the nerves of then-king Saul and was also a brave warrior who, as a shepherd boy, killed the well-armed Philistine giant Goliath using only stones from a catapult.

David ruled first in **Hebron** within the territory of Judah. Eventually, he captured **Jerusalem**, making it his capital, and because this was a city of the non-Israelite Jebusites, not part of any tribal territory, it was more acceptable as a capital for all the tribes. The Ark of the Covenant was brought to Jerusalem by David, although it was his son **Solomon** who built the **Temple** there because David's warrior status made him unsuitable to erect the House of God.

According to the Jewish tradition, David was the one true king, and his descendants, the House of David, represent the authentic royal line. The Kings from any other genealogical line were therefore regarded as upstarts, as was the case of the **Hasmonean** kings who were priests from the tribe of Levi, and because of this, they were denigrated by the **Talmudic** rabbis. The daily liturgy includes prayers for the restoration of the reign of the Davidic House. There is also an aggadic teaching in the Talmud to the effect that "David king of Israel is alive and lives on," which is included in the liturgy for the sanctification of the new moon.

The **Messiah** will be a descendant of the House of David, and down the ages, Messianic claimants have tried to establish their Davidic pedigree through their paternal line. The later **Kabbalistic** tradition explains that the greatest king of Israel, and his Messianic descendant, had to come in part from a Moabite tribe despised because of its evil ways, for only thus could they overcome the power of evil itself.

The Book of Psalms, or at least much of its contents, is ascribed to David, the "sweet singer of Israel." Because he is so highly regarded as an ideal devotee of God, the Talmudic rabbis try to explain away his lapses, particularly his "adulterous" relationship with Bath Sheba, so they should not be seen as the major sins they seem at first sight. The primary Jewish symbol, the six-pointed star, known as the **Magen David**, the "Shield of David" or more commonly the "Star of David," is named after him, although there is no historical evidence for this association.

DAYAN (JUDGE). *See* SANHEDRIN.

DAYAN, MOSHE (1915–81). A distinguished **Israeli** general and political figure who learned his military skills with the special squads organized by Orde Wingate and lost an eye while fighting for the British in Syria. His black eye patch became his trademark, making him instantly recognizable on the international scene. Dayan fought in the **Haganah** during Israel's **War of Independence** as commander of the **Jerusalem** region. During the **Sinai Campaign** of 1956, he was chief of staff and minister of defense during the **Six-Day War** of 1967. Although affiliated to the Labor Party, he served as foreign minister under the right-wing government of **Menachem Begin** and was involved in the Camp David peace agreement. He ended his life in political isolation, with his many amorous affairs and his predilection for "collecting" antiquities, leaving a stain on his reputation.

DAY OF ATONEMENT (HEBREW YOM KIPPUR). A fast on the 10th day of the Hebrew month Tishri, usually falling in late September, which is the holiest day of the Jewish year. It is a day of complete rest, like the **Sabbath**. In **Temple** times, a whole series of sacrificial rituals were performed on Yom Kippur. A goat, known in English as a scapegoat, was selected by lot to be sent into the wilderness bearing the sins of **Israel**. The High Priest used to enter the Holy of Holies of the Temple bearing incense, and no one else was allowed in during the rest of the year. According to Rabbinic tradition, a rope had to be tied around the waste of the High Priest, so that should he collapse while inside, he could be drawn out by the rope. The High Priest also had to be married to be able to confess his own sins, the sins of his family, as well as the sins of all Israel, so a second wife was on standby for him should his wife die.

After the Temple was destroyed, the sacrificial system ceased, and the Temple practices were merely recited as part of the liturgy of the day. Since the **Bible** describes Yom Kippur as a time of afflicting one's soul (Leviticus 16:29), the fasting continued, as did the prohibition on leather shoes, washing for pleasure, and sexual relations.

Prior to the fast, Jews visit the graves of their parents or other close relatives. There is also a ritual that many people perform on the day before the fast called kapparot, which involves swinging a chicken around the head and declaring that this should be a substitute for oneself. There were strong objections to this ritual from some leading **rabbis**, who regarded it as of pagan origin, but it is still popular among ultra-**Orthodox** Jews. Others use money to waive around their heads and then give it to charity. It is customary for people to bathe in a ritual bath, **mikveh**, as an act of purification before the fast.

The fast day begins the evening before with the recital of Kol Nidrei, the annulment of religious vows sung to a haunting tune. People dress in white, men even wearing a shroudlike white garment called a kittel and a white prayer shawl, **tallit**, even though this is not usually worn at night. There is a theory that the annulment of vows was introduced into the liturgy for the sake of those **Marrano** Jews, who, having been forcibly converted to Christianity and sworn allegiance to the church, wished to have their vows annulled.

People light a memorial candle for the dead members of their family, and memorial prayers are recited during the day in **synagogue**. The liturgy has the theme of confession of sins, which is repeated throughout the services on the day, and of repentance, which is needed for atonement. There are various biblical readings, including the Book of Jonah, which deals with repentance. In many communities at the end of the fast, the ram's horn, shofar, is blown. *See also* CALENDAR; JEWISH RITUAL YEAR.

DAY OF JUDGEMENT. *See* MESSIAH (HEBREW MASHIACH); NEW YEAR FESTIVAL (HEBREW ROSH HASHANAH, LITERALLY "HEAD OF THE YEAR").

DEAD SEA. *See* DEAD SEA SCROLLS; ESSENES; QUMRAN.

DEAD SEA SCROLLS. A vast group of manuscripts found in caves near the Dead Sea from 1947 on. The first cache of scrolls came to light when a Bedouin shepherd stumbled on some clay pots in a cave near **Qumran**. Many of the scrolls have been published and worked on by scholars, but there is still much work that needs to be done. Some of the scrolls are the earliest **biblical** texts in existence; others represent the internal texts of the Qumran community or series of communities, including books of rules like the *Manual of Discipline*.

The scrolls, the earliest of which date before the Common Era, have provided an insight into Jewish life in **Palestine** and the emergence of Christianity itself. From the excavations at the nearby site of Khirbet Qumran, it seems that the community that lived there and to whom some, if not all, of the scrolls belonged was an **Essene**-type community, well organized with ascetic tendencies and keen on ritual purity through ritual bathing. Many questions about the nature of the sect that produced the scrolls, and about the meaning of some of the scrolls, remain unanswered. *See also* CAIRO GENIZAH.

THE DEARBORN INDEPENDENT **(NEWSPAPER).** *See* ANTI-DEFAMATION LEAGUE (ADL).

DEBORAH (BIBLICAL FIGURE). *See* WOMEN IN JUDAISM.

DECALOGUE. *See* TEN COMMANDMENTS (OR DECALOGUE).

DEGANIAH (FIRST KIBBUTZ). *See* KIBBUTZ (HEBREW, "COLLECTIVE," PLURAL KIBBUTZIM); WAR OF INDEPENDENCE (HEBREW MILCHEMET HA-AZTMAUT).

DEMBOWSKI, BISHOP NICHOLAS. *See* FRANK, JACOB (1726–91); TALMUD.

DEREKH ERETZ (HEBREW, "WAY OF THE LAND"). *See* HIRSCH, SAMSON RAPHAEL (1808–88); NEO-ORTHODOXY.

***DER JUDENSTAAT* (EARLY ZIONIST MANIFESTO).** *See* HERZL, THEODOR (1860–1904); ZIONIST CONGRESS.

DIASPORA. A word of Greek origin meaning "dispersion" and used for Jews outside of the **Land of Israel**. Because, for the last 2,000 years, most Jews have lived in the Diaspora, the major developments of Jewish life and culture have taken place there, usually under the influence of Christian and Muslim host cultures.

The beginnings of Diaspora Jewish life can be traced back to the fall of the kingdom of Judea to the **Babylonians** in 586 BCE. The Babylonian policy was to take the leadership and sections of the population into exile from their conquered homeland, thus preventing rebellion. This happened to a large number of Judeans, who were resettled in the Babylonian Empire. A similar thing had happened to the northern kingdom of **Israel** when it was conquered by the Assyrians in 722 BCE. Some of the 10 tribes who lived there were taken into Assyrian exile, but we have little knowledge of the Diaspora life of these tribes, and their captivity gave rise to the legend of the **Ten Lost Tribes**.

After the destruction of the Second **Temple** by the Romans in 70 CE and the crushing of the **Bar Kokhba** revolt in 135 CE, the center of Jewish life gradually moved from the troubled area of **Palestine** to the Babylonian Diaspora. This became the center of Jewish life for almost a millennium. It was challenged for dominance by **Sephardi** Jewish life in Muslim Spain from the 10th century and then by the **Ashkenazi** European Diaspora throughout the Middle Ages in Central and Eastern Europe.

In the 19th century, the center of gravity of Diaspora life began to move westward to Germany and France, as the **Enlightenment** freed Jews from their isolation in spiritual and physical **ghettos**, and then in the early 20th century to Great Britain and the United States. It is only since the foundation of the State of Israel in 1948, which today contains nearly half the world population of Jews, that the focus of Jewish religious and cultural life has changed, and though the Diaspora has continued, it is the **Holy Land** as much as the large communities of North America that are shaping Judaism and Jewish life. *See also* ZIONISM.

DIETARY LAWS. Among the distinctive features of Jewish life are a series of dietary laws that determine what is **kosher** (the **Ashkenazi** pronunciation of the **Hebrew** word *kasher* meaning "fit," or suitable to eat) and what is not kosher. Like much of the **halakhah**, these laws go back to prescriptions in the **Bible** that have been developed and expanded down the ages. The main dietary laws affect the eating of meat and fish.

Thus in Deuteronomy, chapter 14, kosher animals are defined as those that chew the cud and have a cloven hoof. This includes cattle, sheep, goats, and deer but excludes even animals having only one of these characteristics, such as the pig, which has a cloven hoof but does not chew the cud, or the camel, which chews the cud but does not have a cloven hoof. Only the milk of kosher animals is itself kosher.

Before kosher animals can be eaten, they must be slaughtered by a trained slaughterer, known as a shochet, who will cut their neck and windpipe with a knife. The slaughtered animal has to be examined to ensure that it is not diseased before it is certified as kosher. Because Jews are prohibited from eating blood, the meat is then soaked, salted with coarse salt, and left on a draining board to remove any loose blood. After that, it is rinsed to remove the salt. Another method of removing the blood is by grilling the lightly salted meat over an open flame. The latter method is always used for liver, which has too much blood to remove by the washing method.

The Pentateuch lists 24 species of birds that are not kosher. These are mostly birds of prey, but because not all of these types of birds can be identified today, the only birds that are eaten as kosher are those that have been eaten by one or another Jewish community in the past. Birds also need ritual slaughter and removal of the blood as with quadrupeds. The eggs of a kosher bird are themselves kosher as long as they are not fertilized. Jews will examine eggs after they are cracked to see if there are any blood specks attached to the yoke, which would render them not kosher.

Kosher fish are defined as sea creatures having fins and scales. This excludes all types of shellfish, which are not kosher, and also fish not having removable scales, as well as such sea mammals as whales. Unlike animals and birds, fish do not have to be ritually slaughtered nor is there any need to remove their blood.

There is also a set of prohibitions on cooking or eating meat and milk together, based on the Rabbinic understanding of the thrice-repeated prohibition on not cooking a kid in its mother's milk (Exodus 23:19, 34:26, and Deuteronomy 14:21). **Orthodox** Jews wait several hours after eating meat before having cheese or milk dishes to strictly fulfill this commandment.

Some Jews will keep these laws stringently, as well as those prohibiting the eating of insects—so vegetables have to be thoroughly washed—and the ingestion of **Gentile** wine or cooked foods. Many Jews, however, only keep the dietary laws in part, for instance merely avoiding shellfish or pork. Reform Jews may consider all kosher laws as antiquated and not relevant to contemporary religion.

In the State of **Israel**, the official organs of the state, such as army bases, are committed to maintaining kosher food regulations. Secular Israeli Jews do not wish to be bound by these laws, and so outside of religious areas in Israel, it is possible to buy a variety of non-kosher products. Occasionally, when pork is sold in butcher shops, it is euphemistically described as "white meat."

The dietary laws have had a profound effect on Jewish identity because they have forced Jews to socialize among themselves. Being unable to share the food of outsiders has acted as a symbolic barrier, not only between Jews and Gentiles, but even between different subgroups of Jews on the basis of the community that eats together stays together. Thus ultra-Orthodox Jews may not rely on the kosher standards of other religious Jews, or Ashkenazi and **Sephardi** Jews may apply some of the dietary laws differently. The ritual slaughter practiced by **Chasidic** Jews was declared not kosher at one time, though today the objections of the **Mitnaggedic** opponents of Chasidism are muted. *See also* RABBI (HEBREW, "MY MASTER").

DISPERSION. *See* DIASPORA.

DISPUTATIONS. Christianity saw itself as a missionary religion, so it regarded as an affront the refusal of "stiff-necked" Jews who lived among Christians to accept the Christian religion. As a means of converting Jews to the "true" faith in the Middle Ages, public disputations were arranged by the Christian authorities, and Jews were forced to attend. The general format for these disputations was for a number of Christian scholars, often led by a Jewish apostate, to put the case for Christian teaching that Jesus was the **Messiah** and the son of God. They often argued that Jewish literature, particularly the **Talmud**, actually supported Christian teaching, but it was willfully misinterpreted by Jews. Local **rabbis** were called upon to defend their faith but sometimes had to be careful not to attack Christianity, the host religion, too strongly. The tradition of disputations began with that of Paris in 1240, which was followed by the burning of copies of the Talmud. They continued in Europe for several hundred years. *See also* BARCELONA, DISPUTATION OF; FRANK, JACOB (1726–91).

DISRAELI, BENJAMIN (1804–81). British prime minister of Jewish origin and novelist. Disraeli was converted to Christianity at the age of 13, when his father, Isaac, left the **Sephardi** congregation in London over a trivial matter and had his children baptized. In 1837, Disraeli was elected to Parliament, and after serving in various cabinet roles, he became Tory prime minister for the first time in 1868. He served in this role once again from 1874; during this second period, he acquired shares in the Suez Canal with the support of the **Rothschilds**. He was also made Earl of Beaconsfield by Queen Victoria, with whom he had established a close relationship. Disraeli was proud of his Jewish origins, and a number of his novels contain Jewish themes. Some, like *Alroy*, are indeed centered around Jewish characters. In 1847, he supported Lionel de Rothschild's attempt to enter Parliament without taking a Christian oath. Disraeli was criticized for his foreign policy, which took into consideration the position of the Jews in Ottoman Turkey and Russia. Indeed, at the Congress of Berlin in 1878, he supported the clause demanding equal rights for Jews in the Balkans.

DOENMEH. When the **Messianic** figure **Shabbetai Tzvi** was forced to convert to Islam in 1666, a small number of his Turkish–Jewish followers also apostatized. Like their master, they kept their Messianic Jewish beliefs in secret while outwardly practicing Islam. They were known as Doenmeh, a Turkish word meaning "converts," and lived mostly in Salonika. Although their number may have been as high as 15,000 in the early years of the 20th century, they were split into three main groups. After the exchange of population between Turkey and Greece in 1924, most of the Doenmeh moved to Istanbul, though only one of the three groups, the most radical one at that, actually survived; members of the other two were **assimilated** into wider Turkish society. It is rumored that some of the Doenmeh, having lived double lives as Muslims, played leading roles in the Young Turk Movement, which brought secularism into the heart of Islamic Turkey. *See also* NATHAN OF GAZA (1643–80).

DREIDL (YIDDISH, "SPINNING TOP"). *See* CHANUKAH.

DRESS. *See* ENLIGHTENMENT (HEBREW HASKALAH); HEAD COVERING; HIRSCH, SAMSON RAPHAEL (1808–88); NETUREI KARTA (ARAMAIC, "GUARDIANS OF THE CITY"); NEW YEAR FESTIVAL (HEBREW ROSH HASHANAH, LITERALLY "HEAD OF THE YEAR"); OATH MORE JUDAICO; OMAR, COVENANT OF; PURIM; TALLIT (ARAMAIC, "PRAYER SHAWL"); TZADDIK (HEBREW, "RIGHTEOUS ONE," PLURAL TZADDIKIM).

DREYFUS, ALFRED (1859–1935). *See* DREYFUS CASE.

DREYFUS CASE. Alfred Dreyfus (1859–1935) was a captain in the French army who was falsely accused of spying for Germany. The evidence against Dreyfus was very weak, but he was a Jew and therefore suspect in the eyes of the French intelligence service. He was sentenced to Devil's Island after a court martial. Dreyfus was retried again after an independent investigation by George Picquart, the new head of the intelligence service, raised serious doubts about his guilt. There was also a public outcry by some French intellectuals maintaining Dreyfus's innocence, including the novelist Emile Zola, who published a newspaper article entitled "J'accuse!" Nevertheless, Dreyfus was still found guilty and was only eventually pardoned and exonerated in 1906.

The overt **anti-Semitism** of the Dreyfus Case among army officers, politicians, and the anti-Dreyfus mobs had a profound effect on the wider Jewish community. It brought home the strength of anti-

Jewish feeling even in a country as **enlightened** as France. **Theodor Herzl**, who covered the Dreyfus case as a journalist, is reputed to have formulated his ideas about **Zionism** and the need for a Jewish state from his experience.

DRUZE. *See* ISRAEL; ISRAEL DEFENSE FORCE. (IDF)

– E –

EASTER. *See* OMER (HEBREW, "SHEAF" OF BARLEY); SHTETL.

ECKSTEIN, ZEV. *See* KASZTNER, RUDOLF (1906–57).

EDICT OF EXPULSION (SPAIN). *See* INQUISITION.

EDWARD I, KING. *See* CROMWELL, OLIVER (1599–1658).

EFIKOMEN (RITUAL FOOD). *See* PASSOVER (HEBREW PE-SACH).

EICHMANN, ADOLPH (1906–62). Nazi officer of Austrian origin in charge of the policy of Jewish extermination. Eichmann was a supposed expert on Jewish matters, knowing some **Yiddish** and **Hebrew**, and in 1941 became the head of the **Gestapo** section responsible for Jewish affairs, a position that he retained until the end of World War II. He was behind the efficient policy of deportation and extermination, particularly after the Wannsee Conference of 1942, even when the German war effort needed the resources that were devoted to the **Final Solution**. Having escaped to South America after the defeat of Germany, he was abducted from Argentina in 1960 by **Israeli** secret service agents and brought to trial in Israel. **David Ben Gurion**, the Israeli prime minister, wanted a show trial to bring home to Israeli youth the horrors of the **Holocaust**. In 1962, having been found guilty, Eichmann was hanged in Israel. *See also* ARENDT, HANNAH (1906–75); BRAND, JOEL (1906–64); KASZTNER, RUDOLF (1906–57); TZADDIK (HEBREW, "RIGHTEOUS ONE," PLURAL TZADDIKIM).

EICHMANN IN JERUSALEM **(BOOK).** *See* ARENDT, HANNAH (1906–75).

EL AL (AIRLINE). *See* SABBATH (HEBREW SHABBAT).

ELDAD HA-DANI (9TH CENTURY). Mysterious figure who claimed to be from the tribe of Dan, one of the **Ten Lost Tribes**, and was thus known as "ha-Dani," the Danite. Eldad is the source of many of the legends of these tribes, whom he claimed had their own independent kingdom in East Africa. Some of them did not make contact with other Jews because they lived beyond the river **Sambatyon**, a river that was impassable on weekdays and quiescent only on the **Sabbath** when Jews could not travel. Eldad reported various ritual practices of the Lost Tribes to the Jews of **Babylon**, North Africa, and Spain when he traveled among them, but though some scholars dismissed his traveler's tales as fiction or accused him of being a **Karaite**, he was referred to as a reliable source by others. Certainly, his account of Jewish independent states was of great comfort to Jews living under **anti-Semitic** persecution. *See also* REUVENI, DAVID (15TH–16TH CENTURIES).

ELIJAH (PROPHET). *See* KABBALAH; LURIA, ISAAC (1534–72).

ELIJAH OF VILNA (1720–97). Known as the Vilna Gaon, Elijah was the leading sage of East European Jewry in the premodern period. Although a number of young men produced by the **Talmudic** education system showed aspects of genius, Elijah was quite exceptional even among them. According to legend, at the age of eight he had already outgrown his teachers. He spent his life in devoted study of the Talmud and **Kabbalistic** mysticism, reputedly only sleeping two hours a night. Although he held no official position in the Vilna community, he was highly respected as the ideal Rabbinic sage, and his views were sought on important matters. It was Elijah who led the opposition to the nascent **Chasidic Movement**, signing **cherem** documents of excommunication against them on the suspicion that they were heretical and followers of **Shabbetai Tzvi**. The **Mitnaggedic Movement** grew up around his followers, and the Lithuanian **yeshivah** education system, the model for all advanced rabbinic studies, was founded by Elijah's main disciple, **Chaim of Volozhin**.

ELUL (MONTH). *See* CALENDAR.

EMANATION. *See* KABBALAH.

EMANCIPATION. In the 18th century, the spirit of the **Enlightenment** influenced Jewish communities in Europe, and many Jews wished to become emancipated and accepted as full citizens of their host countries. **Napoleon Bonaparte**, in his attempt to unify and modernize French society, insisted that a condition of granting Jews equal rights was a reform of their attitude of exclusiveness. He called together a **Sanhedrin** of clerical and lay leaders to tackle these issues, and this led to granting Jews full civil rights in France in 1831.

There was considerable opposition from Christians to accepting Jews as equals and some resistance among **Orthodox** Jews to emancipation, which they considered a threat to Jewish religion. Indeed, at least one **Chasidic** leader, Shneur Zalman of Liadi, founder of Lubavitch Chasidism, encouraged his followers to spy for the czar during Napoleon's invasion of Russia. This was not out of patriotism, because Jews were severely discriminated against in Czarist Russia, but out of fear of the consequences of Napoleon's policy of emancipation. The approach to emancipation in Germany was driven by the fall of the **ghetto** walls and the exposure to German culture, leading to the granting of civil rights in 1848. Eventually, Jews were emancipated in all European countries. *See also* ASSIMILATION.

ENLIGHTENMENT (HEBREW HASKALAH). The modernist movement within Judaism, which began in the late 18th century, took its inspiration from the European Enlightenment. Haskalah emphasized rationality and the adoption of secular knowledge, which conflicted with the attitudes of traditional Judaism. Its followers were known as maskilim ("enlightened ones"), and in many communities clashes took place between traditionalists and maskilim.

Ultimately, **Reform Judaism**, **Conservative Judaism**, **Neo-Orthodoxy**, and **Zionism** were the progeny of the Haskalah, while its traditional opponents, especially **Chasidism** and the ultra-**Orthodox** in Eastern Europe, froze those aspects of Judaism that were threatened by modernity, including preserving the dress worn in Eastern Europe in the late 18th and early 19th centuries as normative Jewish dress. *See also* MENDELSSOHN, MOSES; WOMEN IN JUDAISM.

ENTEBBE. A rescue operation undertaken by the **Israel** Air Force on 4 July 1976 to release Israeli passengers hijacked by **Palestinian** terrorists while on an Air France plane and taken to Entebbe Airport in Uganda. Although the distance from Israel to Uganda was approximately 2,500 miles, the daring operation was a success. There was only one casualty among the Israeli troops, that of the commander of the raid, Lt. Colonel Yoni Netanyahu, brother of Binyamin Netanyahu, the future prime minister of Israel, as well as the deaths of two hostages. One hostage was later killed by Ugandan troops while in hospital. Although criticized for infringing on Ugandan sovereignty, the rescue operation was also highly praised for its planning and implementation. *See also* ISRAEL DEFENSE FORCE (IDF); PERES, SHIMON (1923–).

EPHRAIM (TRIBE). *See* ISRAEL; SAMARITANS.

ERETZ YISRAEL (HEBREW, "LAND OF ISRAEL"). *See* IS-RAEL; LAND OF ISRAEL (HEBREW ERETZ YISRAEL).

ESHKOL, LEVI. *See* MEIR, GOLDA (ORIGINALLY MYERSON, 1898–1978).

ESSENES. A religious community that flourished in **Palestine**, particularly around the Dead Sea, for several centuries until just after the destruction of the **Temple** in **Jerusalem** in 70 CE. According to contemporary reports, especially that of the Jewish historian **Josephus Flavius**, the Essenes were an ascetic community who lived a semimonastic life of ritual and spiritual purity, sharing everything in common. These were mostly communities of men, though evidence from the **Qumran** Community associated with the **Dead Sea Scrolls** seems to indicate the presence of **women**. It is not clear whether the beliefs of the Essenes were the same as those of the Qumran settlers, or whether the latter were merely an independent Essene-like sect. *See also* MIKVEH; PHARISEES.

ESTHER, BOOK OF. *See* HAMAN; JEWISH RITUAL YEAR; PROSELYTES (HEBREW GERIM, SINGULAR GER); PURIM.

ESTHER, FAST OF. *See* JEWISH RITUAL YEAR.

ESTHER, QUEEN (BIBLICAL FIGURE). *See* HAMAN; JEWISH RITUAL YEAR; PURIM; WOMEN IN JUDAISM.

ETHIOPIA. Formerly known as Abyssinia, a country in northeast Africa where most of the population is Monophysite Christian aligned with the Coptic Church of Egypt. According to Ethiopian legend, the royal line of Ethiopian kings comes from a son born of the union of King **Solomon** and the Queen of Sheba when she visited the wise **Hebrew** king from her home in Ethiopia (I Kings 10). There has certainly been Hebraic influence on Ethiopian culture, and although the origin of the **Falashas**—the black Jews of Ethiopia—is somewhat obscure, there are a number of biblical references to Ethiopia. There are also Semitic elements in its language and religious practices. Male circumcision is practiced among Ethiopian Christians, and Saturday, the Jewish **Sabbath**, is also regarded as a Sabbath day. There is even an Ethiopian legend that the holy Ark of the Covenant, which was housed in the **Temple** in **Jerusalem**, was taken secretly to Ethiopia.

ETROG (CITRUS FRUIT). *See* TABERNACLES (HEBREW SUKKOT).

EUCHARIST. *See* HOST DESECRATION.

EVE (BIBLICAL FIGURE). *See* HEBRON.

EXCOMMUNICATION. *See* CHEREM.

EXILARCH (ARAMAIC RESH GALUTA, "HEAD OF THE EXILE"). The leader of **Babylonian** Jewry. The exilarch was a descendant of the **Davidic** line and was recognized by the government as well as by the Jewish community throughout the Babylonian Empire and the **Diaspora**. There are no reliable data as to when the institution began, though there is some evidence that its origins go back to the role assigned to the exiled king of **Judah**, as recorded in the Book of Kings (II Kings 25:27–30). It is possible that the formal institution of an exilarch gradually emerged from a less-formal attitude toward Babylonian Jewish leadership.

As life in the **Holy Land** deteriorated after the revolts against Rome were crushed and the **Temple** was destroyed, a large part of the authority attaching to the leader of **Palestinian** Jewry, the Nasi, shifted to the exilarch. Some exilarchs were scholars, and their leadership was both religious and social. Others were not respected for their learning but were regarded essentially as political leaders. Inevitably, there were disputes between the exilarch and the **rabbis** of Babylonia, particularly with the geonim, the heads of the **yeshivah** academies.

The most bitter leadership disputes were between candidates for succession to the position of exilarch. The position was sought after because with it came the power to appoint judges, raise taxes, inflict corporal punishment, and live in luxury close to the secular powers. In the 8th century, a major schism occurred when **Anan ben David** was passed over for the position of exilarch in favor of his younger brother. Anan broke away from the Rabbinic establishment and eventually became the founding father of the **Karaite** Movement. *See also* JUDAH THE NASI.

EXILE (HEBREW GALUT). The experience of exile is a central theme of Jewish identity and the Jewish self-image. The suffering of the **Israelite** slaves in Egypt, followed by the **Exodus** and journey to the **Promised Land**, became a paradigm of all future exile and redemption. Thus the **Babylonian** captivity, after the Babylonians conquered the Kingdom of **Judah** in 586 BCE, was followed by the return of the exiles and the building of the Second **Temple** in **Jerusalem**. Jews were able to survive their long exile after the destruction of the Jewish life in **Palestine** as a consequence of the revolts against Rome of 67–70 CE and 132–35 CE because they awaited **Messianic** redemption and the ingathering of the exiles from the **Diaspora**. The experience of exile was even interpreted by Jewish mystics in the **Kabbalah** as a reflection of the exile of God Himself, so that history was given a theological dimension. **Zionism** meant the negation of exile by the return of the Jewish people to their homeland. *See also* LURIA, ISAAC (1534–72).

EXODUS. The biblical story of the redemption of the **Israelites** from Egyptian slavery and their journey through the Sinai Desert to the **Promised Land** is known as the Exodus. It is celebrated by Jews through ritual, drama, and literature, particularly during the **Passover**, and is a paradigm of God's role in history. **Moses**, through whose agency the Exodus came about, is credited with uniting the various tribes of Semites into one people, **Israel**, sharing a common destiny. *See also* TEN COMMANDMENTS (OR DECALOGUE).

EZRA, BOOK OF. *See* ARAMAIC.

– F –

FAITLOVITCH, JACQUES. *See* FALASHAS (ALSO KNOWN AS BETA ISRAEL).

FALASHAS (ALSO KNOWN AS BETA ISRAEL). The black Jews of **Ethiopia** whose religion is more **Bible**-based than that of the majority of their coreligionists. The origin of the Falashas is obscure, some scholars maintaining that they were native Ethiopians who had **assimilated** Jewish elements from Yemenite Jews who had settled among them. According to the Falashas' own traditions, the black Jews are the descendants of the entourage of Hebrews who returned with the Queen of Sheba after she visited King **Solomon**. There was virtually no contact between Falasha Jews and the rest of **Diaspora** Jewry until modern times, although reports of their existence were provided by **Eldad Ha-Dani** in the 9th century and by various medieval travelers. There is also some evidence indicating that **David Reuveni** in the 16th century was actually a Falasha.

Since the 16th century, a number of leading **rabbis** in the Diaspora, and later on in **Israel**, have recognized the Falashas as **Jews** and members of the tribe of Dan, one of the **Ten Lost Tribes**. The first to do so was a leading **Sephardi** rabbi and head of the Jewish community in Cairo, David Ibn Abi Zimra (1479–1573), who recognized that Falasha religion lacked many of the Rabbinic developments of the postbiblical era but still permitted intermarriage with them as long as they were willing to accept the Rabbinic interpretation of Judaism.

The **Alliance Israélite Universelle** sent an emissary, Joseph Halévy (1827–1917), to Ethiopia in 1868 to report on the condition of the Falashas. Halévy, together with his pupil Jacques Faitlovitch (1881–1955), began a process of education among the Falashas of Ethiopia. Faitlovitch brought back two Falasha students to be educated in Europe so they could be sent back as teachers to Ethiopia and eventually set up schools in some of the areas of Falasha settlement.

The majority of the Falashas has either made their own way to Israel, often undergoing great suffering en route, or has been brought on **aliyah** by the **Jewish Agency.** The Israeli government has also airlifted many of the one-time Ethiopian black Jews, who were converted to Christianity by missionaries in the 19th century, to Israel, but this has been much more controversial. The integration of both groups of Falashas into Jewish society in Israel has been a slow and difficult process.

The Israeli chief rabbinate, while accepting the main body of Falashas as Jews, has insisted that they should undergo a ceremony of renewal of the Jewish Covenant, involving a ritual purification bath in a **mikveh** and a symbolic removal of a drop of blood from the place of circumcision. This has been widely resented by Falashas, who view it as an unnecessary conversion to Judaism for people who are already Jews. They also want their own traditional priests to receive recognition on a par with that granted to rabbis.

Other factors that have complicated their full acceptance, even by secular Israeli society, are the more primitive lifestyles of the Falashas who have come from traditional villages to a technological, sophisticated world almost overnight. There are also issues of the prevalence of HIV and AIDS in those parts of Africa inhabited by Falashas and the fear among Israelis that many Falashas may already have been infected before they came to Israel.

FEDAYEEN (TERRORIST GROUPS). *See* SINAI CAMPAIGN.

FEISAL, EMIR. *See* WEIZMANN, CHAIM (1874–1952).

FERDINAND, KING. *See* INQUISITION; SEPHARDIM; TORQUEMADA, TOMAS DE (1420–98).

FESTIVALS. *See* CALENDAR; CHANUKAH; CRUSADES; ISRAEL INDEPENDENCE DAY (HEBREW YOM HA-ATZMAUT); JEWISH RITUAL YEAR; LAG B'OMER; NEW YEAR FESTIVAL (HEBREW ROSH HASHANAH, LITERALLY "HEAD OF THE YEAR"); PASSOVER (HEBREW PESACH); PENTECOST (HEBREW SHAVUOT); PURIM; TABERNACLES (HEBREW SUKKOT); TEMPLE (HEBREW BET HA-MIKDASH); TZADDIK (HEBREW, "RIGHTEOUS ONE," PLURAL TZADDIKIM).

FINAL SOLUTION. The name given to the Nazi policy of exterminating the Jews, in other words the Final Solution of the Jewish Problem. In the period leading up to the Wannsee Conference of 1942, various methods were used for ridding Nazi-controlled areas of their Jews. Forced emigration was one option, but there were no countries willing to take large numbers of Jewish refugees. The Wannsee Conference empowered **Adolph Eichmann** to implement the murder of the Jews, initially by such methods as mass shooting, but eventually by the more efficient method of mass gassing in death camps. It is estimated that 6 million Jews were massacred by the Nazis and their Polish, Ukrainian, Lithuanian, and other allies in the **Holocaust**. *See also* ANTI-SEMITISM; AUSCHWITZ; BERGEN-BELSEN; BRAND, JOEL (1906–64); BUCHENWALD; FRANK, ANNE (1929–45); GESTAPO (GEHEIME STAATS-POLIZEI); GHETTO; HITLER, ADOLPH (1889–1945); HOLOCAUST REMEMBRANCE DAY (HEBREW YOM HASHOAH); JUDENREIN (GERMAN, "FREE OF JEWS"); KASZTNER, RUDOLF (1906–57); KORCZAK, JANUSZ (PSEUDONYM OF HENRYK GOLDSZMIDT, 187–1942); KRISTALLNACHT (GERMAN, "NIGHT OF BROKEN GLASS"); MARTYRDOM (HEBREW KIDDUSH HASHEM, "SANCTIFICATION OF (GOD'S) NAME"); POGROM; WARSAW GHETTO UPRISING; YAD VASHEM.

FOOD. *See* BNAI B'RITH (HEBREW, "SONS OF THE COVENANT"); CHANUKAH; CHEREM; DAY OF ATONEMENT (HEBREW YOM KIPPUR); DIETARY LAWS; GENTILE (HEBREW GOY, PLURAL GOYIM, "NATION" OR "PEOPLE"); JOSEPH; KOSHER ("FIT FOOD," HEBREW KASHER, KASHRUT); MITNAGGEDIC MOVEMENT (HEBREW, "OPPONENTS"); MIZRACHI (ABBREVIATION OF MERCAZ RUCHANI, "SPIRITUAL CENTER"); NEW YEAR FESTIVAL (HEBREW ROSH HASHANAH, LITERALLY "HEAD OF THE YEAR"); NINTH OF AV, FAST OF (HEBREW TISHA B'AV); PASSOVER (HEBREW PESACH); PENTECOST (HEBREW SHAVUOT); PURIM; RABBI (HEBREW, "MY MASTER"); SALANTER, ISRAEL (1810–83); SEVENTEENTH OF TAMMUZ; SHTETL; SYNAGOGUE (HEBREW BET KNESSET).

FORD, HENRY. *See* ANTI-DEFAMATION LEAGUE (ADL).

FRANK, ANNE (1929–45). Young German Jewish girl who kept a diary of the two years she, her family, and some other Jews spent in hiding in Amsterdam, only to be eventually betrayed to the **Gestapo** by an unknown Dutch acquaintance and deported to **Auschwitz** and subsequently to **Bergen-Belsen**, where she died. Her diary, which was rescued by her father after the war and published in Dutch, has been translated into many languages, dramatized, and made into films. It has become a poignant symbol of the **Holocaust** because it puts a human face on what is often described as an inhuman hell. *See also* FINAL SOLUTION.

FRANK, JACOB (1726–91). Polish Jewish sectarian and follower of **Shabbetai Tzvi**. Frank believed that his soul was a reincarnation of the soul of Shabbetai Tzvi, and he was destined for greatness. He and his followers were persecuted by the Jewish community in Poland because of their anti-nomianism and were put in **cherem**. They sought the protection of the Catholic Church, claiming they had much in common with Christianity. The local bishop, Nicholas Dembowski, ordered a **disputation** between the Frankists and the Rabbanites in 1757 at the Polish town of Kamieniec, following which many copies of the **Talmud** were burned. The Frankists outwardly converted to Catholicism in a mass baptism in 1759 in order to protect themselves while privately still subscribing to a form of **Zohar**-inspired Messianic Judaism, with Jacob Frank as the **Messiah**. *See also* CHASIDIC MOVEMENT (ALSO HASIDIC); KABBALAH; MESSIANIC MOVEMENTS; ORAL TORAH; TZADDIK (HEBREW, "RIGHTEOUS ONE," PLURAL TZADDIKIM).

– G –

GABBAI (WARDEN). *See* SYNAGOGUE (HEBREW BET KNESSET).

GALUT. *See* EXILE (HEBREW GALUT).

GAMBLING. *See* CHANUKAH.

GEDALIAH (GOVERNOR OF JUDEA). *See* JEWISH RITUAL YEAR.

GEDALIAH, FAST OF. *See* JEWISH RITUAL YEAR.

GEHEIME STAATS-POLIZEI. *See* GESTAPO (GEHEIME STAATS-POLIZEI).

GEIGER, ABRAHAM. *See* HIRSCH, SAMSON RAPHAEL (1808–88).

GENIZAH (HEBREW, "HIDDEN REPOSITORY"). A storeroom for old holy texts, often attached to a **synagogue**, that may act as a temporary repository for these texts until they are eventually buried. Objects were stored in a genizah because texts bearing the name of God could not be destroyed and had either to be stored away or buried. This was extended to cover any religious text and even non-specifically religious texts written in **Hebrew** characters. A genizah was also used for storing heretical or religiously problematic texts that needed to be taken out of circulation. The best known genizah is the **Cairo Genizah**, but the store of texts known as the **Dead Sea Scrolls** were also presumably a genizah because Jews were known to hide away holy texts when undergoing persecution.

GENTILE (HEBREW GOY, PLURAL GOYIM, "NATION" OR "PEOPLE"). From biblical times, a distinction is made between **Jews** and Gentiles, whether the Jews were known as Hebrews or **Israelites**. The origins of these distinctions were the differentiation between the pagan beliefs of the nations of the world and the monotheism of the descendants of **Abraham**, with whom God had established His Covenant.

Over time, this distinction widened as the sense of Jewish identity became stronger and more structured and as Judaism had to contend with missionary religions like Christianity and Islam. Judaism needed to draw the boundaries of Jewish identity more sharply by erecting barriers not merely against idolatrous paganism, but also against the remnants of idolatry that Jews found in Christianity. These barriers were even meant to distinguish Jewish belief from the monotheism of Islam.

This led **Moses Maimonides** to formulate Thirteen Principles of Jewish faith that differentiate Jews from Gentiles and without which someone could not be considered a faithful child of the Covenant. They involve the belief in the existence and unity of a perfect, incorporeal God, who is eternal and the only object of human worship. God inspires prophets, of whom **Moses** was the greatest. God's **Torah**, in the form of the Pentateuch, was given to Moses, and it cannot be changed. God is aware of man's deeds and rewards and punishes those who keep or disregard his commandments. At the end of days, He will send the **Messiah**, and there will be the **resurrection** of the dead.

Clearly, some of these principles are a polemic against Christian and Islamic teachings. According to Maimonides, any Jew who denies even one of these principles is a Jewish heretic. Other thinkers strongly criticized Maimonides' list and proposed alternatives. Nevertheless, the Thirteen Principles made their way into the **synagogue** service in the form of liturgical hymns. Those who objected to the rather philosophical dimension of Maimonides' principles, such as members of the **Chasidic Movement**, simply omit these hymns from their prayer books.

The prevention of intermarriage between Jews and Gentiles was one of the main concerns of the **halakhah**, originally because wives or husbands of another religion would lead Jews astray, and even spouses who subscribed to monotheism would be a problem unless they converted to Judaism as **proselytes**. Judaism introduced a series of rituals to preserve the barriers between Jews and Gentiles and thus discourage such intermarriages. It developed certain food laws, such as the ban on Gentile wine and Gentile-cooked food, to prevent oversocializing. *See also* DIETARY LAWS; KOSHER ("FIT FOOD," HEBREW KASHER, KASHRUT); YAD VASHEM.

GEONIM (BABYLONIAN AUTHORITIES). *See* EXILARCH (HEBREW RESH GALUTA, "HEAD OF THE EXILE").

GERIM (HEBREW, "CONVERTS," SINGULAR GER). *See* PROSELYTES (HEBREW GERIM, SINGULAR GER).

GESTAPO (GEHEIME STAATS-POLIZEI). Nazi secret police organization with a principal task of dealing with Jews and ultimately implementing the **Final Solution**. Members of the Gestapo participated in the murder squads charged with the mass shooting of Jews and others. The herding of large numbers of Jews into **ghettos**, from which they could be deported to concentration camps for slave labor or to death camps for extermination, was also the direct responsibility of the Gestapo. The extensive powers of the Gestapo over the confiscation of property, and particularly over life and death, made them the most feared element within the Nazi state apparatus. *See also* AUSCHWITZ; EICHMANN, ADOLPH (1906–62); FINAL SOLUTION; HOLOCAUST.

GHETTO. Originally, an area reserved for Jews, usually with the proviso that they could not live outside its boundaries or the walls that surrounded it. The first such official ghetto was erected in Venice in 1516, when Jews were forced to live in a walled area near an iron foundry, which is what the word *ghetto* means. Subsequently, any such restricted quarter for Jews was referred to as a ghetto, whether it existed to protect Jews from **pogroms** and marauding mobs or to prevent Jews open access to their host societies. The **Enlightenment** meant the emergence of Jews into European society and the fall of the ghetto walls. In modern times, the Nazis confined Jews to urban ghettos in most of the big towns in Europe conquered by them prior to their deportation to concentration camps or to death camps. *See also* ANTI-SEMITISM; WARSAW GHETTO UPRISING.

GILGUL (TRANSMIGRATION OF SOULS). *See* FRANK, JACOB (1726–91); KABBALAH; ZOHAR.

GINSBERG, ASHER HIRSCH. *See* ACHAD HA-AM (HEBREW, "ONE OF THE PEOPLE").

GOLDEN CALF. *See* TEN COMMANDMENTS (OR DECALOGUE).

GOLDMANN, NAHUM. *See* CONFERENCE ON JEWISH MATERIAL CLAIMS AGAINST GERMANY.

GOLDSTEIN, BARUCH. *See* HEBRON.

GOLDSZMIDT, HENRYK. *See* KORCZAK, JANUSZ (PSEUDONYM OF HENRYK GOLDSZMIDT, 1878–1942).

GOLIATH (PHILISTINE GIANT). *See* DAVID.

GOY. *See* GENTILE (HEBREW GOY, PLURAL GOYIM, "NATION" OR "PEOPLE").

GRAETZ, HEINRICH (1817–91). German Jewish historian. Graetz received his doctorate for a thesis on "Judaism and Gnosticism" and for a time studied Judaica with **Samson Raphael Hirsch**, one of Germany's leading **Orthodox rabbis**. He spent most of his life lecturing and writing about the history of the Jews as a deeply committed Jew influenced by the rational ideas of the **Enlightenment**. In his magnum opus, the 11-volume *History of the Jews*, he presented the whole of Jewish history until the mid–19th century, emphasizing the ethical monotheism that characterized Jewish life down the ages in contrast to what he regarded as the often cruel history of Christianity.

GREGORY IX, POPE. *See* INQUISITION.

GRUENWALD, MALKIEL. *See* KASZTNER, RUDOLF (1906–57).

GRYNSZPAN, HERSCHEL (1921-?). Young Jewish assassin of Ernst von Rath, the third secretary of the German embassy in Paris, on November 7, 1938. Von Rath died on November 9, and the Nazi government used the killing as a pretext for anti-Jewish measures in Germany, including the destruction of hundreds of **synagogues**, known as the infamous **Kristallnacht** (the "Night of Broken Glass," November 9–10). Grynszpan was eventually captured by the Germans, but rather than being put on trial, he simply disappeared and is assumed to have been killed by the **Gestapo**, although there is speculation that he survived. The accepted view, expressed by Grynszpan himself on his arrest by French police, is that he was angry at the German deportation of Jews of Polish origin, including his parents, in 1938. There is some evidence, however, that von Rath had actually been Grynszpan's homosexual lover and that the assassination was a crime of passion rather than a political act.

GUARDIANS OF THE CITY. *See* NETUREI KARTA (ARAMAIC, "GUARDIANS OF THE CITY").

***GUIDE FOR THE PERPLEXED* (PHILOSOPHICAL WORK).** *See* MAIMONIDES, MOSES (1135–1204).

GYPSIES. *See* AUSCHWITZ; BABI YAR; HOLOCAUST.

– H –

HA-ARI. *See* LURIA, ISAAC (1534–72).

HAGANAH (HEBREW, "DEFENSE"). The main military organization of **Palestinian** Jews until the establishment of the **Israeli** army in 1948. The Haganah was founded during the British Mandate period because the British were incapable of preventing Arab attacks on Jewish settlements. It came into its own during the Arab riots of 1929 and 1936, when it saved some areas from the worst excesses of Arab massacres. The Haganah was not primarily anti-British. After World War II, however, when the British refused to allow refugees from **Holocaust** Europe into Palestine, it took a more militant anti-British stance. During the **War of Independence**, the Haganah was indispensable in preventing Israel from being overrun by Arab forces and eventually became the main part of the new Israeli army, the **Israel Defense Force**. *See also* ALLON, YIGAL (1918–80); DAYAN, MOSHE (1915–81); YADIN, YIGAL (1917–84).

HAGGADAH (RITUAL TEXT). *See* PASSOVER (HEBREW PESACH).

HAIDAMACKS. Ukrainian peasant bands, often led by priests, that terrorized Jewish communities in Polish-controlled Ukraine during the 18th century. The relatively affluent Jews were an easy target for the impoverished Haidamacks, who murdered and pillaged often with little interference from the local people. Christian **anti-Semitism** enabled the priests to stir up the mobs, who not only attacked Jewish merchants but sometimes massacred whole towns, including women and children. This happened in the fortified city of Uman, where the Polish authorities gave in to the Haidamacks, vainly hoping to be spared, and the whole Jewish community was slaughtered, most while seeking refuge in the **synagogue**. Eventually, Polish and Russian troops crushed the Haidamack rebellion. *See also* CHMIELNICKI MASSACRES; POGROM.

HAIR. *See* BAR MITZVAH/BAT MITZVAH ("COMING OF AGE"); HEAD COVERING; LAG B'OMER; NETUREI KARTA (ARAMAIC, "GUARDIANS OF THE CITY").

HAJ (ARABIC "PILGRIMAGE"). *See* MESHED.

HALAKHAH (HEBREW, "THE WAY"). Term used of correct practice in ritual, ethical, and social behavior. Halakhah bases itself on biblical commandments, mitzvot, but through the various processes of the **Oral Torah**, it has expanded into many new patterns of living. Thus, it not only includes different interpretations of the practical application of scriptural texts, but it also incorporates a whole structure of rabbinic additions; the many different customs, minhag, of individual communities; and the rulings of rabbinic authorities down the ages.

Although most **Orthodox** Jews generally follow the halakhah as codified in the **Shulchan Arukh** and its commentaries, there are considerable differences between **Ashkenazi**, **Sephardi**, and Yemenite communities as to which halakhic traditions they follow. **Conservative Judaism** has modified the halakhah in line with modern thinking on many issues, and **Reform Judaism** has developed its own guidelines for religious behavior that differs from traditional halakhic norms. *See also* AGUDAT ISRAEL (ALSO KNOWN AS AGUDAH); ANAN BEN DAVID, (8TH CENTURY); BAR MITZVAH/BAT MITZVAH ("COMING OF AGE"); CALENDAR; CHASIDIC MOVEMENT (ALSO HASIDIC); DIETARY LAWS; GENTILE (HEBREW GOY, PLURAL GOYIM, "NATION" OR "PEOPLE"); JEW (HEBREW YEHUDI); JEWISH RITUAL YEAR; KARAITES; KOSHER ("FIT FOOD," HEBREW KASHER, KASHRUT); MAIMONIDES, MOSES (1135–1204); MIKVEH; MISHNAH; NEO-ORTHODOXY; PHARISEES; RABBI (HEBREW, "MY MASTER"); SABBATH (HEBREW SHABBAT); SADDUCEES; SAMARITANS; SANHEDRIN; TALMUD; TORAH (HEBREW, "TEACHING"); YESHIVAH (HEBREW, "PLACE OF SITTING," PLURAL YESHIVOT).

HALEVI, JUDAH. *See* KHAZARS.

HALÉVY, JOSEPH. *See* FALASHAS (ALSO KNOWN AS BETA ISRAEL).

HALIVNI, DAVID WEISS. *See* JEWISH THEOLOGICAL SEMINARY (JTS).

HAMAN. Biblical figure and villain of the Book of Esther. Haman is the prototype **anti-Semite** whose desire to destroy the Jews is based on a trivial loathing. In the story, Haman's plans are thwarted by God, who plays a background role and is never explicitly mentioned in the book, and by the Jewish Persian queen Esther and her relative Mordecai. Jews celebrate their victory over the Persian followers of Haman every year at the festival of **Purim**, a carnival-like festival that is also a response to the countless Hamans, from biblical times to **Adolph Hitler**, who may undertake **pogroms** but whose plans to commit total genocide against Jews in some **Final Solution** are ultimately frustrated.

HAMBURG TEMPLE. *See* REFORM JUDAISM.

HA-NADIV (HEBREW "THE BENEFACTOR"). *See* ALLIANCE ISRAÉLITE UNIVERSELLE (AIU).

HANUKKAH. *See* CHANUKAH.

HARVARD UNIVERSITY. *See* NUMERUS CLAUSUS (LATIN, "CLOSED NUMBER").

HASIDISM. *See* CHASIDIC MOVEMENT (ALSO HASIDIC).

HASKALAH. *See* ENLIGHTENMENT (HEBREW HASKALAH); MENDELSSOHN, MOSES (1729–86).

HASMONEANS. Family name of the **Maccabean** priests who led a successful revolt against the Seleucid Greek rulers of the **Holy Land** in 165 BCE, as recorded in the Apocryphal Books of Maccabees and by the 1st century CE Jewish historian **Josephus**. The Seleucid policy was to Hellenize their empire, introducing worship of Greek gods. They desecrated the **Temple** in **Jerusalem** and prohibited the practice of Jewish religion.

Though there were Hellenizing Jews who went along with this policy, it was unacceptable to various groups of Jewish religious zealots. United by the Hasmoneans, they rebelled and, after a series of guerrilla-type battles, drove the Greek rulers out. The Hasmoneans were priests, and not of the **Davidic** line, yet they assumed the role of kings and governed the Holy Land for more than a hundred years, from the establishment of the Hasmonean Dynasty by Simon Maccabeus in 140 BCE until **Herod** the Great. Jewish religion survived because of their revolt and subsequent independent Jewish rule in the Holy Land. The Hasmonean victory is celebrated in the annual Jewish festival of **Chanukah**. *See also* JUDAH MACCABEE (2ND CENTURY BCE).

"HA-TIKVAH" (HEBREW, "THE HOPE"). National anthem of the State of **Israel** expressing the hope of the Jewish people to return to their homeland. "Ha-Tikvah" was written by Naphtali Herz Imber at the end of the 19th century as a **Zionist** poem, and it was soon set to music to the tune of a Moldavian folk song that was eventually included in "Ma Vlast" by the Czech composer Bedrich Smetana. At the 18th **Zionist Congress** in 1933, "Ha-Tikvah" was adopted as the official Zionist anthem, having been sung enthusiastically at previous congresses.

An English translation of the words of "Ha-Tikvah" is as follows:

As long as deep within the recesses of the heart / The soul of a Jew still yearns,
And forward to the edges of the East / An eye toward Zion turns,
Then our hope is not lost, / The hope which is two millennia old,
To be a free people in our own land, / In the land of Zion and Jerusalem.

The anthem has been a bone of contention between secular Zionists and the **Orthodox** community because some of the latter object to these words and sing a modified version with more of a religious gloss. Thus they replace the phrase "to be a free people" with the words "to be a holy people."

HAVDALAH ("RELIGIOUS CEREMONY"). *See* SABBATH (HEBREW SHABBAT).

HEAD COVERING. One of the distinctive features of traditional Jewish life is the style of clothing that the religion imposes on its adherents. This is specifically true of head covering. Thus all **Orthodox, Conservative**, and some **Reform** Jewish males cover their heads at times of prayer, and the former also wear a head covering at other times. It is also incumbent on Orthodox married **women** to cover their hair, although this does not apply to single women.

The head covering for men usually consists of a small skullcap known by various **Hebrew** or **Yiddish** names, such as a kippah (Hebrew), a kappel, or a yarmulka (Yiddish). The style of these skullcaps differs among groups of Jews and is often regarded as a mark of group identity. Thus many Modern Orthodox Jews and religious **Zionists** wear a knitted skullcap, more right-wing charedi Jews wear black cloth skullcaps, and **Chasidic** Jews often wear a black velvet skullcap. Above the skullcap, a variety of hats are found in different Jewish subgroups. Black hats of assorted shapes and sizes are worn by **Mitnaggedic** Jews and other charedi Jews, while Chasidim don fur-lined hats, known as streimels or spodaks for their **Sabbath** and festival attire in imitation of the Polish aristocratic dress of the 19th century. **Sephardi** and Oriental Jews used to wear turbans and colored or decorated skullcaps, but today, under **Ashkenazi** influence, the head gear of young Sephardim does not differ significantly from that worn by Ashkenazim.

Orthodox married women either wear a wig or a head scarf, known in Yiddish as a sheitel or a tichel respectively, or they wear a hat. There are different reasons for head covering for men and women. The reason Orthodox men cover their heads is because it is a mark of respect indicating that they are in God's presence. Married women, by contrast, cover their hair because their hair is regarded as a naked part of their body that should not be exposed to men other than their husbands.

HEBREW. A Semitic language with ancient and modern forms. The original language of most of the **Bible**, recognized by Jews as Scripture, is in ancient Hebrew, with a small amount written in **Aramaic**. The **Mishnah** and some early postbiblical texts are in a Hebrew clearly distinct from the language even of the later books of the Bible, while the modern Hebrew spoken and written in the State of **Israel** is itself a distinct form of the language. Hebrew, like other Semitic languages such as Aramaic and Arabic, is written from right to left and uses the Masoretic script, although there are more ancient Hebrew scripts, such as that used in the **Samaritan** scrolls of the **Torah**. It is regarded by religious Jews as a holy tongue, the original language through which God created the world. *See also* ACADEMY OF THE HE-

BREW LANGUAGE (HEBREW VAAD HA-LASHON HA-IVRIT); BEN YEHUDAH, ELIEZER (1858–1922); BRIT IVRIT OLAMIT (HEBREW, "WORLD HEBREW COVENANT"); GENIZAH (HEBREW, "HIDDEN REPOSITORY"); LADINO; YIDDISH.

HEBREWS. *See* FALASHAS (ALSO KNOWN AS BETA ISRAEL); GENTILE (HEBREW GOY, PLURAL GOYIM, "NATION" OR "PEOPLE"); ISRAEL; JEW (HEBREW YEHUDI); SAMARITANS.

HEBREW UNION COLLEGE (HUC). Reform rabbinical seminary founded in Cincinnati in 1875, with branches later opening in New York (1922), Los Angeles (1954), and Jerusalem (1963). The HUC was established by Isaac Mayer Wise, a leading light of **Reform Judaism** in the United States and one of its main architects. The HUC is an institution that includes **women** in its student body and ordained its first female **rabbi** in 1972. It encourages free inquiry, and apart from the training of Reform rabbis, the HUC has won an international reputation for its academic publications and research program.

Reform Judaism was originally antagonistic toward **Zionism**, believing that Jews should be full members of their host countries while professing the Jewish religion. That situation changed after the **Holocaust** and the foundation of the State of **Israel**. Currently, rabbis in training have to spend a year in the Israel branch of the HUC, specializing in **Hebrew** and knowledge of the **Land of Israel**.

HEBREW UNIVERSITY OF JERUSALEM. A major academic institution in **Israel** opened in 1925 by Arthur James Balfour, the author of the **Balfour Declaration**. Present at the opening were British and Jewish dignitaries, including **Chaim Weizmann**, president of the **Zionist** Organization; the British chief rabbi **Joseph Herman Hertz**; the **Ashkenazi** chief rabbi of the **Holy Land** Rabbi **Abraham Isaac Kook**; and his **Sephardi** counterpart Rabbi Jacob Meir. The idea of founding such an institute had been discussed from even before the first **Zionist Congress** of 1897, but although the idea was muted at several Zionist Congresses, it was only after the British were given a Mandate for **Palestine** that it came to fruition in 1918 with the laying of foundation stones on Mt. Scopus.

The university began on a small scale in 1925 and gradually expanded its faculties. The idea behind it was to have an academic institution in which the language of instruction was **Hebrew** and the study of Judaica would have pride of place with scientific and liberal arts subjects. Refugees from Nazi Germany greatly enhanced the academic standing of the university, which was also augmented by the development of a major library, the Jewish National Library, and the Hadassah teaching hospital.

After the **War of Independence**, the campus on Mt. Scopus was unusable because it was isolated and surrounded by Palestinian territory, and a group of doctors and nurses traveling there were attacked and killed. The campus relocated to Givat Ram on the Jewish side of **Jerusalem**, and the Hadassah teaching hospital eventually relocated to En Kerem. After the **Six-Day War**, the Mt. Scopus campus was accessible once again, and both campuses were fully used. The university was not without controversy and was opposed by ultra-**Orthodox** Jews as an affront to the holy city. Rabbi Kook was criticized for attending the opening ceremony and was accused of saying that the university was an example of **Torah** emanating from Zion, although he denied ever having made such a remark.

HEBRON. Holy city to the south of **Jerusalem**. The cave of Machpelah in Hebron is the traditional burial place of Adam and Eve, as well as of the biblical **Patriarchs** and three of the Matriarchs. It is a place of **pilgrimage** for Jews from **Israel** and from the **Diaspora**. As it is sacred to both Jews and Muslims, it has been subject to many clashes between **Palestinians** and Jews. In 1929, Arab gangs massacred the Jews there, including students at the Hebron **yeshivah**, and **synagogues** were desecrated. During the Arab revolt of 1936, the Jewish community had to be evacuated to prevent another massacre. After the **Six-Day War** of 1967, Jews returned to the Hebron area and continued to live in troubled relationship with the local inhabitants. In 1994, a Jewish settler in Hebron, Baruch Goldstein, opened fire on Palestinian Arabs in a Hebron mosque, killing 29 worshippers. *See also* DAVID; MIZRACHI (ABBREVIATION OF MERCAZ RUCHANI, "SPIRITUAL CENTER").

HEIDEGGER, MARTIN. *See* ARENDT, HANNAH (1906–75).

HEROD. King of Judea from 37 BCE until 4 CE. Herod was a descendant of Idumean **proselytes** who had been forcibly converted

to Judaism by the **Hasmoneans**. He married Mariamne of the Hasmonean family but killed off any of the remaining Hasmoneans who
threatened his reign, including Mariamne herself, as well as a number
of his own sons. Herod was only able to establish his position with
Roman backing and was never totally accepted by all the Jews. He
was often in dispute with the **Pharisees**, particularly those members
of the Rabbinic establishment in the **Sanhedrin**. He only gained their
acquiescence in his activities by murder, killing off those Sanhedrin
members who preferred the Hasmoneans. Herod was a great builder,
rebuilding the **Jerusalem Temple** as well as various towns in honor
of his Roman patrons, fortresses, and palaces. Parts of the **Wailing
Wall** around the Temple Mount in Jerusalem are all that remain today
of Herod's Temple.

HERTZ, JOSEPH HERMAN (1872–1946). Chief rabbi of the British Commonwealth from 1913 until his death. Hertz was educated
at the newly founded **Jewish Theological Seminary** in New York,
which was opened in 1887 and originally took in **Orthodox** students,
although it later became a **Conservative** institution. After serving
congregations in the United States and South Africa, he became the
British chief rabbi and an outspoken leader of British Orthodoxy for
33 years. Hertz was a committed **Zionist**, a position out of favor with
the Anglicized leadership of the United Synagogue, and attended the
opening of the **Hebrew University** in 1925. He was critical of British
policy in **Palestine**. Hertz stood up for Modern Orthodoxy against
Reform and Liberal Judaism, editing a **Bible** text with commentaries
still widely in use today and in which he defended the Mosaic au-
thorship of the Pentateuch. This work, as well as his commentary on
the prayer book and his *Book of Jewish Thoughts*, were anathema to
the ultra-Orthodox because of his inclusion of the opinions of many
Gentile thinkers in them.

HERUT (POLITICAL PARTY). *See* REVISIONIST ZIONISTS.

HERZL, THEODOR (1860–1904). Founder of political **Zionism** and
secular prophet of the State of **Israel**. Herzl was a journalist and while
covering the **Dreyfus Case** in Paris became convinced that the only
solution to the rampant **anti-Semitism** in Europe was the creation
of a homeland for the Jews. His idea was that a Jewish state would

be set up with the support of the world powers, and so he eventually made contact with German, Turkish, and British governments. In his contacts with the Ottoman Empire, he promised financial help if the **Holy Land** could be assigned to Jews. He was, however, unable to raise the massive economic resources needed, though he tried to gain support from the **Rothschild** family and other Jewish financiers, with the argument that only thus could their wealth be safeguarded.

Nothing came of his fundraising, so Herzl published a book, *Der Judenstaat* (1896), which became a manifesto for his dream of a Jewish state. He convened the first **Zionist Congress** in 1897 in Basel, Switzerland, which marked the beginning of the **World Zionist Organization** (WZO), of which Herzl was elected president. Herzl chaired the next five congresses until his death in 1904. Herzl met the German Kaiser Wilhelm II in the Holy Land in 1898 and the Ottoman sultan in 1901, without any real success.

In his novel *Altneuland* (1902), he depicted what a Jewish country could be like. Herzl's inspiration led directly to the modern State of **Israel**, and he wrote in his diary after the first Zionist Congress that in Basel he had founded the Jewish state "maybe in another five years but certainly in 50 years." That was in August 1897. In November 1947, the United Nations voted in favor of a Jewish state in a divided Palestine, and the state was declared in May 1948.

HEXAGRAM. *See* MAGEN DAVID (HEBREW, "SHIELD OF DAVID" OR "STAR OF DAVID").

HIGH PRIEST. *See* DAY OF ATONEMENT (HEBREW YOM KIPPUR); REVISIONIST ZIONISTS; SANHEDRIN; TEMPLE (HEBREW BET HA-MIKDASH).

HILLEL. *See* JUDAH THE NASI.

HILLEL FOUNDATION. *See* BNAI B'RITH (HEBREW, "SONS OF THE COVENANT").

HIRSCH, SAMSON RAPHAEL (1808–88). Rabbi and rejuvenator of **Orthodox** Jewish life in Germany. As a student, Hirsch was close to Abraham Geiger, who was later to become a leader of **Reform Judaism** and was also a role model for **Heinrich Graetz**, the historian.

After serving in some major rabbinic positions, Hirsch put himself forward as a candidate for the British chief rabbinate but was unsuccessful. He came to Frankfurt on the Main to be the rabbi of a small Orthodox community and stayed there from 1851 until his death in 1888. In Frankfurt, he shaped the nature of the German Orthodox response to the **Enlightenment**, modernity, and Reform Judaism.

This response, known as **Neo-Orthodoxy**, was based on the Rabbinic teaching that **Torah** should be combined with the way of the land, derekh eretz. For Hirsch, this meant a total commitment to the practice and outlook of Orthodox Judaism but at the same time an affirmation of the best of German culture that was available for Jews. He rejected any affiliation with Reform, which wished to modify traditional Judaism in the light of modern values. While Hirsch introduced modern elements in such areas as Jewish dress and vernacular sermons, he rejected anything that involved a basic change to **halakhah** and was antagonistic toward **Zionism**.

HISTADRUT (TRADE UNION BODY). See MEIR, GOLDA (ORIGINALLY MYERSON, 1898–1978).

HISTORY OF THE JEWS **(GRAETZ).** See GRAETZ, HEINRICH (1817–91).

HITLER, ADOLPH (1889–1945). Chancellor of Germany from 1933 and the dominant power behind Nazi racist ideology and its genocidal policies in the **Holocaust**. Hitler felt aggrieved, like many Austrians and Germans, at the Treaty of Versailles at the conclusion of World War I. He blamed the Jews for the defeat and humiliation and regarded "International Jewry" as a demonic force poisoning all the nations of the world. Already in the mid-1920s, his book *Mein Kampf* ("My Struggle") was replete with **anti-Semitism** and the dangers of the "Jewish peril."

Hitler built this ideology of race and anti-Semitism into the National Socialist outlook that guided the Nazi conquest of most of Europe. The **Nuremberg Laws** of 1935 began the process of Aryanization of the German Reich by removing German citizenship from Jews and prohibiting Jews and Aryans from engaging in sexual relations. In his speeches, Hitler blamed the Jews for the ills of German society, and the roots of the **Final Solution** can be traced to the prejudice and propaganda for which he was mainly responsible. His message was readily received not only by Germans and Austrians but by many anti-Semites, particularly in Poland and the Ukraine, who were ready to assist in the Nazi extermination of the Jews.

The policy of genocide evolved from an initial policy of ridding Germany of her Jews. Once the number of Jews under Nazi control grew exponentially with the conquest of Central and Eastern Europe, the policy changed to extermination. Although signed documentary evidence for Hitler's role in this policy shift is absent, there is no doubt that he was instrumental in the genocide that followed. A surviving record of the Wannsee Conference of 1942 indicates that the notion of a Final Solution was agreed on, and there was no ambiguity in Hitler's rhetoric about Jewish annihilation and of making Europe **Judenrein**. *See also* AUSCHWITZ; BERGEN-BELSEN; BUCHENWALD; EICHMANN, ADOLPH (1906–62); GESTAPO (GEHEIME STAATS-POLIZEI); GHETTO; HAMAN; HOLOCAUST REMEMBRANCE DAY (HEBREW YOM HASHOAH); HUSSEINI, HAJ AMIN (1893–1974); KRISTALLNACHT (GERMAN, "NIGHT OF BROKEN GLASS"); MARTYRDOM (HEBREW KIDDUSH HASHEM, "SANCTIFICATION OF (GOD'S) NAME"); POGROM; PROTOCOLS OF THE ELDERS OF ZION; WARSAW GHETTO UPRISING; YAD VASHEM.

HIV. *See* FALASHAS (ALSO KNOWN AS BETA ISRAEL).

HOLOCAUST. Term most widely used to characterize the extermination of the Jews by the Nazis and their allies before and during World War II. Among Jews, this genocidal series of events is known as the Shoah, a Hebrew word meaning "catastrophe," as the word *Holocaust* originally means a completely burned offering and is not considered appropriate to be applied to mass murder. It is estimated that 6 million Jews, as well as gypsies, homosexuals, political prisoners, and prisoners of war, died as a result of Nazi activity.

The **Final Solution** of the Jewish "problem" became, for the Nazi hierarchy, the ultimate liquidation of the Jews through starvation, shooting, and gassing in death camps. The Holocaust has left a deep and abiding impression on Jewish consciousness, particularly in the State of **Israel**. The fact that **anti-Semitic** hatred could lead to such terrible consequences in mid-20th-century Europe has enhanced the **Zionist** belief that Jews can never be safe as a minority, even in the most cultured of **Gentile** countries. *See also* AUSCHWITZ; BERGEN-BELSEN; BRAND, JOEL (1906–64); BUCHENWALD; EICHMANN, ADOLPH (1906–62); FRANK, ANNE (1929–45); GESTAPO (GEHEIME STAATS-POLIZEI); GHETTO; GRYN-SZPAN, HERSCHEL (1921–?); HAMAN; HITLER, ADOLPH (1889–1945); HOLOCAUST REMEMBRANCE DAY (HEBREW YOM HASHOAH); HUSSEINI, HAJ AMIN (1893–1974); IRON GUARD; JUDENREIN (GERMAN, "FREE OF JEWS"); KAPO; KASZTNER, RUDOLF (1906–57); KIELCE POGROM; KORC-ZAK, JANUSZ (PSEUDONYM OF HENRYK GOLDSZMIDT, 18748–1942); KRISTALLNACHT (GERMAN, "NIGHT OF BRO-KEN GLASS"); MAGEN DAVID (HEBREW, "SHIELD OF DA-VID" OR "STAR OF DAVID"); MARTYRDOM (HEBREW KID-DUSH HASHEM, "SANCTIFICATION OF (GOD'S) NAME); NUREMBERG LAWS; PARTISANS; POGROM; PROTOCOLS OF THE ELDERS OF ZION; SZENES, HANNAH (1921–44); WARSAW GHETTO UPRISING; YAD VASHEM.

HOLOCAUST REMEMBRANCE DAY (HEBREW YOM HAS-HOAH). A day set aside in the State of **Israel** to remember the victims of the Nazi **Holocaust** and to commemorate those involved in revolts against the Nazis, particularly the **Warsaw Ghetto Uprising**. The date chosen by the Israel parliament was the Hebrew date of the 27th of Nisan. It falls five days after the end of **Passover** in the **Omer** period traditionally assigned for mourning the death of **martyrs** in the past. The Warsaw Ghetto Uprising began at the beginning of the Passover, but as Passover is a joyful festival, it was not considered an appropriate time for such a remembrance day, so it was delayed.

HOLY LAND. According to the **Bible**, the **Land of Israel**, known by the Romans as **Palestine** and in ancient times as Canaan, was promised by God to **Abraham** and his seed. It was toward this land that **Moses** led the Israelites through the desert after the **Exodus** from slavery in Egypt. Having conquered and settled the land under Joshua, **Jerusalem** became its capital under King **David**, and his son, King **Solomon**, built the **Temple** there. The holiness of the land was thus a product of both the divine promise and its historical role as the location of the central sanctuary of Judaism.

Ten of the Hebrew tribes were exiled from the Holy Land when the northern kingdom of **Israel** was conquered by the Assyrians in 722 BCE, while the two tribes in the southern kingdom of **Judah** were exiled to **Babylonia** in 586 BCE. At least some of the inhabitants of Israel never returned to the Holy Land, and legend has it that they are the **Ten Lost Tribes** who will return in the **Messianic** Age. Many of the Judeans did return after the Persians conquered the Babylonian Empire. They rebuilt Jerusalem and the Temple and reestablished Jewish life in the Holy Land, which also became a place of **pilgrimage** for those **Jews** in the **Diaspora** who would come to Jerusalem for the pilgrimage festivals, particularly the **Passover**.

The Romans crushed a rebellion of the Jews against their rule in Palestine and destroyed the Temple in 70 CE. They also put down a second rebellion under **Bar Kokhba** in 135 CE. Jewish life in Palestine became more difficult, and Jews were forbidden to live in Jerusalem. Though their leaders produced works of major significance, such as the **Mishnah**, the center of religious activity gradually shifted away from the Holy Land to the Babylonian Diaspora and then to areas of the Roman Empire in Europe.

The Holy Land remained strongly implanted in the consciousness of Diaspora Jews. They turn toward the Temple every day in prayer, praying for it to be rebuilt and for God to dwell once more in Jerusalem. They request God to gather the Jewish People from the four corners of the earth and return them to Zion.

Although Jews down the ages made an effort to go on **aliyah** to the Holy Land, it was only with the rise of **Zionism** in the late 19th century that a new kind of mass immigration occurred. Because, however, the Zionist ideology was a secular, nationalist one, there was considerable opposition from **Orthodox** circles to the desecration of the Holy Land by unholy pioneers who did not keep the commandments. By not waiting for God to return the exiles to their homeland in His time, they were regarded as negating the divine role in redemption. *See also* PROMISED LAND.

HOLY OF HOLIES. *See* DAY OF ATONEMENT (HEBREW YOM KIPPUR); TEMPLE (HEBREW BET HA-MIKDASH); WAILING WALL (HEBREW KOTEL HA-MAARAVI, "WESTERN WALL").

HOMOSEXUALITY. *See* GRYNSZPAN, HERSCHEL (1921–?); HOLOCAUST.

HOSHANA RABBA (MINOR FESTIVE DAY). *See* TABERNACLES (HEBREW SUKKOT).

HOST DESECRATION. Accusation against Jews that they stole the wafers used in the Eucharist ceremony and stabbed them or otherwise desecrated them. The background to this accusation was the Catholic belief that, in the mass, the consecrated wafers became the actual body of Jesus and that Jews, having once crucified him, were intent on causing him harm again. Jews were widely viewed as a malevolent force in Christian society, and when these **anti-Semitic** accusations were directed against them in the Middle Ages, they were persecuted and killed. It is significant that claims of host desecration first began to surface in the mid–13th century, soon after the Catholic Church officially adopted the belief in transubstantiation. *See also* BLOOD LIBEL.

HUGH OF LINCOLN, SAINT. *See* BLOOD LIBEL.

HURVITZ, JOSEPH JOSEL. *See* MUSAR MOVEMENT.

HUSSEINI, HAJ AMIN (1893–1974). Mufti of **Jerusalem** and **Palestinian** leader. Husseini played a major role in anti-Jewish attacks by Palestinian Arabs in the 1920s and 1930s and in the Arab rebellion of 1936 against British Mandate rule in Palestine. He was imprisoned for a short time by the British, and eventually, during World War II while in exile, he collaborated with **Adolph Hitler** and the Nazis in their plans to exterminate the Jews. *See also* ARAB REFUGEES; FINAL SOLUTION; HOLOCAUST.

HYKSOS. *See* JOSEPH.

– I –

I AND THOU **(BOOK).** *See* BUBER, MARTIN (1878–1965).

IBN ABI ZIMRA, DAVID. *See* FALASHAS (ALSO BETA ISRAEL).

IDOLS. *See* GENTILE (HEBREW GOY, PLURAL GOYIM, "NATION" OR "PEOPLE"); MITNAGGEDIC MOVEMENT (HEBREW, "OPPONENTS"); TEN COMMANDMENTS (OR DECALOGUE).

IDUMEANS. *See* HEROD; PROSELYTES (HEBREW GERIM, SINGULAR GER).

IMBER, NAPHTALI HERZ. *See* "HA-TIKVAH" (HEBREW, "THE HOPE").

INDIA. *See* BENE ISRAEL.

INQUISITION. The Inquisition was set up in the early 13th century by Pope Gregory IX to root out heresy. It was mostly concerned with Christian heterodoxy, although it did engage in burning the **Talmud** in 1242. Its main involvement with **Jews**, however, began in Spain in the late 15th century.

The Christian conquest of Spain led to the forced conversion of a large number of Jewish communities in 1391. This left many Jewish **conversos** living a double life as **Marranos**, outwardly Christian but secretly continuing Jewish practice. They were able to live this way because they were in touch with those Jews who had not been converted. The Inquisition, which was set up in Spain in 1481, tried to prevent the backsliding of these converts.

In 1469, Isabella, heiress to the throne of Castile, married Ferdinand, heir to the throne of Aragon, and this led some 10 years later to the unifying of the two kingdoms. As devout Catholic monarchs, they encouraged the Inquisition to deal with the problem of the Jewish converts, and the Inquisition started to investigate conversos suspected of Judaizing. It was obvious to the inquisitors that they could not eradicate Jewish heresies from the conversos as long as practicing Jews still lived in their midst. After **Tomas de Torquemada** was appointed inquisitor general in 1483, thousands of conversos were condemned by the Inquisition for practicing Judaism in secret. Many of them were tortured or sentenced to a cruel death by being burned at the stake, and all their possessions were confiscated.

When Granada, the last area of Muslim rule in Spain, fell to the Catholic armies in 1492, the need for religious unity of the kingdom was paramount, and this unity was threatened not only by the Jewish presence in Spain, but also by the Judaizing conversos. An edict of expulsion of the Jews was issued by Ferdinand and Isabella under the influence of the Spanish Inquisition to help deal with the problem of backsliding conversos. Any Jews who accepted Christianity were allowed to stay, their numbers adding to the potential Judaizers investigated by the Inquisition.

A considerable number of the conversos, who had remained true to Jewish faith, managed to return to Judaism when they eventually fled Spain and rejoined **Sephardi** communities in Europe, South America, and the Orient, as long as they could avoid the long reach of the Inquisition. *See also* LADINO.

INTERMARRIAGE. *See* DIETARY LAWS; GENTILE (HEBREW GOY, PLURAL GOYIM, "NATION" OR "PEOPLE"); HITLER, ADOLPH (1889–1945); KAIFENG; MITNAGGEDIC MOVEMENT (HEBREW, "OPPONENTS"); NAPOLEON BONAPARTE (1769–1821); NUREMBERG LAWS; ROTHSCHILD FAMILY; SASSOON FAMILY; SOLOMON (10TH CENTURY BCE).

INTERNATIONAL JEWRY. *See* ALLIANCE ISRAÉLITE UNIVERSELLE (AIU); ANTI-DEFAMATION LEAGUE (ADL); HITLER, ADOLPH (1889–1945); PROTOCOLS OF THE ELDERS OF ZION.

IRGUN TZEVAI LEUMI (HEBREW, "NATIONAL ARMY ORGANIZATION," KNOWN AS THE IRGUN). A right-wing militant underground organization associated with **Vladimir Jabotinsky** and **Revisionist Zionism** that was founded in 1931 and believed in attacking Arab and British interests in **Palestine**. Among its activities, the Irgun, headed by **Menachem Begin**, blew up the King David Hotel, the center of British control of Palestine, and killed many people in an attack on the Arab village of Deir Yasin. When it refused to unconditionally surrender the arms-carrying ship the *Altalena*, the **Haganah** blew up the Irgun ship off the Tel Aviv beach on **David Ben Gurion**'s orders.

IRON GUARD. Romanian **anti-Semitic** party that was behind attacks on **synagogues** and led **pogroms** against Jews before and during World War II. The ideology of the Iron Guard was inspired by Christian antagonism to Jews and nationalist beliefs that Jews were an alien element in Romanian society. Although the power of the Iron Guard was broken in 1944 when anti-Nazi forces took over the country, its members continued in existence in exile in various European locations.

ISABELLA, QUEEN. *See* INQUISITION; SEPHARDIM; TORQUE-MADA, TOMAS DE (1420–98).

ISLAM. *See* ANTI-SEMITISM; ASHKENAZIM (SINGULAR ASH-KENAZI); AUTO-DA-FÉ ("ACT OF FAITH"); BIBLE; CONVER-SOS; CRUSADES; DAMASCUS BLOOD LIBEL; DIASPORA; DOENMEH; HUSSEINI, HAJ AMIN (1893–1974); INQUISITION; ISRAEL; JERUSALEM; KHAZARS; KOSHER ("FIT FOOD," HEBREW KASHER, KASHRUT); MAIMONIDES, MOSES (1135–1204); MARTYRDOM (HEBREW KIDDUSH HASHEM, "SANCTIFICATION OF (GOD'S) NAME"); MESHED; MESSI-ANIC MOVEMENTS; MOUNTAIN JEWS; NATHAN OF GAZA (1643–80); OMAR, COVENANT OF; PILGRIMAGE (HEBREW ALIYAH LE-REGEL, "ASCENT BY FOOT"); PROSELYTES (HEBREW GERIM, SINGULAR GER); REUVENI, DAVID (15TH–16TH CENTURIES); SABBATH (HEBREW SHABBAT); SAMARITANS; SEPHARDIM; SHABBETAI TZVI (1626–76); SYNAGOGUE (HEBREW BET KNESSET); TORQUEMADA, TOMAS DE (1420–98); WAILING WALL (HEBREW KOTEL HA-MAARAVI, "WESTERN WALL").

ISRAEL. Name given to **Jacob**, the third **Patriarch**, in the **Bible** after he wrestled with an angel (Genesis 32) and was then applied to his descendants, who are known as the children of Israel, or more commonly Israelites. The term *Israel* can thus mean the people of Israel, otherwise known as Hebrews or **Jews**. It can also refer to the **Land of Israel**, eretz yisrael, also commonly called the **Holy Land** or the **Promised Land**, as this is the land of the Israelites.

The 12 tribes of Israel entered what was then known as the land of Canaan under the leadership of Joshua, the successor to **Moses**. After fighting a series of battles, they settled different parts of the country in tribal groups, often engaging in ongoing clashes with the surrounding nations and with non-Israelite tribes who continued to live among them in the land. It was only during the rule of King **David** that the Israelite tribes were completely united with **Jerusalem**, a city that had not belonged to any tribal territory, as their capital. This tribal unity continued during the reign of David's son **Solomon** (10th century BCE), but after the death of the latter, the land was divided between two Israelite tribal groups.

Ten of the tribes, led by the Joseph subtribes of Manasseh and Ephraim, broke away to form the northern kingdom, which adopted the name Israel and had Samaria as its capital, while the remaining two tribes, under the leadership of the tribe of Judah, to which David and Solomon belonged, formed the southern kingdom of Judah in the area around Jerusalem. These two warring kingdoms kept the Land of Israel disunited until the northern kingdom was destroyed by the Assyrians in 722 BCE, and the northern tribes were dispersed in the Assyrian empire, giving rise to the legend of the **Ten Lost Tribes**. Unlike the southern kingdom, which was destroyed by the **Babylonians** in 586 BCE and rebuilt by the returning Judean exiles from Babylonia, the northern kingdom of Israel was never formally reconstituted until modern times. The whole land, however, was still referred to as the Land of Israel and the Jewish people as the People of Israel.

When a new Jewish state came into being in 1948 on a portion of the Holy Land, the name Israel was chosen in line with accepted usage. The modern State of Israel is bounded by the Arab states of Lebanon and Syria to the north, Jordan to the east, and Egypt to the south. Although it has fought wars in the past with all its neighbors, Israel has signed peace treaties with Egypt and Jordan and is currently engaged in a very troubled effort to achieve a peace agreement with the **Palestinians**.

As in the past, one of the greatest challenges facing the State of Israel has been how to unite the many different "tribes" of Jews who were either already living in the Holy Land or who have made **aliyah** to its territory in the last century or so. These modern "tribal" groups are divided into Western and Oriental Jews, **Ashkenazim** and **Sephardim**, **Chasidim** and **Mitnaggedim**, Ultra-Orthodox, **Orthodox**, **Conservative** and **Reform** Jews, **Falashas**, Yemenites, Persians, **Bene Israel**, **Karaites**, and **Samaritans**.

Another major challenge is to build bridges with Druze, Bedouin Arabs, Muslim, and Christian Palestinians, who together make up about a fifth of Israel's population. Some of these latter groups are themselves subdivided into factions only united by their opposition to the government of Israel. *See also* AGUDAT ISRAEL

(ALSO KNOWN AS AGUDAH); ALLIANCE ISRAÉLITE UNI-VERSELLE (AIU); BALFOUR DECLARATION; BRITISH IS-RAELITES; DIASPORA; EXILE (HEBREW GALUT); HEBREW; ISRAEL DEFENSE FORCE (IDF); ISRAEL INDEPENDENCE DAY (HEBREW YOM HA-ATZMAUT); KNESSET (HEBREW, "ASSEMBLY"); MIZRACHI (ABBREVIATION OF MERCAZ RUCHANI, "SPIRITUAL CENTER"); PILGRIMAGE (HEBREW ALIYAH LE-REGEL, "ASCENT BY FOOT"); SINAI CAMPAIGN; SIX-DAY WAR; ZIONISM.

ISRAEL AIR FORCE. *See* COHEN, ELI (1924–65); ENTEBBE; SIX-DAY WAR.

ISRAEL BEN ELIEZER. *See* BAAL SHEM TOV, ISRAEL BEN ELIEZER (1700–60); CHASIDIC MOVEMENT (ALSO HASIDIC).

ISRAEL DEFENSE FORCE (IDF). The **Israeli** army, known as the Israel Defense Force, came into being in 1948 with the foundation of the State of Israel, incorporating members of the **Haganah, Palmach**, and other military groups. Although the backbone of the IDF is a small professional army, it mostly consists of Jewish, Druze, and Bedouin Arab civilians on reserve duty. *See also* ASHKENAZIM (SINGULAR ASH-KENAZI); COHEN, ELI (1924–65); DAYAN, MOSHE (1915–81); ENTEBBE; RABIN, YITZCHAK (1922–95); SIX-DAY WAR; WAR OF INDEPENDENCE (HEBREW MILCHEMET HA-ATZMAUT).

ISRAEL INDEPENDENCE DAY (HEBREW YOM HA-ATZ-MAUT). The fifth day of the **Hebrew** month of Iyyar is Independence Day for the State of **Israel**. It was on this day on Friday, May 14, 1948, according to the secular calendar, that the new state was declared by **David Ben Gurion**. It is a public holiday in Israel, and for some Jews in Israel and the **Diaspora**, it is a semireligious occasion with special prayers thanking God for the miracle of return to the **Promised Land** and national independence. The day before Independence Day is Remembrance Day for the fallen in Israel's wars.

ISRAELITES. *See* ALIYAH (HEBREW, "GOING UP," PLURAL ALIYOT); BRITISH ISRAELITES; EXODUS; GENTILE (HE-BREW GOY, PLURAL GOYIM, "NATION" OR "PEOPLE");

HOLY LAND; ISRAEL; JERUSALEM; JEW (HEBREW YEHUDI); JEWISH RITUAL YEAR; JOSEPH; MOSES; PASSOVER (HEBREW PESACH); PENTECOST (HEBREW SHAVUOT); PROMISED LAND; SABBATH (HEBREW SHABBAT); SAMBATYON; TABERNACLES (HEBREW SUKKOT); TALLIT (ARAMAIC, "PRAYER SHAWL"); TEMPLE (HEBREW BET HA-MIKDASH); TEN COMMANDMENTS (OR DECALOGUE).

ISSERLES, MOSES. *See* CARO, JOSEPH (1488–1575); SHULCHAN ARUKH (HEBREW, "LAID TABLE").

IYYAR (MONTH). *See* CALENDAR; ISRAEL INDEPENDENCE DAY (HEBREW YOM HA-ATZMAUT); JEWISH RITUAL YEAR; LAG B'OMER.

– J –

JABOTINSKY, VLADIMIR (1889–1940). Right-wing **Zionist** leader who believed that a Jewish state in **Palestine** should be on both sides of the Jordan River. While this was rejected by mainstream Zionism, Jabotinsky's encouragement of self-defense had considerable influence in inspiring Jewish militancy against Palestinian Arabs and in anti-British Jewish terrorist groups. He began his career in Russia when he decided that the only way to counter **pogroms** was by organizing Jewish self-defense groups, an activity he continued in **Jerusalem** in the 1920s. He was an advocate of total boycott of Nazi Germany in the 1930s and supported illegal **aliyah** into Mandate Palestine. Jabotinsky was one of the founders of the **Revisionist Zionist** Movement and, for a while, was the head of the **Irgun Tzvai Leumi**. *See also* BEGIN, MENACHEM (1913–92); BETAR (ACRONYM OF BERIT TRUMPELDOR); TRUMPELDOR, JOSEPH (1880–1920).

"J'ACCUSE!" (ARTICLE BY EMILE ZOLA). *See* DREYFUS CASE.

JACOB. Biblical **Patriarch** and grandson of **Abraham** whose story is found in the Book of Genesis. There, it is related that Jacob acquired the name **Israel** after wrestling with an angel, and thus his descendants came to be known as the children of Israel. Jacob married two wives, Leah and Rachel, and had two concubines, with whom he fathered 12 sons and 1 daughter. According to the Bible, these sons subsequently formed the 12 tribes of Israel. The stories of jealousy and infighting among the sons from different mothers, particularly the animosity toward **Joseph**, a son of Rachel, reflect the tribal clashes in later Israelite history. After the reign of King **Solomon** of the tribe of **Judah**, the Israelite tribes split into 2 groups, with 10 of the tribes, led by the Joseph tribes, seceding from those led by Judah to form the northern state of Israel. It was these tribes that later became the **Ten Lost Tribes** of Jewish legend.

JERUSALEM. Holiest city for the Jewish religion and the site of both the First and Second **Temples**. The city was conquered by King **David**, who made it his capital and brought the Ark of the Covenant there. His son, King **Solomon**, built the First Temple on one of the hills of Jerusalem, and this became the central sanctuary for all Israelites, further uniting the Israelite tribes. When, after Solomon's death, the monarchy split into the northern kingdom of **Israel** and the southern kingdom of **Judah**, Jerusalem remained the Judean capital until it was conquered and burned down by the **Babylonians** in 586 BCE. The Judeans taken into captivity to Babylon preserved the memory of Jerusalem as expressed in Psalm 137: "If I forget you, O Jerusalem, let my right hand forget (its power). Let my tongue cleave to the roof of my mouth if I do not remember you; if I do not raise (the thought of) Jerusalem above my chief joy." The city and Temple were rebuilt by returning exiles some 70 years later, and Jerusalem remained the Holy City of Judaism until its destruction by the Romans in 70 CE.

Jews in the **Diaspora** and the **Land of Israel** turn toward Jerusalem in prayer and utter invocations for it to be rebuilt three times a day. It was only in the middle of the 19th century that Jews once again made up the majority of the city's inhabitants. After the Israeli **War of Independence**, the city was divided between a Jewish and a **Palestinian** section and was reunited under Jewish control when the Arab areas were conquered in the **Six-Day War** of 1967. Today, it is Israel's capital and largest city, with a population of approximately 750,000 inhabitants, housing the **Knesset**, the Israeli parliament, the **Hebrew University** and many government buildings.

Jerusalem is not only holy to Jews, but also to Christians and Muslims. It contains some of the most important sacred sites of Christian-

ity associated with the life and death of Jesus. The Islamic tradition sees the Temple Mount in Jerusalem as the site of Mohammed's night journey to the "furthest mosque" mentioned in the Koran, and it thus became the third most sacred place in Islam after Mecca and Medina. For Palestinian Arabs, Jerusalem is the obvious place for the future capital of any Palestinian state, and because of its centrality for Jews, this has been one of the main problems in peace negotiations between Israelis and Palestinians. *See also* HEROD.

JESUITS. *See* KAIFENG.

JESUS. *See* ANTI-SEMITISM; ARAMAIC; BARCELONA, DISPUTATION OF; BIBLE; DISPUTATIONS; HOST DESECRATION; JERUSALEM; MARTYRDOM (HEBREW KIDDUSH HASHEM, "SANCTIFICATION OF (GOD'S) NAME"); MESSIANIC MOVEMENTS; PHARISEES; SHTETL; TALMUD; WANDERING JEW.

JEW (HEBREW YEHUDI). The term *Jew* delineates an ethnic religious community also known at different times as **Israelites** or Hebrews. Although the exact definition of who is a Jew has led to controversies, traditionally it was someone who was a child of the covenant between God and the descendants of the biblical **Patriarchs**. The term *Jew* first came into use after the **Babylonian** conquest of **Judah** in 586 BCE, when the inhabitants taken away into exile were known as Judeans. This is what the Hebrew word *yehudi* means.

The classical Jewish position was that someone was a Jew if born of a Jewish mother or if they were a **proselyte** who had converted to the religion. **Reform Judaism** has introduced a patrilineal definition of *Jew*, so that someone with only a Jewish father but a **Gentile** mother would be considered a Jew. **Anti-Semites** have their own ways of identifying Jews, which may be in terms of race or "blood." These are categories that Jews do not recognize as having any relevance for Jewish identity because of the great variety of Jewish types ranging through black, brown, yellow, and pink skin colors, all of whom may be **halakhically** Jewish. *See also* ABRAHAM; ASHKENAZIM (SINGULAR ASHKENAZI); ASSIMILATION; BENE ISRAEL; BRITISH ISRAELITES; CONVERSOS; DOENMEH; ESSENES; FALASHAS (ALSO KNOWN AS BETA ISRAEL); KARAITES; KHAZARS; KRIMCHAKS; LAW OF RETURN;

MESHED; MOUNTAIN JEWS; NEW CHRISTIANS; NUMERUS CLAUSUS (LATIN, "CLOSED NUMBER"); NUREMBERG LAWS; OMAR, COVENANT OF; SAMARITANS; SEPHARDIM; TEN LOST TRIBES; WANDERING JEW.

JEWISH AGENCY. An international organization originally called the Jewish Agency for **Palestine**, which was set up in 1929 by **Chaim Weizmann** on behalf of the **World Zionist Organization** to deal with practical issues involved in the settlement of Jews in Palestine. In Mandate Palestine, the agency, made up of Zionists and non-Zionists, was the main body representing Jewry in the **Holy Land**, and in 1948, **David Ben Gurion**, as the head of the Jewish Agency, officially declared an independent State of **Israel**. The agency continued to exist after the founding of the state to deal with the absorption of immigrants, agricultural developments in Israel, and education of **Diaspora** Jews. *See also* MEIR, GOLDA (ORIGINALLY MYERSON, 1898–1978).

JEWISH BRIGADE. A uniquely Jewish brigade within the British army that fought in World War II and was made up mostly of **Palestinian** Jewish volunteers. It came about because of pressure from the **Zionist** establishment in Palestine to have Jews represented as Jews in the fight against Nazi Germany. Although it was disbanded after the war, the army experience provided military training for Palestinian Jews in skirmishes with Palestinian gangs and in the **War of Independence** with their Arab neighbors in 1948. *See also* ISRAEL DEFENSE FORCE (IDF).

JEWISH DEFENSE LEAGUE (JDL). An American vigilante association founded by Rabbi Meir Kahane in 1968 to take a militant role in the defense of Jews and to combat prejudice and **anti-Semitism**. The JDL was based in New York, but it eventually spread to **Israel**, where it began a political party under the name Kach. Kahane was elected to the **Knesset** on a far right-wing ticket in 1984. His party was eventually barred for its racist views, and Kahane was assassinated by an Arab in New York in 1990.

JEWISH FIGHTING ORGANIZATION (WARSAW). *See* WARSAW GHETTO UPRISING.

JEWISH IDENTITY. *See* ASSIMILATION; BENE ISRAEL; BRITISH ISRAELITES; CANTONISTS; CONSERVATIVE JUDAISM; CONVERSOS; EXILE (HEBREW GALUT); FALASHAS (ALSO KNOWN AS BETA ISRAEL); GENTILE (HEBREW GOY, PLURAL GOYIM, "NATION" OR "PEOPLE"); JEW (HEBREW YEHUDI); KAIFENG; KARAITES; REFORM JUDAISM; SAMARITANS; TEN LOST TRIBES.

JEWISH LEGION. *See* REVISIONIST ZIONISTS.

JEWISH MUSEUM, PRAGUE. *See* MOLCHO, SOLOMON (1500–32).

JEWISH NATIONAL FUND (HEBREW KEREN KAYEMET LEYISRAEL, JNF). The fundraising arm of the **World Zionist Organization**. The JNF began in 1901 to acquire land, mostly agricultural land, in **Palestine** for Jewish use. After the founding of the State of **Israel** in 1948, the funds raised by the JNF among **Diaspora** communities were mostly used for improving the quality of the land in Israel and planting forests, as well as supporting **Zionist** educational and cultural activities. It still plays a major role in Israel's development, and the blue-and-white JNF charity box is a cherished item in many Diaspora homes. Jews who drop their small change into the box feel they are expressing solidarity with the Jewish state and the Jewish People. Fundraising for JNF causes is also done on a much larger scale with dinners, balls, and **synagogue** appeals organized throughout Diaspora communities by local Zionists.

JEWISH NATIONAL LIBRARY. *See* HEBREW UNIVERSITY OF JERUSALEM.

JEWISH RITUAL YEAR. The Jewish ritual year contains 12, and sometimes 13, lunar months that make up the Jewish **calendar**. In the **Bible**, the months usually do not have names, and the names currently in use were borrowed from the **Babylonians**. The year begins in the autumn at the beginning of the seventh month, Tishri, with the **New Year Festival**; the next day, the third of Tishri, is the Fast of Gedaliah, which remembers the assassination of Gedaliah, the Babylonian appointed governor of Judea. The first 10 days of Tishri are known as the

Ten Days of Penitence, culminating in the fast of the **Day of Atonement**, and are followed 5 days later by the festival of **Tabernacles**.

The next festival is **Chanukah**, which falls toward the end of the ninth month, Kislev, and is an eight-day postbiblical festival of light. In the next month, Tevet, there is the fast of the 10th of Tevet, which remembers the attack on **Jerusalem** by the Babylonians when the city was besieged.

Two months later, on 14 Adar, is the carnival festival of **Purim** celebrating the events recounted in the Book of Esther. This is preceded by a fast known as the Fast of Esther. In a leap year, there is an extra month, Second Adar, in which case the festival of Purim is in this leap month.

The month after Adar is Nisan, the first month according to the biblical reckoning, on the 15th of which the festival of **Passover** falls. The period of 49 days from Passover to the festival of **Pentecost**, which falls in the month of Sivan, is known as the **Omer**. This is a period of semimourning remembering the Crusades and persecution down the ages. Just after the end of the Passover is **Holocaust Remembrance Day** on 27 Nisan and a **Zionist** festival, **Israel Independence Day**, on 5 Iyyar. This latter is celebrated by many religious people as an expression of the divine miracle of the return of Jews to their homeland. The minor festival of **Lag B'Omer** is on 18 Iyyar.

Pentecost is the third of the pilgrimage festivals and celebrates the giving of the **Ten Commandments** to the Israelites at Mt. Sinai. It is a one-day festival in Israel, falling on the sixth of Sivan, and two days in the **Diaspora**. The ritual year ends with a strict mourning period associated with the destruction of the **Temple** in Jerusalem, beginning with the fast of the **Seventeenth of Tammuz** in the 10th month, and ending with the fast of the **Ninth of Av**, the saddest day of the Jewish year, in the 11th month.

JEWISH THEOLOGICAL SEMINARY (BRESLAU). *See* YESHI-VAH (HEBREW, "PLACE OF SITTING," PLURAL YESHIVOT).

JEWISH THEOLOGICAL SEMINARY (JTS). A seminary for the training of **rabbis** and educators as part of **Conservative Judaism**. The seminary was started in 1887 as a place to train rabbis of all traditional persuasions, including **Orthodoxy**, and indeed, one of its first graduates was **Joseph Herman Hertz**, future British chief rabbi.

When in 1902 **Solomon Schechter** was appointed as head of the JTS, however, it soon became a specifically Conservative institution, with a major library, internationally known scholars, and an important graduate school. Schechter also founded the United Synagogue of America, modeled on the British United Synagogue, to bring together Conservative congregations for whom the graduates of the seminary could act as rabbis.

Unlike a **yeshivah**, where the concentration of studies is on the **Talmud** and its commentaries, the seminary had a broad curriculum from the outset, including secular studies. The seminary has a training school for cantors and opened a branch, the University of Judaism, in Los Angeles in 1947 and a training school for rabbis in Jerusalem in 1984. It admitted **women** to its rabbinical program in 1983, despite some opposition in Conservative circles. This led to a breakaway group led by David Weiss Halivni, a prominent teacher at the JTS, setting up an opposition movement, the Union for Traditional Judaism.

THE JEWISH WAR **(BOOK).** *See* JOSEPHUS FLAVIUS (1ST CENTURY CE).

JEWS COLLEGE (LONDON). *See* YESHIVAH (HEBREW, "PLACE OF SITTING," PLURAL YESHIVOT).

JEW SUESS. *See* OPPENHEIMER, JOSEPH (1698–1738, KNOWN AS JEW SUESS).

THE JOINT. *See* AMERICAN JEWISH JOINT DISTRIBUTION (JDC, OR THE JOINT).

JOSELMANN, JOSEPH, OF ROSHEIM (1478–1554). *See* JOSEPH JOSELMANN OF ROSHEIM (1478–1554).

JOSEPH. Biblical character, son of **Jacob** and his wife Rachel. According to the biblical account in the Book of Genesis, Joseph was a favorite son of his father and, having been given a coat of many colors as a sign of his father's affection, aroused the jealousy of his brothers, who eventually sold him into slavery in Egypt. There, Joseph rose to a high position in charge of the Egyptian economy.

When his brothers came from the land of Canaan during a famine looking for food in Egypt, he set various tests for them before revealing himself to them. He encouraged his father, brothers, and family to come and live with him, and thus the sojourn of the **Israelites** in Egypt began. They eventually became slaves of the Egyptians when a new dynasty of pharaohs arose. It is assumed that this reflects the situation when the Hyksos, a Semitic ethnic group, were expelled from Egypt in the 16th century BCE.

Though in later Jewish history, after the reign of King **Solomon**, the Joseph subtribes led the other tribes in a break away from the tribe of **Judah**, Joseph nevertheless was held up in Rabbinic literature as the exemplar of a righteous man, **tzaddik**, because of his resistance to the seduction of his master's wife in Egypt and because he preserved his affection for his family and humility despite his high office. *See also* TEN LOST TRIBES.

JOSEPH, KING (LEGENDARY FIGURE). *See* REUVENI, DAVID (15TH–16TH CENTURIES).

JOSEPH JOSELMANN OF ROSHEIM (1478–1554). One of the most important **Court Jews** in Germany who represented Jewish interests, particularly of the Jews in Alsace, and obtained documents of protection for German Jews from Emperor Charles V. His efforts to save Jews extended beyond the German borders, and he was active in combating expulsion orders and accusations of **blood libel** and **host desecration**, as well as engaging in **disputations** about the nature of Judaism. *See also* OPPENHEIMER, JOSEPH (1698–1738, KNOWN AS JEW SUESS); ROTHSCHILD FAMILY; SASSOON FAMILY; WAHL, SAUL (1541–1617).

JOSEPHUS FLAVIUS (1ST CENTURY CE). Jewish historian. Josephus was a commander of the Galilee rebel militia during the zealot revolt against Roman rule in **Palestine**. When the Galilean rebels were defeated in 67 CE, Josephus and the remainder of his force took refuge in a cave, where they planned to kill each other rather than fall into Roman hands. Josephus arranged to be the last one alive and then surrendered to the Romans. He spent the rest of his life in Rome and, perhaps out of a sense of guilt, wrote a series of major works in Greek: *The Jewish War*, about the war against Rome; *The Antiquities*

of the Jews, about Jewish history; *Life*, an autobiographical justification of his actions; and *Against Apion*, a defense of Judaism against
anti-Semitic criticisms.

JOSHUA (BIBLICAL FIGURE). *See* HOLY LAND; ISRAEL;
PROMISED LAND; PURIM.

JUDAH (HEBREW YEHUDAH). Biblical character, son of **Jacob**
and his wife Leah, and according to the biblical account, founder of
the tribe named after him. Judah married a Canaanite woman, which
may reflect the composition of the tribe in later times. His was the
largest of the tribes and source of the Davidic line of kings. King
David and King **Solomon** ruled over the confederation of the 12
tribes, but the competition between the Judah and **Joseph** tribes led
to a split after Solomon's death into the northern kingdom of **Israel**,
with Samaria (*see* SAMARITANS) as its capital, and the southern
kingdom of Judah, with **Jerusalem** as its capital. The name *Jew* is
the English for yehudi, meaning a Judean, a member of the tribe or
kingdom of Judah.

JUDAH MACCABEE (2ND CENTURY BCE). A **Hasmonean** warrior who led the revolt of the **Maccabees** against the Seleucid Greek
rulers of **Palestine** after the death of his father Mattathias. Judah,
through a strategy of guerrilla warfare, managed to defeat the more
powerful armies of the Seleucid king Antiochus Epiphanes and in 164
BCE reconquered **Jerusalem** and rededicated the **Temple**. His victory
is celebrated by Jews each year in the festival of **Chanukah**. Judah
was eventually killed in battle but attained the status of a folk hero.

JUDAH THE NASI. Palestinian rabbinical leader in the late 2nd century CE. A descendant of the **Davidic** line and of the 1st–century CE
sage Hillel, Judah became the nasi, the official head of Jewry in the
Holy Land, and ruled in royal style. Various **Talmudic** stories tell of
Judah's close association with the Roman leadership, even with an
unidentified Roman emperor known as Antoninus. Judah's rule was
not without opposition from some of his colleagues who objected to
his strong leadership, yet he was also elevated by the Jewish tradition to quasi-saintly status and was known as Rabbenu Ha-Kadosh,
"Our Holy **Rabbi**." Judah and his colleagues were responsible for

producing the first official work of the **Oral Torah**, the **Mishnah**. *See also* EXILARCH (ARAMAIC RESH GALUTA, "HEAD OF THE EXILE").

JUDEA. *See* ALIYAH (HEBREW, "GOING UP," PLURAL ALIYOT); BABYLONIA; DIASPORA; HEROD; HOLY LAND; ISRAEL; JERUSALEM; JEW (HEBREW YEHUDI); JEWISH RITUAL YEAR; JUDAH (HEBREW YEHUDAH); PROSELYTES (HEBREW GERIM, SINGULAR GER); SANHEDRIN; TEMPLE (HEBREW BET HA-MIKDASH); YADIN, YIGAL (1917–84).

JUDENREIN (GERMAN, "FREE OF JEWS"). Nazi term used to refer to areas where the Jewish population had been killed or transported to concentration camps. The aim of the **Final Solution** policy of the Nazis implemented during the **Holocaust** was to make all of Europe Judenrein.

JUDGMENT OF SOLOMON. *See* SOLOMON (10TH CENTURY BCE).

– K –

KABBALAH. The Jewish mystical tradition. Mysticism had a profound effect on Jewish life from the late Middle Ages down to the period of the **Enlightenment**. The high point of the early Kabbalah was the dissemination of the **Zohar**, a work produced in Spain in the late 13th century CE that developed the idea of the 10 Sefirot, the interfaces between God and the created world, through which the world had emanated from the Godhead and was controlled by Him. The Zohar also gave an important role to the feminine side of God, Shekhinah; to the reality of evil; and to the idea of the transmigration of souls, gilgul.

The next great turning point in the development of Kabbalah took place in the 16th century with teachings of **Isaac Luria** (1534–72). Luria gained the reputation of a holy man to whom the prophet Elijah appeared. He taught that, during the process of emanation, the divine light was too powerful for the vessels that were meant to contain it, and the vessels shattered. This caused sparks of the divine light to become entrapped in the shells of the broken vessels, and it is up to man to rectify this by freeing these sparks. The entrapped sparks are the source of evil in the world.

The idea of rectification of the world by man had a strong **Messianic** element because man can bring about Messianic redemption if he can free the trapped sparks. The consequences of Lurianic Messianism in the centuries after Luria were dramatic, leading to major Messianic movements, such as that surrounding **Shabbetai Tzvi** in the mid–17th century, which was based on Lurianic ideology, and its aftermath in the Frankist Movement around the quasi-Messianic figure of **Jacob Frank**. *See also* CHASIDIC MOVEMENT (ALSO HASIDIC); TZADDIK (HEBREW, "RIGHTEOUS ONE," PLURAL TZADDIKIM).

KACH (POLITICAL PARTY). *See* JEWISH DEFENSE LEAGUE (JDL).

KAHANE, MEIR. *See* JEWISH DEFENSE LEAGUE (JDL).

KAIFENG. A city in central China that was home to a community of **Jews** from the mid-12th century CE until the modern era. The first Jewish settlers came as merchants from Persia and gradually **assimilated** to Chinese ways. They had a **synagogue** and scrolls of the **Bible**, but in the course of time, they lost any knowledge of **Hebrew** and by the 19th century had only preserved a rudimentary form of Judaism. The community was discovered by a Jesuit missionary in the early 17th century, who met a Kaifeng Jew in Beijing. The latter assumed that the Jesuits were fellow Jews. Subsequent Jesuit missionaries collected documents and details of the way of life of the Kaifeng Jewish community. Although there are several hundred Chinese families in Kaifeng who still claim Jewish origin, they are indistinguishable from the local Han Chinese through intermarriage and assimilation of Confucian culture.

KAPO. A concentration camp inmate who was appointed by the SS to be in charge of other prisoners. The kapos sometimes were Jews but most often were common criminals and feared for their cruelty in applying camp rules. They were given extra privileges and were thus highly motivated to keep the prisoners in their charge in order, even by sadistic methods. *See also* AUSCHWITZ; BERGEN-BELSEN; BUCHENWALD; HOLOCAUST.

KAPPAROT (RITUAL). *See* DAY OF ATONEMENT (HEBREW YOM KIPPUR).

KAPPEL. *See* HEAD COVERING.

KARAITES. A sect that takes a literalist approach to the **Bible**. The Karaite Movement began in **Babylonia** in the 8th century CE and consisted of followers of **Anan ben David** and members of other heterodox groups. They rejected the **Talmud** and its associated literature of Rabbinic Judaism and would not accept the authority of the Babylonian Rabbinic establishment. This led to a literature of polemics on both sides and eventually to the alienation of Karaite **Jews** from the Rabbanite majority. During the Nazi era, a number of East European Jewish scholars were asked about the Jewish identity of the Karaites by the Germans. In order to save Karaites from the fate of European Jewry in the **Holocaust**, the scholars unanimously replied that Karaites were not of Jewish racial origin, and the Nazis did not persecute them. *See also* ORAL TORAH; RABBI (HEBREW, "MY MASTER"); SADDUCEES.

KASHRUT (DIETARY LAWS). *See* DIETARY LAWS; KOSHER ("FIT FOOD," HEBREW KASHER, KASHRUT); RABBI (HEBREW, "MY MASTER").

KASZTNER, RUDOLF (1906–57). Hungarian journalist and **Zionist** leader involved in the rescue of Jews from Nazi-occupied Europe. Kasztner worked as assistant to Otto Komoly, the head of the underground Rescue Committee. They, together with **Joel Brand**, entered into negotiations with the Nazi and Hungarian fascists. Brand was sent on a mission by **Adolph Eichmann** to try to arrange the exchange of trucks for Jews, known as "blood for goods." Meanwhile, Komoly and Kasztner managed to effect the rescue of several thousand Jews who were first taken to concentration camps before journeying by train to safety in Switzerland. Some of those on the trains were relatives of Kasztner. While Komoly was killed by Hungarian fascists of the Arrow Cross, Kasztner survived with his family.

After the war, Kasztner came to **Israel**, where he received a government position. He was publicly accused of collaboration with the Nazis by a Hungarian survivor, Malkiel Gruenwald, and the government sued for libel. In the court case in 1955, the judge found that the accusations were essentially true and that Kasztner had "sold his soul to the devil." Among the evidence against Kasztner was documentary proof that at the Nuremberg trials he had written in favor of a Nazi officer whom he had negotiated with, a fact that Kasztner originally denied. This verdict brought shame on the Israeli government, and they appealed. In March 1957, Kasztner was assassinated by Zev Eckstein, a young right-wing Zionist who was associated with the **Stern Gang** underground and also worked with the Israeli secret service, Shin Bet. The Israeli high court eventually exonerated Kasztner in January 1958, and the **Holocaust** museum at **Yad Vashem** included him in their exhibits. *See also* TZADDIK (HEBREW, "RIGHTEOUS ONE," PLURAL TZADDIKIM).

KATZENELLENBOGEN, SAMUEL JUDAH. *See* WAHL, SAUL (1541–1617).

KEDOSHIM ("HOLY MARTYRS"). *See* MARTYRDOM (HEBREW KIDDUSH HASHEM, "SANCTIFICATION OF (GOD'S) NAME").

KEREN KAYEMET LEYISRAEL. *See* JEWISH NATIONAL FUND (HEBREW KEREN KAYEMET LEYISRAEL, JNF).

KHAZARS. A Turkic nation living in southern Russia, many of whom converted to Judaism sometime in the mid-8th century CE. It is assumed that this conversion was a way of asserting Khazar independence from Christian Russia in the northwest and from Muslim expansion in the east. Indeed, the Jewish poet Judah Halevi wrote a work, *The Kuzari* (early 12th century), set in the time of the Khazar conversion where the Khazar king questions representatives of Judaism, Christianity, and Islam before being convinced of the truth of the first.

The Khazar Empire was defeated by the Russians in the 10th century, and the Khazars finally disappeared as an independent people in the 13th century, although some may have joined existing Jewish communities. Theories, mostly promoted by **anti-Semites** to deny the **Israelite** origin of **Ashkenazi** Jews, have circulated since the 19th century that the bulk of Ashkenazi Jews were descended from the Khazars. There is no historical or DNA support for this idea, although it is still popular in some Arab states. It was taken up by the novelist Arthur Koestler in his work *The Thirteenth Tribe* (1976). *See also* BRITISH ISRAELITES; KRIMCHAKS; MOUNTAIN JEWS; PROSELYTES (HEBREW GERIM, SINGULAR GER).

KIBBUTZ (HEBREW, "COLLECTIVE," PLURAL KIBBUTZIM). A collective agricultural settlement in **Israel** originally with a socialist or Marxist ideology. The first kibbutz, Deganiah, was founded in 1909 by a group of young **Zionist** socialist pioneers who made **aliyah** from Russia, intent on founding a utopian-type community in the **Holy Land**. The early kibbutzim were secular and held all kibbutz property in common, as well as organizing families into community units where childrearing was shared by everyone. In the course of time, religious Zionist kibbutzim affiliated with **Mizrachi** were also established, and the Kibbutz Movement evolved from utopian communities into more pragmatic societies with greater privacy for their members, ownership of private property, and an industrial as well as an agricultural economy. Although some of those in the elite ranks of the Israeli army and of Israeli politics are still products of the kibbutz, its role in Israeli society in general has diminished greatly from the early days of the state. *See also* ISRAEL DEFENSE FORCE (IDF).

KIDDUSH (HEBREW, "SANCTIFICATION"). *See* BAR MITZVAH/BAT MITZVAH ("COMING OF AGE"); SABBATH (HEBREW SHABBAT).

KIDDUSH LEVANAH (HEBREW, "SANCTIFICATION OF THE MOON"). *See* CALENDAR; DAVID.

KIELCE POGROM. In July 1946, there was an attack on Jewish refugees who had returned from concentration camps and Russia to the Polish town of Kielce. The **pogrom** was orchestrated by local police and Polish **anti-Semites** and resulted in the death of 42 Jews and injuries among many of the several hundred other Jews in the town. This attack on **Holocaust** survivors led to shock and panic among the remaining Jews in Poland, who realized that they could not simply return to their homes and that anti-Semitism was still a powerful force among the Polish population. Many Jews escaped westward and managed to join groups of illegal immigrants making **aliyah** to **Palestine**. *See also* BERICHAH (HEBREW, "FLIGHT").

KINOT ("DIRGES"). *See* NINTH OF AV, FAST OF (HEBREW TISHA B'AV).

KIPPAH. *See* HEAD COVERING.

KISHINEV POGROMS. A series of **anti-Semitic** attacks in the Russian city of Kishinev orchestrated by government officials, police, and a local mob. The first **pogrom** in 1903 began when rumors spread that the Jews had murdered a Christian child, a modern version of the medieval **blood libel**. Some 49 Jews were killed, hundreds were injured, and many Jewish homes and businesses were looted and burned down. The second pogrom in 1905 was perpetrated by a nationalist mob and, although on a smaller scale, led to the murder of 19 Jews, with many injured and much looting. The pogroms were widely reported and led to the mass emigration westward of Russian Jews, not only from Kishinev itself, but also from other parts of the **Pale of Settlement** in the Russian Empire.

KISLEV (MONTH). *See* CALENDAR; CHANUKAH; JEWISH RITUAL YEAR.

KITTEL (YIDDISH, "SHROUD"). *See* DAY OF ATONEMENT (HEBREW YOM KIPPUR).

KNESSET (HEBREW, "ASSEMBLY"). The parliament of the State of **Israel** made up of 120 members who are elected by a system of proportional representation to serve a maximum period of 4 years. Votes are cast for party lists, and the number of individuals on the list elected to the Knesset depends on the proportion of votes each party achieves. The nature of the electoral system means that small parties often have power out of all proportion to their numbers when they join in a coalition government because no one party of the right, center, or left has been able to attain a clear majority of seats on its own. *See also* ASHKENAZIM (SINGULAR ASHKENAZI).

KOESTLER, ARTHUR. *See* KHAZARS.

KOHANIM (HEBREW, "PRIESTS," SINGULAR KOHEN). *See* TEMPLE (HEBREW BET HA-MIKDASH).

KOLEL (ACADEMY FOR MARRIED STUDENTS). *See* YESHIVAH (HEBREW, "PLACE OF SITTING," PLURAL YESHIVOT).

KOL NIDREI (ANNULMENT OF VOWS). *See* DAY OF ATONEMENT (HEBREW YOM KIPPUR).

KOMOLY, OTTO. *See* KASZTNER, RUDOLF (1906–57).

KOOK, ABRAHAM ISAAC (1865–1935). Mystic and first **Ashkenazi** chief **rabbi** of the **Holy Land**. Although not a member of any **Zionist** organization, Kook believed fervently in Jewish settlement of the **Land of Israel**, and he emigrated from Eastern Europe to become the rabbi of Jaffa in 1904. He was appointed chief rabbi of the Ashkenazi community in **Palestine** in 1921. Unlike most other **Orthodox** rabbis, Kook was tolerant of the secular Zionist pioneers, believing that, like the **Temple** workmen of old, they had to perform the building work before the structure became fully sanctified. His attitude was severely criticized by the ultra-Orthodox, but he set the pattern for cooperation between religious and secular Zionists in the modern State of **Israel**.

Kook was influenced by **Kabbalah**, and his mystical outlook led him to view the return of Jews to the Land of Israel after a 2,000-year **exile** and the recognition granted them by the **Balfour Declaration** as the beginning of **Messianic** redemption. Through his writings and teachings, he has become the spiritual father of the Settler Movement in Israel, whose members believe that it is a religious duty for Jews to settle in all areas of the Holy Land. *See also* HEBREW UNIVERSITY OF JERUSALEM; MIZRACHI (ABBREVIATION OF MERCAZ RUCHANI, "SPIRITUAL CENTER"); REVISIONIST ZIONISTS.

KORAN (ISLAMIC SCRIPTURE). *See* BIBLE; JERUSALEM.

KORCZAK, JANUSZ (PSEUDONYM OF HENRYK GOLDSZMIDT, 1878–1942). Pediatrician and author born in Warsaw to an **assimilated** Jewish family and who died in the concentration camp of Treblinka. Korczak was a doctor who wrote a number of books about the care of children, which won him an international reputation. In 1911, he became the director of the Warsaw orphanage, which he ran in such a manner that children would be able to develop their independence.

He visited **Palestine** and investigated the way children were treated on a **kibbutz**. He had the opportunity of leaving Poland but decided to stay. In 1940, after the Nazi conquest of Poland, Jews, and Korczak's orphanage with them, were herded into the Warsaw **ghetto**. Although he was offered refuge outside the ghetto, Korczak stayed with his orphanage when they were taken to Treblinka, and he was murdered there with the children and other staff members. His love of children and his choice of **martyrdom** during the **Holocaust** have created a heroic legend around the man and his life.

KOSHER ("FIT FOOD," HEBREW KASHER, KASHRUT). The most general term used by **Ashkenazi** Jews for food fit to be eaten according to the **halakhah**. This may refer to kosher types of animals, birds, and fish, as well as to the way they are slaughtered and prepared. The kosher food laws are central to both Ashkenazi and **Sephardi** forms of **Orthodox** Judaism, although there are differences between them about how strictly some of these laws are to be applied. Many **Conservative** Jews also maintain kosher standards, at least in their homes, though they may not apply them very strictly to food eaten in restaurants. **Reform** Jews, on the whole, regard kosher restrictions as antiquated and, like secular Jews, do not abide by them. They may, however, eat kosher-style food that has cultural associations with traditional kosher food, even if it is not actually kosher.

Kosher food is eaten by some **Gentiles**, particularly by Muslims, who share with Jews the prohibition on pork products, and by those Christians who either wish to keep biblical food laws or who believe that the extra supervision involved in kosher food production means that the food is of a higher quality than nonkosher products. *See also* BNAI B'RITH (HEBREW, "SONS OF THE COVENANT"); CHEREM; DIETARY LAWS; MITNAGGEDIC MOVEMENT (HEBREW, "OPPONENTS"); MIZRACHI (ABBREVIATION OF MERCAZ RUCHANI, "SPIRITUAL CENTER"); RABBI (HEBREW, "MY MASTER").

KOTEL HA-MAARAVI (WESTERN WALL). *See* WAILING WALL (HEBREW KOTEL HA-MAARAVI, "WESTERN WALL").

KRIMCHAKS. A distinctive subcommunity of Jews who lived in the Crimea, the majority of whom were killed by the Nazis during the **Holocaust**. The Krimchak language, now barely spoken, was a Jewish dialect of Tartar written in **Hebrew** script with admixtures of Hebrew, **Aramaic**, **Ladino**, and **Yiddish**. The Krimchak community had its own folklore and its own prayer rite and was made up of early Jewish settlers of the Crimea who had absorbed **Khazar** converts, refugees from Byzantium, and **Ashkenazi** Jewish captives of the Tartars, whom they ransomed.

KRISTALLNACHT (GERMAN, "NIGHT OF BROKEN GLASS"). The night of November 9–10, 1938, is known by this name because during that night more than 200 **synagogues**, Jewish-owned businesses, and private homes belonging to Jews were smashed, set on fire, and destroyed by mobs led by Nazi instigators. Thirty-six Jews were killed, many others were injured, and thousands of Jews in Germany and Austria were arrested and sent to concentration camps. The official excuse for this **pogrom** was the shooting of Ernst von Rath, a diplomat in the German embassy in Paris, by a Jewish student, **Herschel Grynszpan**. Von Rath died of his wounds on November 9. *See also* HOLOCAUST.

KUZARI **(BOOK).** *See* KHAZARS.

– L–

LADINO. A variety of Jewish–Spanish dialects, with some **Hebrew** and **Aramaic** elements, spoken by the **Sephardi** exiles from Spain after 1492 throughout North Africa, the Ottoman Empire, the Netherlands, Italy, and parts of Northern Europe. The various native languages in these countries had an effect on local versions of Ladino. Like **Yiddish**, Ladino was usually written in Hebrew characters, and over the centuries, a considerable Ladino culture evolved, comprising religious texts, poetry, translations, and a developed musical tradition. There was also a secular literature of plays and fiction.

The main centers of Ladino speakers were destroyed in Greece and the Balkans during the **Holocaust**, and today, though there are still thousands of immigrants to **Israel** who can speak basic Ladino, it is in serious decline as a living language.

LAG B'OMER. The 33rd day of the **Omer** period, which falls on the 18th of the Hebrew month Iyyar. While the Omer period is one of semimourning, Lag B'Omer is a joyous day as the anniversary of the death of the 2nd–century CE mystic and sage Simeon bar Yochai. It is a favorite day for weddings, which are not allowed during parts of the Omer, depending on different customs. Since Simeon bar Yochai is the spiritual hero of the **Zohar**, it is customary to go on a pilgrimage to the site of his grave in Meron in the Galilee. There, crowds chant texts from the Zohar and build bonfires into which the hair of three-year-old boys is thrown after their hair is cut. *See also* JEWISH RITUAL YEAR.

LAND OF ISRAEL (HEBREW ERETZ YISRAEL). That area of the Middle East lying between Syria to the north and Egypt to the southwest that was mentioned in the **Bible** as promised to the people of **Israel**. It is otherwise known as the **Holy Land** or the **Promised Land**. The Romans called it **Palestine** in the 2nd century CE. In 1948, the new country, brought into being by the United Nations in part of Palestine, called itself the State of Israel.

LANGUAGE. *See* ACADEMY OF THE HEBREW LANGUAGE (HEBREW VAAD HA-LASHON HA-IVRIT); ARAMAIC; ASH-KENAZIM (SINGULAR ASHKENAZI); ASSIMILATION; BEN GURION, DAVID (1886–1973); BEN YEHUDAH, ELIEZER (1858–1922); BIROBIDZHAN; BRIT IVRIT OLAMIT (HEBREW, "WORLD HEBREW COVENANT"); BUND (SHORT FORM OF ALGEMEINER YIDDISHER ARBETER BUND); ETHIOPIA; HE-BREW; HEBREW UNIVERSITY OF JERUSALEM; KRIMCHAKS; LADINO; MOUNTAIN JEWS; SEPHARDIM; YESHIVAH (HE-BREW, "PLACE OF SITTING," PLURAL YESHIVOT); YIDDISH.

LAW OF RETURN. Law passed by the **Knesset** in 1950 affirming the right of every Jew, with a few exceptions, to come to **Israel** and be granted citizenship. Though this law was in line with the ideals of **Zionism**, it has proved highly controversial because it raises the question of who is a **Jew**, about which there are significantly different views. The law has been amended several times to define a Jew as someone born of a Jewish mother or converted to Judaism but also to include the spouses, children, and grandchildren of Jews who might not be regarded as Jews by any of the Jewish denominations. According to the Israeli Supreme Court, the Law of Return would not apply to Jews who have voluntarily adopted another religion.

LEAGUE OF NATIONS. *See* PALESTINE; ZIONISM.

LEAH (BIBLICAL FIGURE). *See* JACOB; JUDAH (HEBREW YE-HUDAH); PATRIARCHS.

LECHI. *See* STERN GANG (HEBREW LOCHAMEI CHERUT YIS-RAEL OR LECHI).

LEON, MOSES DE. *See* ZOHAR.

LESSING, GOTTHOLD. *See* MENDELSSOHN, MOSES (1729–86).

LIBERAL JUDAISM. *See* HERTZ, JOSEPH HERMAN (1872–1946).

LIFE **(BOOK).** *See* JOSEPHUS FLAVIUS (1ST CENTURY CE).

LIKKUD (POLITICAL PARTY). *See* ASHKENAZIM (PLURAL ASHKENAZI); REVISIONIST ZIONISTS.

LOCHAMEI CHERUT YISRAEL. *See* STERN GANG (HEBREW LOCHAMEI CHERUT YISRAEL OR LECHI).

LOVE OF ZION. *See* CHIBBAT TZION (HEBREW, "LOVE OF ZION").

LUBAVITCH CHASIDISM. *See* CHASIDIC MOVEMENT (ALSO HASIDIC); EMANCIPATION; MESSIAH (HEBREW MASHIACH); MITNAGGEDIC MOVEMENT (HEBREW, "OPPONENTS").

LULAV (ARAMAIC, "PALM BRANCH"). *See* TABERNACLES (HEBREW SUKKOT).

LURIA, ISAAC (1534–72). Kabbalist who created a new dimension in Kabbalah. Luria, whose full name was Isaac Luria Ashkenazi, was known by Kabbalists as Ha-Ari, "the lion," an acrostic of the **Hebrew** "the divine Rabbi Isaac." By association, his disciples were known as the "lion cubs." He grew up in Egypt, where his study of Kabbalah led him to spend seven years on an island in the Nile. There, he continued his study of the **Zohar**. There is a legend that some secret Kabbalistic manuscripts came into his hands and the prophet Elijah revealed himself to him.

Luria moved to the town of Safed in the Galilee region of the **Holy Land** in 1570, where he gathered around himself a small group of disciples to whom he taught his new ideas on Kabbalah. He wrote very little himself, apart from a few hymns, so all of his recorded teachings are from the pen of his disciples, written down in different versions. His main disciple was Chaim Vital, whose interpretation of Luria's teaching became the standard one for Kabbalists.

Lurianic Kabbalah taught that, when the world emanated from the Godhead, the vessels that were meant to contain the divine light were unable to contain them and broke. Sparks of the divine light were trapped in the broken shells of the vessels, and these shells are the source of evil in the world. Man has the power, through mystical contemplation in prayer and performing the commandments, to rectify this situation and return these sparks to their source. When this process is complete, the **Messianic** Age will dawn. This mystical Messianism had a profound effect on Judaism in post-Lurianic times, leading to the messianic movements associated with **Shabbetai Tzvi** and **Jacob Frank**. *See also* CHASIDIC MOVEMENT (ALSO HASIDIC).

– M –

MACCABEE, JUDAH (2ND CENTURY BCE). *See* JUDAH MACCABEE (2ND CENTURY BCE).

MACCABEES. Name applied to the **Hasmonean** family who led an uprising against the Seleucid Greek rulers of **Palestine** in the 2nd century BCE. There is no general agreement about the origin or meaning of the name, though one of the most successful military leaders of the revolt was known as **Judah Maccabee**. In modern times, the name has been adopted by Jewish sporting organizations and **Israeli** football clubs. *See also* CHANUKAH.

MACHAL (VOLUNTEERS). *See* WAR OF INDEPENDENCE (HEBREW MILCHEMET HA-ATZMAUT).

MACHPELAH, CAVE OF. *See* HEBRON; PILGRIMAGE (HEBREW ALIYAH LE-REGEL, "ASCENT BY FOOT"); SARAH.

MAGEN DAVID (HEBREW, "SHIELD OF DAVID" OR "STAR OF DAVID"). Six-pointed star, or hexagram, that has come to be a Jewish symbol found on Jewish gravestones, **synagogues**, and the flag of the State of **Israel**. Although it is unclear how it is associated with King **David** or when it first became a specifically Jewish symbol, it was widely used on **Kabbalistic** charms in the 14th century. The Star of David, usually yellow in color, was imposed by the Nazis on Jews, who had to wear it as an identifying badge. The Red Star of David, Magen David Adom, is the name and symbol of the Israeli equivalent of the Red Cross.

MAGEN DAVID ADOM. *See* MAGEN DAVID (HEBREW, "SHIELD OF DAVID" OR "STAR OF DAVID").

MAGGID (DAEMON). *See* CARO, JOSEPH (1488–1575); MARTYRDOM (HEBREW KIDDUSH HASHEM, "SANCTIFICATION OF (GOD'S) NAME).

MAGGID MESHARIM (MYSTICAL DIARY). *See* CARO, JOSEPH (1488–1575).

MAIMONIDES, MOSES (1135–1204). Philosopher and **halakhic** codifier. Maimonides was born in Cordova, Spain, but fled as a teenager with his father Maimon and family, eventually ending up in North Africa. They were escaping from a fanatical Muslim sect, the Almohads, who forcibly converted Jews to Islam. There is some evidence from Muslim sources that Maimonides' family themselves underwent such a forced conversion, but this has been strongly denied by Jewish scholars.

Maimonides spent most of his adult life as a physician in Egypt, becoming one of the personal doctors to the sultan's court. He was also the head of the Jewish community of Fostat, Old Cairo, and was active in undermining **Karaite** influence in Egypt. Maimonides is best known for his many works on medicine, philosophy, and Judaica, as well as his correspondence with Jews from far and wide who sought his help and advice.

One of his letters is about those Jews who faced forced conversion. Maimonides encouraged them to return to Judaism and reminded the Jewish community of the need to accept them back. Another of his letters is to the Jews of the Yemen, who wanted to know whether a messianic figure there was indeed the true **Messiah**. Maimonides explained to them that there were many pseudomessiahs who should not be followed.

The two most important of Maimonides' works are his **Hebrew** code of Jewish law, known as the Mishneh Torah, and his philosophical reinterpretation of Judaism, *The Guide for the Perplexed*, written originally in Arabic. Both of these proved to be highly controversial works. His code, which influenced **Joseph Caro**'s code, the **Shulchan Arukh,** to the point that Caro often cites Maimonides verbatim, was criticized because Maimonides does not quote his sources and he includes philosophical material in it about the belief in God that is not found in the **Talmud**. Criticism was also directed against Maimonides' views that magic and sorcery are only believed in by childish people who lack a rational outlook because these are referred to in the Talmud as having efficacy. *The Guide* came in for even more severe criticism because it reinterprets Judaism in Aristotelian terms, which proved shocking to those of a more traditional outlook who had no understanding of philosophy.

One of the distinctive contributions of Maimonides to Jewish theology was his formulation of Thirteen Principles of Jewish Faith, which he included in his Arabic commentary on the **Mishnah**. These he thought were the minimum series of beliefs necessary for a Jew to avoid heresy. They served to distinguish Judaism from **Gentile** beliefs, such as those found in Christian and Muslim religion. Maimonides' principles, however, were not acceptable to a number of his Rabbinic colleagues, who either regarded them as too minimalist because they held that all of the teachings of the **Torah** are necessary beliefs or as demanding too much of the Jewish believer simply to be included among the **Orthodox**.

In the period following Maimonides, some of his disciples took his philosophical approach to extremes, reinterpreting both the biblical stories and the commandments as philosophical symbols. This led to a strong reaction on the part of traditionalists, who proclaimed a **cherem** against Maimonides' writings, and their complaints to the Catholic authorities led to the burning of Maimonides' books. Later, when the church burned copies of the Talmud, they regretted this involvement of the Catholic authorities and saw the burning of the Talmud as a punishment for their own mistreatment of Maimonides' works. *See also* CONVERSOS; MARTYRDOM (HEBREW KIDDUSH HASHEM, "SANCTIFICATION OF (GOD'S) NAME").

MANASSEH (TRIBE). *See* ISRAEL; SAMARITANS.

MANASSEH BEN ISRAEL (1604–57). Dutch **Marrano** and mystic whose efforts were responsible for the return of Jews to England after a gap of more than 300 years. Manasseh was inspired by reports that Jewish tribes, descendants of the **Ten Lost Tribes**, had been found in South America. He argued that, according to biblical prophecy, the age of the **Messiah** would entail the ingathering of the Jews from the furthest corners of the earth to the **Holy Land**. Because England was one such "corner of the earth" (Angle Terre), the return of Jews there would hasten **Messianic** redemption. He presented a "Humble Address" to **Oliver Cromwell** in 1655, petitioning him on this subject. Although this petition was not immediately successful, it set in motion a process that allowed Jews freedom of religion in England within a year. *See also* SAMBATYON.

MANNA. *See* SABBATH (HEBREW SHABBAT).

MANUAL OF DISCIPLINE. *See* DEAD SEA SCROLLS.

MAPPAH (HEBREW, "TABLECLOTH"). *See* SHULCHAN ARUKH (HEBREW, "LAID TABLE").

MARCHESHVAN (MONTH). *See* CALENDAR.

MARIAMNE (HASMONEAN QUEEN). *See* HEROD.

MAROR (RITUAL FOOD). *See* PASSOVER.

MARRANO. A pejorative term, thought to derive from the Portuguese for "swine," used of Jews who secretly retained their Jewish religion after having been forced to convert to Roman Catholicism during the 14th and 15th centuries in the Iberian peninsula. Though persecuted by the **Inquisition**, small groups of converted Jews continued to practice marrano religion into modern times. In some areas of Portugal, efforts have been made recently by younger members of marrano families to openly return to Judaism. *See also* AUTO-DA-FE ("ACT OF FAITH"); CONVERSOS; CROMWELL, OLIVER (1599–1658); DAY OF ATONEMENT (HEBREW YOM KIPPUR); INQUISITION; MANASSEH BEN ISRAEL (1604–57); MARTYRDOM (HEBREW KIDDUSH HASHEM, "SANCTIFICATION OF (GOD'S) NAME"); MOLCHO, SOLOMON (1500–32); NEW CHRISTIANS; REUVENI, DAVID (15TH–16TH CENTURIES); SEPHARDIM; TORQUEMADA, TOMAS DE (1420–98).

MARRIAGE. *See* GENTILE (HEBREW GOY, PLURAL GOYIM, "NATION" OR "PEOPLE"); LAG B'OMER; MESHED; MINYAN (HEBREW, "NUMBER"); MISHNAH; NAPOLEON BONAPARTE (1769–1821); NUREMBERG LAWS; OMER (HEBREW, "SHEAF" OF BARLEY); RABBI (HEBREW, "MY MASTER").

MARTYRDOM (HEBREW KIDDUSH HASHEM, "SANCTIFICATION OF (GOD'S) NAME"). Religious conflict with Greek and Roman paganism led to the formulation of ideas about martyrdom in the **Talmud**. The conclusions reached were applied in later times when **Jews** were called upon to maintain their faith in Christian and Muslim countries. This was particularly true in the Middle Ages, when Christianity frequently offered Jews the choice of conversion or persecution and death. Thus, many communities chose death rather than apostasy during the period of the **Crusades**, and **Marranos** in the Iberian Peninsula continued to practice Judaism, knowing this could mean torture and being burned alive after investigation by the **Inquisition**.

Less frequently, martyrs in Islamic countries chose death rather than forced conversion to Islam. This was because the **halakhah** did not view Islam with the same suspicion as it viewed Christian belief in the divinity of Jesus, which was anathema to Jewish monotheists. Many Jews fled Spain and parts of North Africa in the 12th century in the face of the fanatical Almohad sect's alternative of death or conversion, having undergone nominal Islamicization. There is some evidence that the family of **Moses Maimonides** was among them. The Jews of **Meshed** in Iran, apart from a few martyrs who chose death, converted en masse to Islam while secretly retaining Jewish religious practices.

It was regarded as a great privilege to be able to die as a martyr with a prayer on one's lips, and martyrs are referred to as kedoshim, "holy ones." Rabbi **Joseph Caro** desired to die such a holy martyr's death and was told by his angelic guide (maggid) that he would merit this, but it was not to be. The term *holy ones* eventually came to be applied to all Jews who died because they were Jews, even though their death was not voluntary, such as the kedoshim of the **Holocaust**.

MARXISM. *See* BUND (SHORT FORM OF ALGEMEINER YID-DISHER ARBETER BUND); KIBBUTZ (HEBREW, "COLLEC-TIVE," PLURAL KIBBUTZIM); YEVSEKTSIYA.

MASHIACH. *See* MESSIAH (HEBREW MASHIACH).

MASKILIM. *See* ENLIGHTENMENT (HEBREW HASKALAH).

MASONRY. *See* BNAI B'RITH (HEBREW, "SONS OF THE COV-ENANT").

MATRIARCHS. *See* HEBRON; PATRIARCHS; PILGRIMAGE (HE-BREW ALIYAH LE-REGEL, "ASCENT BY FOOT"); PROS-ELYTES (HEBREW GERIM, SINGULAR GER); SARAH.

MATTATHIAS (HASMONEAN LEADER). *See* JUDAH MACCA-BEE (2ND CENTURY BCE).

MATZAH (HEBREW, "UNLEAVENED BREAD"). *See* PASS-OVER (HEBREW PESACH).

MECCA. *See* JERUSALEM; MESHED.

MECHITZAH (HEBREW, "PARTITION"). *See* SYNAGOGUE (HEBREW BET KNESSET).

MEDINA. *See* JERUSALEM.

MEGILLAH (HEBREW, "SCROLL"). *See* PURIM.

***MEIN KAMPF (MY STRUGGLE,* BOOK).** *See* HITLER, ADOLPH (1889–1945).

MEIR, CHIEF RABBI JACOB. *See* HEBREW UNIVERSITY OF JERUSALEM.

MEIR, GOLDA (ORIGINALLY MYERSON, 1898–1978). First female prime minister of **Israel**. She fled with her family from Russia in 1906 to the United States, and in 1921, Golda Meir emigrated with her husband to **Palestine** to join a **kibbutz**. In 1934, she was elected to the executive of the Histadrut, the workers trade union body, and some 10 years later became acting head of the **Jewish Agency**.

Golda Meir was sent to negotiate secretly with King Abdullah of Jordan before **David Ben Gurion** declared the establishment of the State of Israel to persuade him not to attack the state. She was unsuccessful in her mission. After a stint as a diplomat in Moscow, she joined the Israeli government first as minister of labor and then for nine years as foreign minister. She became prime minister when the previous incumbent, Levi Eshkol, died in 1969 and stayed in that position despite problems with her coalition partners until after the Yom Kippur War of 1973. She, together with her defense minister **Moshe Dayan** and other cabinet colleagues, was blamed for the deficiencies of the war. She resigned her position in June 1974. As prime minister, she was rumored to hold cabinet meetings in her kitchen. *See also* WOMEN IN JUDAISM.

MELENIK. *See* SOLOMON (10TH CENTURY BCE).

MEMORIAL FOUNDATION FOR JEWISH CULTURE. *See* CONFERENCE ON JEWISH MATERIAL CLAIMS AGAINST GERMANY.

MENDELSSOHN, MOSES (1729–86). Leading intellectual force behind the Jewish **Enlightenment**, Haskalah, in Germany. Although Mendelssohn was self-taught in secular subjects, he won a prize for one of his philosophical essays while in Berlin. He was admired both by **Gentile** leaders of the Enlightenment, such as Gotthold Lessing, as well as by Jews far and wide.

Mendelssohn translated the **Bible** into German printed in **Hebrew** characters for his coreligionists to encourage them to abandon **Yiddish** and to speak a polished German. With the aid of his disciples, he began a revolution in Jewish education. His efforts to modernize Jews led many German Jews to **assimilate** and adopt Protestant Christianity, for which he was heavily criticized by traditionalists. Yet, that was not his intention, and he himself remained an **Orthodox** Jew living successfully in the worlds of both **halakhah** and Haskalah.

MENSTRUATION. *See* BLOOD LIBEL; MIKVEH; SHTETL; WOMEN IN JUDAISM.

MERCAZ RUCHANI ("SPIRITUAL CENTER"). *See* MIZRACHI (ABBREVIATION OF MERCAZ RUCHANI, "SPIRITUAL CENTER").

THE MERCHANT OF VENICE **(PLAY).** *See* USURY.

MESHED. A Muslim holy city in the north of Iran. There was a flourishing Jewish community there in the 18th century, but in 1839, a Shiite mob attacked the Jewish quarter of the town and burned down the **synagogue**. The Jews themselves were only saved from a **martyr**'s death by being forcibly converted to Islam. They lived as secret Jews, openly professing Islam but maintaining strict Jewish practice in private, until they were able to leave and openly resume their faith. They married only among themselves, with two sets of marriage contracts, a Muslim one and a Jewish one, and even went on the Haj pilgrimage to Mecca to prove they were "good" Muslims. Most of the Meshedi Jews now live in **Israel** or the United States. *See also* CONVERSOS.

MESSIAH (HEBREW MASHIACH). A descendant of King **David** who, in the future, will be a new king over **Israel** in an era of redemption. He will gather exiled Jews from the **Diaspora** to the **Promised Land**; usher in a period of peace, justice, and harmony; and, after wars and cataclysms involving the defeat of heathen nations, will unveil his kingdom in Zion and **Jerusalem**, where the Third **Temple** will be established. There are many different teachings found in Judaism about the Messiah, the **Resurrection** of the dead, and the Day of Judgment that will accompany the Messianic Age.

The Messianic hope was an important support for Jews facing persecution, **pogroms**, forced conversion, and extreme **anti-Semitism**. Although in modern times **Reform Judaism** has replaced the belief about a human Messiah with the idea of a new age of harmony for mankind, it is still held in a traditional form by many religious Jews. Some **Zionists** believe that the **Holocaust** and the reestablishment of an independent Jewish state in **Palestine** are the beginnings of Messianic redemption, while followers of the Lubavitch **Chasidic** subbranch maintain that their recently deceased leader, Rabbi Menachem M. Schneerson, was the Messiah, and he will return from the dead at the Resurrection. *See also* AGUDAT ISRAEL (ALSO KNOWN AS AGUDAH); ALROY, DAVID (12TH CENTURY); BARCELONA, DISPUTATION OF; BAR KOKHBA (d. 135 CE); CHMIELNICKI MASSACRES; CROMWELL, OLIVER (1599–1658); DISPUTATIONS; DOENMEH; FRANK, JACOB (1726–91); GENTILE (HEBREW GOY, PLURAL GOYIM, "NATION" OR "PEOPLE"); KABBALAH; LURIA, ISAAC (1534–72); MAIMONIDES, MOSES (1135–1204); MANASSEH BEN ISRAEL (1604–57); MESSIANIC MOVEMENTS; MOLCHO, SOLOMON (1500–32); NATHAN OF GAZA (1643–80); NETUREI KARTA (ARAMAIC, "GUARDIANS OF THE CITY"); PHARISEES; REUVENI, DAVID (15TH–16TH CENTURIES); SABBATH (HEBREW SHABBAT); SHABBETAI TZVI (1626–76); SIX-DAY WAR; SYNAGOGUE (HEBREW BET KNESSET); TABERNACLES (HEBREW SUKKOT); TEMPLE (HEBREW BET HA-MIKDASH).

MESSIANIC MOVEMENTS. The belief in the coming of a **Messiah** has led to a series of Messianic movements down the ages. The best known is that surrounding Jesus in 1st–century CE **Palestine**, a movement that eventually became the new religion of Christianity. According to the historian **Josephus Flavius**, there were a number of Messianic figures in that area in the 1st century, and there is some evidence that **Bar Kokhba** in the 2nd century was regarded as the Messiah by his followers. Throughout the Middle Ages, Messianic movements arose in various areas of the **Diaspora**: Arab lands, France, the Ottoman Empire, Persia, Spain, and Yemen. They usually ended in catastrophe and sometimes in apostasy. Thus, **Shabbetai Tzvi** converted to Islam with some of his followers, and **Jacob Frank** converted to Catholicism with all of his followers. *See also* DOENMEH; MAIMONIDES, MOSES (1135–1204).

MI5 (BRITISH SECRET SERVICE). *See* ROTHSCHILD FAMILY.

MIDRASHIC LITERATURE. *See* ORAL TORAH; PENTECOST (HEBREW SHAVUOT).

MIKVEH. A ritual bath that is used by **women** after menstruation before resuming sexual relations with their husbands, by **proselytes** as part of the process of conversion to Judaism, and by Jews to purify themselves prior to certain festivals, in particular before the **Day of Atonement.** In **Temple** times, the mikveh was frequently used by priests to remove minor impurities before engaging in the sacrificial cult. The **Kabbalah** puts a great emphasis on purification by water, as did the ancient sect of the **Essenes.** Many **Chasidic** Jews today bathe in a mikveh each weekday before morning prayers and on Fridays just before the onset of the **Sabbath.**

People must clean themselves physically in a shower or bath before immersion in the mikveh, which is meant to be a purely spiritual cleansing. Thus, the mikveh also served as the communal bathhouse when private bathrooms were uncommon. During the **Black Death,** it is possible that the hygienic qualities of ritual bathing was one of the factors that protected Jews from the worst ravages of the plague. A mikveh is also used for dipping cooking vessels made by **Gentiles** before use by **Orthodox** Jews.

The mikveh is constituted of rainwater, snow, or some other natural water source. Once constituted, then a pool of tap water is attached to the natural water, and the tap water becomes natural water by association. It is the tap water that can be changed and renewed for clean water. There are various technical ways in which the **halakhah** allows the tap water to be in contact with the natural water for the mikveh to be properly constituted.

MIKVEH ISRAEL (HEBREW, "HOPE OF ISRAEL"). *See* ALLI-ANCE ISRAÉLITE UNIVERSELLE (AIU).

MILA 18 (STREET). *See* WARSAW GHETTO UPRISING.

MILCHEMET HA-ATZMAUT. *See* WAR OF INDEPENDENCE (HEBREW MILCHEMET HA-ATZMAUT).

MINHAG (HEBREW, "CUSTOM"). *See* HALAKHAH (HEBREW, "THE WAY").

MINYAN (HEBREW, "NUMBER"). The quorum needed for some forms of public prayer and rituals, like the marriage ceremony, is known as a minyan. It is made up of 10 adult Jewish males over the age of **bar mitzvah**, this being the minimum number of people needed to constitute a community. In Orthodox practice, **women** are not counted in a quorum, but some non-Orthodox communities do count women.

MIRIAM (BIBLICAL FIGURE). *See* WOMEN IN JUDAISM.

MISHKAN (HEBREW, "SANCTUARY"). *See* TEMPLE (HEBREW BET HA-MIKDASH).

MISHNAH. First official text of the **Oral Torah** edited by **Judah the Nasi** in the beginning of the 3rd century CE. There were previous Mishnah collections that were incorporated in the official Mishnah text, which was mainly of a legal and ritual nature. Differing opinions on many of the major issues dealt within the Mishnah are cited, so the Mishnah is by no means a code. Rather, it is a collection of sources and teachings for study and analysis in which Judah the Nasi expressed his opinion as to which views he preferred. The Mishnah as a study text is precisely how the **Talmud** relates to it, as it is structured around the Mishnah text as an extended, wide-ranging commentary.

The Mishnah is divided up into six orders, dealing respectively with agricultural laws, blessings, and prayers; Sabbaths and festivals; marriage and divorce; interpersonal relations; sacrificial matters; and ritual purity, particularly as affecting the **Temple**.

There is some evidence that the Mishnah was not originally written down, there being some resistance to committing oral teachings to writing, but was memorized by scholars with exceptional memories known as tannaim (from the singular tanna, a "repeater"). The name eventually became attached to all Mishnaic **rabbis**, who were called tannaim. *See also* PHARISEES.

MISHNEH TORAH (HALAKHIC WORK). *See* MAIMONIDES, MOSES (1135–1204).

MITNAGGEDIC MOVEMENT (HEBREW, "OPPONENTS"). A movement formed by those East European Jews who were strongly opposed to the **Chasidic Movement**. The spiritual leader of the Mitnaggedim was **Elijah of Vilna** (1720–97), who suspected the Chasidim of Shabbatean tendencies, criticized their lack of commitment to **Torah** study in favor of ecstatic prayer, and viewed the cult of the personality in the adulation of the **tzaddik** as idolatrous.

Although the opposition cooled in the course of time under the leadership of **Chaim of Volozhin** (1749–1821), particularly when the Chasidim became a part of the **Orthodox** establishment in the late 18th and early 19th centuries, some of the more extreme opponents in Lithuania proclaimed a **cherem** in 1772 and again in 1781. Books were burned, anti-Chasidic tracts were published, Chasidic slaughter of animals was declared not **kosher**, and intermarriage with Chasidim was forbidden.

Avigdor, the **rabbi** of Pinsk, complained to the government in the 1790s and 1800, accusing Chasidim of heresy and subscribing to Shabbateanism. He denounced the Chasidic leader Shneur Zalman of Liadi, founder of Lubavitch Chasidism, to the authorities, and the latter was arrested in 1798 and again in 1801 and tried in St. Petersburg. Shneur Zalman was eventually acquitted.

Today, many of the rabbis associated with Lithuanian-style **Talmudic** academies, known colloquially as the **"yeshivah** world," claim to be spiritual descendants of the Mitnaggedim. This is because of their emphasis on the centrality of Torah study for the religious life rather than on any of the more ecstatic values of Chasidism.

MITZVAH (HEBREW, "COMMANDMENT," PLURAL MITZVOT). *See* HALAKHAH (HEBREW, "THE WAY").

MIZRACHI (ABBREVIATION OF MERCAZ RUCHANI, "SPIR-ITUAL CENTER"). A religious **Zionist** organization founded in 1902 that combined Jewish nationalism with religious values. While socialist Zionism was generally antagonistic toward Judaism, seeing it as the remnant of **ghetto** existence in the **Diaspora**, there was a more popular form of longing for Zion among the masses of Eastern Europe and also among some of their **rabbis**.

The Mizrachi dream was of a Jewish state run according to the principles of the **Torah**, and this was shared by the organizers of the **Chibbat Tzion** Movement. Such a state would involve its citizens keeping the **Sabbath** and festivals and maintaining the **dietary laws** of kashrut, along with a thousand other **halakhic** minutiae. The motto of the religious Zionists was "The **land of Israel** for the people of **Israel** according to the Torah of Israel."

Rabbi **Abraham Isaac Kook**, though not an official member of Mizrachi, was nevertheless regarded as the ideological mentor of the movement. After the foundation of the State of Israel, the Mizrachi Party served in Israeli government coalitions, often controlling the Ministry of Religious Affairs, and was a strong supporter of the Israeli chief rabbinate. The **Six-Day War**, which many members of Mizrachi regarded as the onset of the **Messianic** Age, led young Mizrachists to set up the settler movement encouraging Jews to live in all areas of the historic **Holy Land**, even among the **Palestinian** population as in **Hebron**.

MODERN ORTHODOXY. *See* BAR MITZVAH/BAT MITZVAH ("COMING OF AGE"); BNAI B'RITH (HEBREW, "SONS OF THE COVENANT"); BOARD OF DEPUTIES OF BRITISH JEWS; EN-LIGHTENMENT (HEBREW HASKALAH); HEAD COVERING; HERTZ, JOSEPH HERMAN (1872–1946); HIRSCH, SAMSON RAPHAEL (1808–88); KOOK, ABRAHAM ISAAC (1865–1935); MENDELSSOHN, MOSES (1729–86); MIZRACHI (ABBREVIA-TION OF MERCAZ RUCHANI,"SPIRITUAL CENTER"); NEO-ORTHODOXY; ORTHODOX JUDAISM; RABBI (HEBREW, "MY MASTER"); TALLIT (ARAMAIC, "PRAYER SHAWL"); YESHI-VAH (HEBREW, "PLACE OF SITTING," PLURAL YESHIVOT).

MOHAMMED (ISLAMIC PROPHET). *See* JERUSALEM; WAILING WALL (HEBREW KOTEL HA-MAARAVI, "WESTERN WALL").

MOHAMMED ALI (EGYPTIAN PASHA). *See* DAMASCUS BLOOD LIBEL.

MOHEL (HEBREW, "CIRCUMCISER"). *See* SHTETL.

MOLCHO, SOLOMON (1500–32). Portuguese **Messianic** figure. Solomon's family were **Marranos**, but he openly reverted to Judaism after meeting **David Reuveni**, who proclaimed the imminence of the Messianic Age. Molcho circumcised himself and was then forced to flee Portugal for fear of the Catholic authorities. He studied **Kabbalah** on his travels, probably in Salonika, where one of his fellow students was **Joseph Caro**. Caro developed a great liking for Molcho and in later life desired to be a **martyr** like him. Although Molcho seems to have charmed Pope Clement VI in Rome and escaped arrest on a number of occasions, he was eventually turned in to the **Inquisition** in Mantua, found guilty of Judaizing, and burned at the stake after refusing to recant. People believed that Molcho was the Messiah, and he may have come to believe this himself. A robe and the flag of Molcho are in the Jewish Museum in Prague.

MONOTHEISM. *See* ABRAHAM; GENTILE (HEBREW GOY, PLURAL GOYIM, "NATION" OR "PEOPLE"); GRAETZ, HEINRICH (1817–91); MAIMONIDES, MOSES (1135–1204); PROSELYTES (HEBREW GERIM, SINGULAR GER); SARAH; SOLOMON (10TH CENTURY BCE); TEN COMMANDMENTS (OR DECALOGUE).

MONTEFIORE, SIR MOSES (1784–1885). Leading British philanthropist and Jewish elder statesman. Montefiore, born in Italy, became a broker in the city of London and a figure of the English establishment. He was knighted by Queen Victoria. Montefiore was president of the **Board of Deputies of British Jews** for nearly 40 years from 1835 and devoted himself to the welfare of his coreligionists throughout the world. He set up living areas for Jews in **Palestine**; was involved in assisting his coreligionists in the **Damascus Blood Libel**; helped persecuted Jews in Russia, Morocco, and Romania; and tried to resolve the **Mortara Case**. His wealth and great age made him a figure of respect in Britain and abroad.

MOON. *See* CALENDAR; DAVID.

MORDECAI (BIBLICAL FIGURE). *See* HAMAN; PURIM.

MORTARA CASE. In 1853, a Jewish infant, Edgardo Mortara, was secretly baptized in Bologna, Italy, by his Catholic nanny, who was afraid that he might die. When she told this to her priest in 1858, the six-year-old child was taken by the papal authorities to Rome as a Catholic, and they refused to return him to his parents. The case caused a scandal worldwide, and **Sir Moses Montefiore** even journeyed to Rome to persuade the church to release him but without success. The shock among European Jews led directly to the founding of the **Alliance Israélite Universelle** in 1860. *See also* CONVERSOS.

MOSES. The greatest of the **Hebrew** prophets, known in the Jewish tradition as Moshe Rabbenu, "Moses, our teacher." Moses is regarded as the author of the Pentateuch, which he wrote under divine inspiration. The biblical stories about Moses, a major part of the salvation history of **Israel**, are set in the 13th century BCE.

As a Hebrew baby, Moses was hidden by his parents in the bulrushes to avoid Egyptian infanticide, where he was found by the daughter of the pharaoh, who adopted him. Although he grew up in the Egyptian court, Moses became aware of the oppression of his brethren and one day killed an Egyptian slavemaster who was beating a Hebrew slave. He was forced to flee from Egypt to Midian, where God appeared to him on Mt. Horeb in a burning bush and told him to return to Egypt and tell the pharaoh to set the Israelite slaves free.

Moses returned to Egypt, where he was instrumental in unleashing the Ten Plagues on the Egyptians, forcing the Egyptians to free the Israelites. The **Exodus** was led by Moses, who took the people into the desert. When they came to a sea of reeds, mistakenly referred to as the Red Sea, Moses stretched out his staff, and the sea split, so the Israelites crossed on dry land while the pursuing Egyptians were drowned by the returning waters.

At Mt. Horeb, also known as Mt. Sinai, the covenant between God and Israel was sealed, and Moses ascended the mountain, bringing down two tablets with the **Ten Commandments**. In his absence, the Israelites built a golden calf that they worshipped. An angry Moses broke the tablets and punished the participants; then he ascended the mountain once again and brought down another set of tablets.

As a punishment for doubting God's ability to bring them into the **Holy Land**, the generation of the Exodus had to wander for 40 years in the wilderness until they died out. Moses himself was not allowed to enter the **Promised Land** because of his own shortcomings but was merely able to look out over the land across the Jordan River.

Jews celebrate the major elements of the salvation history associated with Moses. They retell the story of slavery in Egypt, the Ten Plagues, and the ultimate redemption in the Exodus during the rituals of the **Passover** seder meal. Strangely enough, however, Moses is hardly mentioned in the Haggadah version of this story. The reason for this is presumably to play down the cult of personality and place the emphasis on God alone. The giving of the Ten Commandments is celebrated at the festival of **Pentecost** and the wandering through the desert at the festival of **Tabernacles**.

MOSHE RABBENU (HEBREW, "MOSES, OUR TEACHER"). *See* MOSES.

MOSQUES. *See* HEBRON; JERUSALEM; SYNAGOGUE (HEBREW BET KNESSET).

MOSSAD (ISRAELI INTELLIGENCE SERVICE). *See* COHEN, ELI (1924–65); EICHMANN, ADOLPH (1906–62).

MOUNTAIN JEWS. A warlike community of Jews living originally in mountainous regions of the East Caucasus and speaking a Jewish Tat dialect, related to Persian, which was originally written in **Hebrew** characters. According to legend, the first Mountain Jews were members of the **Ten Lost Tribes**, but most likely, the community was started by refugees from Byzantine persecution and Persia, with an admixture of **Khazar** converts to Judaism. They suffered under Persian and Muslim rule and were known because the males always wore a sword or dagger in their belts. Under Soviet rule of the Caucasus, the farms of the Mountain Jews were collectivized, but there was no serious interference with their religious traditions because they lived in a sensitive border area. After the collapse of the Soviet Union, most Mountain Jews made **aliyah** to **Israel** or emigrated to the West, where they have lost their distinctive ethnic and religious identity and merged with other Jewish communities.

MUFTI OF JERUSALEM. *See* HUSSEINI, HAJ AMIN (1893–1974); WAILING WALL (HEBREW KOTEL HA-MAARAVI, "WESTERN WALL").

MUNICH CODEX (TALMUD). *See* TALMUD.

MUSAR (HEBREW, "ETHICS"). *See* MUSAR MOVEMENT; SALANTER, ISRAEL (1810–83); YESHIVAH (HEBREW, "PLACE OF SITTING," PLURAL YESHIVOT).

MUSAR MOVEMENT. A movement within **Orthodox** Judaism that emphasized the ethical dimension of religious life. Musar was founded in the mid-19th century by **Israel Salanter** on the basis of teachings going back to **Chaim of Volozhin**, one of the spiritual fathers of the **Mitnaggedim**. Chaim of Volozhin said that people must learn to participate with others in their sufferings, this being a central feature of Judaism.

Salanter originally intended his emphasis on morality within religion to improve the life of the ordinary householder who was subject to the secularizing influence of the **Enlightenment** or to the attraction of **Chasidism**. Salanter even moved to Germany and France to preach there in the very centers of modernity. He eventually extended the scope of Musar to include **yeshivah** students, and a series of gifted followers of Salanter introduced Musar to most of the main yeshivah academies in Lithuania in the face of fierce opposition from some leading **rabbis**.

The Musar yeshivah encouraged its students to spend time on ethical literature and in soul searching rather than merely on **Talmudic** texts. Even in minimalist Musar yeshivot, at least half an hour a day was given over to ethical reflection. Today, many of the great yeshivah academies of the Mitnaggedim at least pay lip service to Musar, and some have a full-time moral tutor who preaches to the whole academy at least once a week on an ethical topic, interweaving themes from Rabbinic literature.

In pre–World War II Eastern Europe, there were two basic models for a Musar yeshivah. One, the Slobodka type, believed that students should dress neatly and learn how to consider others while perfecting themselves in studying Judaism. In the other, more extreme Novardok model, students were encouraged to learn how to overcome egoism by engaging in strange practices that brought them shame in public. For example, they would dress in rags and go out in public to be made fun of, or they would stand in a queue in a pharmacy and when their turn to be served came would ask for something ridiculous in a loud voice, like half a pound of mincemeat. These and many similar exercises were introduced by Joseph Josel Hurvitz, the Alter (Yiddish, "Old Man") of Novardok, who himself had spent years in isolation grappling with his internal demons.

MYERSON, GOLDA (1898–1978). *See* MEIR, GOLDA.

MYSTICISM. *See* ALROY, DAVID (12TH CENTURY); ARAMAIC; BAAL SHEM TOV, ISRAEL BEN ELIEZER (1700–60); CARO, JOSEPH (1488–1575); CHASIDIC MOVEMENT (ALSO HASIDIC); ELIJAH OF VILNA (1720–97); EXILE (HEBREW GALUT); FRANK, JACOB (1726–91); KABBALAH; KOOK, ABRAHAM ISAAC (1865–1935); LAG B'OMER; LURIA, ISAAC (1534–72); MANASSEH BEN ISRAEL (1604–57); NATHAN OF GAZA (1643–80); OMER (HEBREW, "SHEAF" OF BARLEY); ORAL TORAH; SAMBATYON; SHABBETAI TZVI (1626–76); TABERNACLES (HEBREW SUKKOT); TZADDIK (HEBREW, "RIGHTEOUS ONE," PLURAL TZADDIKIM); ZOHAR.

– N –

NACHMANIDES, MOSES. *See* BARCELONA, DISPUTATION OF.

NAMIER, LEWIS. *See* WEIZMANN, CHAIM (1872–1952).

NAPOLEON BONAPARTE (1769–1821). French emperor whose modernizing policies involved the **emancipation**, and in many cases the **assimilation**, of his Jewish subjects. Napoleon called together leading Jewish figures, lay and clerical, in an Assembly of Jewish Notables (1806). They discussed issues raised by Napoleon, such as polygamy, how Jews were meant to behave toward **Gentiles**, intermarriage with Christians, attitudes toward the laws of France, the authority of **rabbis**, and the practice of **usury**. There were deep disagreements among members on some of these issues, but the final answers that emerged were a compromise to please Napoleon. He subsequently summoned together a **Sanhedrin** (1807) with 71 members, two thirds being rabbis, that was modeled on the Sanhedrin court of ancient times to give religious formulation to these answers.

Napoleon abolished **ghettos** throughout his empire, made Judaism one of the official religions of France in 1807, and established the **Consistoire** system. He was even rumored to have favored the establishment of a Jewish state when campaigning in **Palestine**. Napoleon's assimilationist policies were fervently opposed by some **Orthodox** Jews, and during his invasion of Russia, some **Chasidim** actually spied for the czar because of their opposition to Napoleonic **enlightenment**.

NASI (LEADER OF PALESTINIAN JEWRY). *See* EXILARCH (ARAMAIC RESH GALUTA, "HEAD OF THE EXILE"); JUDAH THE NASI.

NASSER, GAMAL ABDEL. *See* SINAI CAMPAIGN; SIX-DAY WAR.

NATHAN OF GAZA (1643–80). Mystic and prophet of the Shabbatean Movement. It was Nathan who persuaded **Shabbetai Tzvi** to declare himself the **Messiah**, and after Shabbetai's forced conversion to Islam in 1666, Nathan continued to propagate the Messianic belief. He defended the conversion of the Messiah and his **Doenmeh** followers to Islam on **Kabbalistic** grounds. After Shabbetai's death, he refused to accept the Messiah's demise and explained it as merely his disappearance from this mundane world to a higher level of existence from whence he would reappear to complete his redemptive work.

NATIONAL ARMY ORGANIZATION. *See* IRGUN TZEVAI LEUMI (HEBREW, "NATIONAL ARMY ORGANIZATION," KNOWN AS THE IRGUN).

NAZIS. *See* ALIYAH (HEBREW, "GOING UP," PLURAL ALIYOT); AMERICAN JEWISH JOINT DISTRIBUTION (JDC, OR THE JOINT); ANTI-SEMITISM; ARENDT, HANNAH (1906–75); ASSIMILATION; AUSCHWITZ; BABI YAR; BERGEN-BELSEN;

BETAR (ACRONYM OF BERIT TRUMPELDOR); BLOOD LI-
BEL; BRAND, JOEL (1906–64); BUND (SHORT FORM OF
ALGEMEINER YIDDISHER ARBETER BUND); CONFERENCE
ON JEWISH MATERIAL CLAIMS AGAINST GERMANY; EICH-
MANN, ADOLPH (1906–62); FINAL SOLUTION; GESTAPO
(GEHEIME STAATS-POLIZEI); GHETTO; GRYNSZPAN, HER-
SCHEL (1921–?); HEBREW UNIVERSITY OF JERUSALEM;
HITLER, ADOLPH (1889–1945); HOLOCAUST; HOLOCAUST
REMEMBRANCE DAY (HEBREW YOM HASHOAH); HUS-
SEINI, HAJ AMIN (1893–1974); IRON GUARD; JABOTINSKY,
VLADIMIR (1889–1940); JEWISH BRIGADE; JUDENREIN (GER-
MAN, "FREE OF JEWS"); KARAITES; KASZTNER, RUDOLF
(1906–57); KORCZAK, JANUSZ (PSEUDONYM OF HENRYK
GOLDSZMIDT, 1878–1942); KRIMCHAKS; KRISTALLNACHT
(GERMAN, "NIGHT OF BROKEN GLASS"); MAGEN DAVID
(HEBREW, "SHIELD OF DAVID" OR "STAR OF DAVID");
NUREMBERG LAWS; PALMACH; PARTISANS; PROTOCOLS
OF THE ELDERS OF ZION; ROTHSCHILD FAMILY; SYNA-
GOGUE (HEBREW BET KNESSET); TZADDIK (HEBREW,
"RIGHTEOUS ONE," PLURAL TZADDIKIM); WAHL, SAUL
(1541–1617); WARSAW GHETTO UPRISING; WEIZMANN,
CHAIM (1874–1952); YAD VASHEM.

NEFESH HACHAIM (MYSTICAL WORK). *See* CHAIM OF VO-
LOZHIN (1749–1821).

NEO-ORTHODOXY. Religious movement in Germany founded by
Samson Raphael Hirsch to preserve an **Orthodox** lifestyle according to the **halakhah** and maintain a belief in the literalness of divine
revelation to **Moses** in the **Torah**, while at the same time participating fully in German culture. Hirsch became the **rabbi** of a small
community in Frankfurt on the Main, which he turned into the center
of the Neo-Orthodox Movement through educational institutions and
publications.

He insisted this movement, with its slogan of "Torah together with
the way of the land," should separate itself completely from **Reform**
Judaism. This was made possible in 1876 by the passing of a law,
Austrittsgesetz, allowing people to break away from the official
Jewish community. Thus, Neo-Orthodox communities were able to

secede completely from those general Jewish communities in which Reform Judaism participated.

NETANYAHU, BINYAMIN. *See* ENTEBBE.

NETANYAHU, COLONEL YONI. *See* ENTEBBE.

NETUREI KARTA (ARAMAIC, "GUARDIANS OF THE CITY"). An extreme **Orthodox** group opposed to **Zionism** and to any compromise with the **Enlightenment** and modernity. Neturei Karta members are so antagonistic toward the State of **Israel** that they join pro-**Palestinian** demonstrations, and those who live in Israel refuse to carry Israeli identity cards or passports, pay taxes to the state, or use any of its facilities. The group, though small in number, is very active and is made up mainly of a small number of **Jerusalem** families plus followers of the Satmar subgroup of **Chasidism.**

Members of Neturei Karta do not negate the return of the Jews to the **Holy Land,** but they believe that this will take place only in God's time when the **Messianic** Age dawns. They reject the secular nationalism, which they see as characterizing Zionism and the State of Israel, as a form of heresy because it negates God's promise of redemption. They disagree with the attitudes of modernity because its secular teachings contradict the literal understanding of the **Bible** and Rabbinic literature.

The dress of Neturei Karta members is similar to that of other members of the ultra-Orthodox community, comprising side curls, long coats, and black hats, but they differ sharply from the majority of ultra-Orthodox Jews who are affiliated with **Agudat Israel.** Neturei Karta followers regard members of Agudah as having sold out to Zionism because they have joined coalition governments in Israel, and they are often more antagonistic toward them than toward religious Zionists of the **Mizrachi** because they have little expectations about the religious standards of the latter. *See also* WOMEN IN JUDAISM.

NEVIIM. *See* BIBLE.

NEW CHRISTIANS. Jews who were converted to Catholicism in Spain, mostly by force in 1391 and 1492, were known as New Christians and were suspected of practicing Judaism in secret. This was the case for many of these **conversos**, who were indeed **Marranos**. Some were caught by the **Inquisition**, while some escaped to Spanish and Portuguese colonies where they could practice their religion more freely. Many attained positions of power in Spain, and in 1485 some of the most prominent New Christians organized the assassination of the leader of the Inquisition in Saragossa to try to hold up his investigation of them.

Thousands of New Christians were tried by the Inquisition and found guilty of Judaizing, and the mass expulsion of Jews from Spain was intended to end the Jewish influence on their forcibly converted brethren. Even those who were genuine converts were discriminated against by their Christian coreligionists in Spain because they were suspect. The conversos in Portugal also faced the wrath of the Inquisition, sometimes more extreme in rooting out Judaizers than its Spanish counterpart. The Portuguese conversos, however, did occasionally manage to ameliorate the activities of the Inquisition through bribery and appeals to the pope. *See also* SEPHARDIM.

NEW TESTAMENT. *See* PHARISEES; SADDUCEES.

NEW YEAR FESTIVAL (HEBREW ROSH HASHANAH, LITERALLY "HEAD OF THE YEAR"). The Jewish New Year festival is a two-day festival at the beginning of the **Hebrew** month of Tishri and usually falls mid-September. It commemorates the creation of the world as recounted in the Book of Genesis and is a day of judgment during which people are judged for their deeds in the past year. The theme of the rituals for this festival is repentance, and during the morning service on both days, a hundred notes are blown on a ram's horn, shofar, to awaken people to repentance.

As a mark of the belief in God's goodness and willingness to forgive, Rosh Hashanah is celebrated in joy, despite being a day of judgment. Jews wear fine clothes and have celebratory meals, which include sweet foods thought to be auspicious for a good and "sweet" new year ahead. Thus, bread, which is usually dipped in salt, is dipped in honey. *See also* CALENDAR; JEWISH RITUAL YEAR.

NICHOLAS II, CZAR. *See* CANTONISTS; PROTOCOLS OF THE ELDERS OF ZION.

NIGHT OF BROKEN GLASS. *See* GRYNSZPAN, HERSCHEL (1921–?); KRISTALLNACHT (GERMAN, "NIGHT OF BROKEN GLASS").

NINTH OF AV, FAST OF (HEBREW TISHA B'AV). The fast of the ninth of the Hebrew month Av usually falls in late July or early August. It commemorates various sad events in Jewish history, the most significant of which is the destruction of the First and Second **Temples**, both of which took place on this date according to Jewish tradition. The First Temple was burned down by the **Babylonians** in 586 BCE, and the Second Temple was destroyed by the Romans in 70 CE.

During the 25 hours of the fast, all food and drink is prohibited, leather shoes are not worn, no sexual relations are to be undertaken, and, until midday, people sit on the ground or on low stools. All of this is how Jews express mourning, and the whole people of Israel are in mourning for the Temple.

The **synagogue** is lit by only a few lights so the congregants recite the prayers in semidarkness. The Book of Lamentations is read as well as a series of dirges known as kinot, which tell in poetic form of the tragedies that have afflicted the Jews down the ages. These include poems about the Temple destruction as well as **martyrdom** during the **Crusades**. Some editions of kinot even include a modern dirge about the **Holocaust**. *See also* CALENDAR; JEWISH RITUAL YEAR; SEVENTEENTH OF TAMMUZ.

NISAN (MONTH). *See* CALENDAR; HOLOCAUST REMEMBRANCE DAY (HEBREW YOM HASHOAH); JEWISH RITUAL YEAR; PASSOVER (HEBREW PESACH).

NOBEL PEACE PRIZE. *See* BEGIN, MENACHEM (1913–92); PERES, SHIMON (1923–); RABIN, YITZCHAK (1922–95).

NOVARDOK YESHIVAH. *See* MUSAR MOVEMENT; SALANTER, ISRAEL (1810–83).

NUMERUS CLAUSUS (LATIN, "CLOSED NUMBER"). The limitation of certain types of people entering education or professions has often been applied to Jews. In premodern Europe, Jews were totally excluded from many areas of life: they were not allowed to own land, the guilds were closed to them, and they could not enter institutes of higher education, which were reserved for Christians. After the 18th-century **Enlightenment**, these restrictions were meant to be lifted, but at least unofficial numerus clausus limitations were imposed, even in the 19th and 20th centuries in democratic societies of the West. Thus, until the second half of the 20th century, Harvard, Yale, and most Ivy League universities in the United States restricted the number of Jewish students and staff. Behind such limitations was resentment or straightforward **anti-Semitism** and also the desire that Jews should not dominate certain professions, like medicine or the liberal arts, which, for cultural and religious reasons, Judaism might favor.

NUREMBERG LAWS. Racial laws passed by the Nazis at a Nuremberg convention in 1935 that restricted Reich citizenship to Aryan people sharing "German blood" and prohibiting marriage between Jews and those of German blood. Many professions were also closed to non-Aryans, and Jews had to have a *J* stamped on their identity cards.

NUREMBERG TRIALS. *See* KASZTNER, RUDOLF (1906–57).

– O –

OATH MORE JUDAICO. Degrading oath that Jews had to take during the Middle Ages when they were involved in a legal case with a Christian. The oath ceremony varied, but in some cases, a Jew was made to stand on a pig's skin, dressed in a humiliating manner, and declare the many curses that would accompany any false statement by him.

OBADIAH OF BERTINORO. *See* SAMBATYON.

OLD TESTAMENT. *See* BIBLE; BRITISH ISRAELITES; PROSELYTES (HEBREW GERIM, SINGULAR GER).

OMAR, COVENANT OF. Regulations applied to Jews and Christians known as dhimmis in Islam and supposedly issued by the second Caliph Omar in the early 7th century that offered them protection but only under very restrictive conditions. These regulations exist in many different versions, all of them involving discrimination against non-Muslims, and were not always strictly applied by Muslim rulers. Among them were severe limitations on the building of **synagogues** by Jews and the need for them to wear distinctive clothing and pay a poll tax.

OMER (HEBREW, "SHEAF" OF BARLEY). The seven-week period between the second day of **Passover**, when a measure of the new barley was offered up in the **Temple**, and the festival of **Pentecost**. The **Bible** commands that each day of this Omer period should be counted (Leviticus 23:15), and the counting of each day is done by **Orthodox** Jews each evening as the Jewish day begins with a blessing.

Due to the **pogroms** and massacres that took place in the Middle Ages, particularly those associated with the **Crusades**, the Omer period, falling in the spring after Easter, became associated with sadness and mourning. Different communities prohibit marriages at different parts of this Omer period. The 33rd day of the Omer, **Lag B'Omer**, which is the death anniversary of the mystic Simeon bar Yochai, interrupts the mourning and is a day of celebration. This is because the **Kabbalah** regards the death of saintly individuals as a marriage between them and God. *See also* CALENDAR; JEWISH RITUAL YEAR; MARTYRDOM (HEBREW KIDDUSH HASHEM, "SANCTIFICATION OF (GOD'S) NAME").

OPPENHEIMER, JOSEPH (1698–1738, KNOWN AS JEW SUESS). One of the wealthiest and most eminent **Court Jews** who was a financial adviser to Karl Alexander, the duke of Württemberg. As with other Court Jews, his fate was tied to the fate of his patron, who was an unpopular ruler. When the duke died, Jew Suess was arrested, his wealth was confiscated, and he was sentenced to death. While awaiting execution, he refused the offer of conversion to Christianity in order to save his life, the efforts of German Jewish communities to ransom him having failed. Jew Suess lived his last year in prison as a devout Jew, having been rather lax in his practice as a Court Jew, and when he was hanged, he died as a Jewish **martyr** with a prayer on his lips. *See also* CONVERSOS; JOSEPH JOSELMANN OF ROSHEIM (1478–1554); ROTHSCHILD FAMILY; SASSOON FAMILY; WAHL, SAUL (1541–1617).

ORAL TORAH. The Rabbinic tradition of interpretation of Scripture was originally passed on orally because there were objections to it being written down, as the written **Torah** was the **Bible**. Eventually the oral teachings were edited in various collections, the first of which was the **Mishnah**, which was originally oral but eventually was written down when the situation in Roman-occupied **Palestine** deteriorated and individuals with developed memories were arrested or killed.

The early phase of the literature of the Oral Torah culminated in the **Jerusalem** and **Babylonian Talmuds** and in Midrashic literature in the form of commentaries on the Bible. The **rabbis** claimed that their interpretations of the Oral Torah were essentially handed down to **Moses** when he received the revelation at Sinai. Though obviously new elements were continuously introduced over centuries of discussion and arguments, it was believed that the principles of the development of the Oral Torah were already given to Moses.

There were a number of sectarian critiques of the Oral Torah, the main one coming from the **Karaite** schism, which began in the 8th century CE. Karaites believed that the Rabbinic traditions of biblical interpretation were mostly incorrect and that Scripture should speak for itself. Throughout the Middle Ages, there was an exchange of polemics between Karaites and Rabbanites about the validity of Oral Torah interpretations.

The other main challenge came from within Judaism. It was the rise of **Kabbalah** involving the mystical interpretations of texts. Though the mainstream of Kabbalah stayed within the boundaries of the Rabbinic tradition, it represented a new way of determining the **halakhah** and interpreting theological material. This was through an intuitive, mystical dimension in place of the rules of hermeneutics and logic used by the Talmud. Shabbateanism [*see* SHABBETAI TZVI (1626–76)] and the Frankist Movement [*see* FRANK, JACOB (1726–91)] took this idea to the point of heresy, fired by Kabbalistic **Messianism**, and ultimately rejected the limitations of the Oral Torah in favor of mysticism and the **Zohar**. *See also* PHARISEES; SADDUCEES.

ORTHODOX JUDAISM. An umbrella term referring to traditional **Jews** who were opposed to the changes introduced by **Reform Judaism** and **Conservative Judaism** and who generally follow the **halakhic** rulings of the **Shulchan Arukh**. The spectrum of orthodoxy is very wide. At one extreme are ultra-Orthodox Jews, charedim, who reject any changes to Jewish life introduced by the **Enlightenment** and modernity, such as members of the **Neturei Karta, Chasidic**

groups, **Agudat Israel**, and the **yeshivah** world. At the other extreme are a large number of Jews who may be called nominally Orthodox because they practice some of the traditional rituals and attend prayers in Orthodox **synagogues** but are otherwise completely modern and somewhat secular in outlook. In between these extremes are Modern Orthodox Jews, who, as their name implies, welcome many cultural aspects of modernity while subscribing to an Orthodox lifestyle and believe in the validity of divine revelation in the **Bible** and **Talmud**, such as **Neo-Orthodoxy** and the **Mizrachi**. *See also* BAR MITZVAH/BAT MITZVAH ("COMING OF AGE"); BOARD OF DEPUTIES OF BRITISH JEWS; HEAD COVERING; HERTZ, JOSEPH HERMAN (1872–1946); GENTILE (HEBREW GOY, PLURAL GOYIM, "NATION" OR "PEOPLE"); HIRSCH, SAMSON RAPHAEL (1808–88); KOOK, ABRAHAM ISAAC (1865–1935); KOSHER ("FIT FOOD," HEBREW KASHER, KASHRUT); LAW OF RETURN; MAIMONIDES, MOSES (1135–1204); MENDELSSOHN, MOSES (1729–86); MIKVEH; MITNAGGEDIC MOVEMENT (HEBREW, "OPPONENTS"); MUSAR MOVEMENT; ORAL TORAH; PHARISEES; PROSELYTES (HEBREW GERIM, SINGULAR GER); RABBI (HEBREW, "MY MASTER"); SABBATH (HEBREW SHABBAT); SALANTER, ISRAEL (1810–83); SANHEDRIN; SCHECHTER, SOLOMON (1847–1915); SHTETL; TALLIT (ARAMAIC, "PRAYER SHAWL"); TORAH (HEBREW, "TEACHING"); TZADDIK (HEBREW, "RIGHTEOUS ONE," PLURAL TZADDIKIM); WOMEN IN JUDAISM.

– P –

PALE OF SETTLEMENT. By a decree of 1791, Jews were only permitted to live in an area of Czarist Russia stretching from the Black Sea to the Baltic known as the Pale of Settlement. They were not allowed to live in the inner portion of Russia so as to preserve the position of native Russians in trade and commerce. The Pale came into existence with the partition of Poland at the end of the 18th century when Russia annexed large parts of that country. Millions of **Yiddish**-speaking Jews were now citizens of Russia, which had few Jews of its own, having officially excluded them several centuries previously. Being restricted to the Pale of Settlement had severe economic consequences for Russian Jews and eventually led to waves of emigration westward in the face of **pogroms** and the many **anti-Semitic** measures of the Czarist government. *See also* BIROBIDZHAN.

PALESTINE. A name for the **Holy Land** based on the biblical word for the land of the Philistines and used by the Romans to refer to a province south of Syria. The exact boundaries of Palestine were not defined, and when the British were officially given the mandate for Palestine by the League of Nations, it included the area across the river Jordan, which the British in 1922 separated off from the rest of Palestine to form an Arab state, now the Kingdom of Jordan. The territory of the State of **Israel**, which came into being in 1948, was in parts of Western Palestine. *See also* JERUSALEM; ZIONISM.

PALESTINE ROYAL COMMISSION. *See* REVISIONIST ZIONISTS.

PALMACH. Commando and special forces unit of the **Haganah**. The Palmach was set up in 1941 as a possible deterrent to the invasion of **Palestine** by the Nazis and their allies. It initially had some support from the British army to carry out sabotage operations against the Vichy French in Syria and Lebanon. It came into its own, however, after World War II while defending Jewish settlements against Arab attack and during the **War of Independence** while fighting on all fronts against invading Arab armies.

The Palmach had its own esprit de corps, with its own songs and tales of heroism. Many of **Israel**'s leading soldiers were products of the Palmach, including **Yigal Allon** (one-time commander), **Moshe Dayan**, and **Yitzchak Rabin**. After some consideration of divergent views, it was decided to merge the Palmach with the **Israel Defense Force**, the army of the newly created State of Israel, in 1948.

PARNAS (HEBREW, "COMMUNITY HEAD"). *See* SHTETL.

PARTISANS. In Nazi-occupied Europe during World War II, various military resistance groups fought against the occupying German army. They mostly hid in forests, swamps, and mountains, where they made forays to harass and sabotage the military occupation.

Individual Jews, or even groups of them, joined general partisan units when they were allowed to, though some nationalist partisans were **anti-Semitic** and were not interested in allowing Jews to save themselves from **Holocaust** genocide. There were also specifically Jewish partisan groups, such as that of the four Bielski brothers under the command of Tuvia Bielski. The Bielskis maintained a camp in the Naliboki forest near the Russian town of Novardok, with living quarters dug out of the earth in which hundreds of noncombatant Jews also took shelter. The Jewish partisans had their own songs, mostly in **Yiddish**, the best known of which begins "Never say that you are on your last journey . . . For our longed for hour will surely come."

PASSOVER (HEBREW PESACH). A spring festival of the barley harvest commemorating the **Exodus** of the Israelites from slavery in Egypt, beginning on the 15th of Nisan and lasting 7 days in Israel and 8 days in the **Diaspora**. The festival is marked by the prohibition of eating leavened bread; instead unleavened matzah is eaten, made simply from dry flour and water, which must be baked within 18 minutes.

On the first night of Passover (the first two nights in the Diaspora), there is a family seder meal, during which the story of the Exodus is recited from an Haggadah text and foods symbolic of the story are eaten. Originally, a Pascal lamb was sacrificed and eaten, a practice still found among **Samaritans**, but this has not been practiced by Jews since the destruction of the Second **Temple**. Instead, a special portion of matzah, known as the efikomen, is eaten at the end of the meal to symbolize the lamb.

Among the other symbolic foods are bitter herbs, maror, eaten to represent the bitterness of slavery, dipped in a mixture of wine, nuts, and fruit, charoset, which symbolizes the mortar. Four cups of wine are drunk during the course of the meal to represent the four expressions of redemption used in the biblical account of the redemption from Egypt. Various foods are dipped in saltwater to represent the tears of the slaves. Passover is the most family-oriented festival, and children try to return home to celebrate it with their parents and grandparents. *See also* CALENDAR; JEWISH RITUAL YEAR; MOSES; OMER (HEBREW, "SHEAF" OF BARLEY); PENTECOST (HEBREW SHAVUOT); PILGRIMAGE (HEBREW ALIYAH LE-REGEL, "ASCENT BY FOOT").

PATRIARCHS. Early biblical figures who are regarded as the fathers of the Jewish people and the Jewish religion. There are three Patriarchs, **Abraham**, Isaac, and **Jacob**, and their wives, **Sarah**, Rebecca, Rachel, and Leah, are known as the four Matriarchs.

PENTATEUCH. *See* ARAMAIC; BAR MITZVAH/BAT MITZVAH ("COMING OF AGE"); BIBLE; GENTILE (HEBREW GOY, PLURAL GOYIM, "NATION" OR "PEOPLE"); HERTZ, JOSEPH HERMAN (1872–1946); MOSES; SAMARITANS; TEN COMMANDMENTS (OR DECALOGUE); TORAH (HEBREW, "TEACHING").

PENTECOST (HEBREW SHAVUOT). A festival 50 days after the beginning of **Passover** at the time of the wheat harvest in the **Land of Israel**, which commemorates the revelation of the **Ten Commandments** at Mt. Sinai. Pentecost is one day in Israel and two in the **Diaspora**, and cheese dishes are traditionally eaten. **Synagogues** are decorated with flowers and greenery, one reason for this being the Midrashic story that Mt. Sinai burst into greenery when the revelation to **Moses** and the Israelites took place.

There was considerable disagreement about the date of Pentecost between the **Pharisees** and the **Sadducees**. This is because the **Bible** indicates that the counting of the **Omer** leading up to Pentecost should begin from the "day after the **Sabbath**" (Leviticus 23:15). While the Rabbanite Jewish tradition, following the Pharisees, took this to refer to the day after the first festival day of Passover, the Sadducees, **Samaritans**, and later on the **Karaites** took it as the day after the Sabbath day, that is, a Sunday, at the beginning of Passover. So for them, Pentecost always falls on a Sunday. *See also* CALENDAR; JEWISH RITUAL YEAR.

PEOPLE OF ISRAEL. *See* ABRAHAM; ISRAEL; JEW (HEBREW YEHUDI); LAND OF ISRAEL (HEBREW ERETZ YISRAEL); MIZRACHI (ABBREVIATION OF MERCAZ RUCHANI, "SPIRITUAL CENTER"); NINTH OF AV, FAST OF (HEBREW TISHA B'AV); PROMISED LAND.

PERES, SHIMON (1923–). Israeli politician and winner of the Nobel Peace Prize together with **Yitzchak Rabin** and Yasser Arafat in 1994. Peres has served in various roles in the Israeli government. He has been leader of the Labor Party and prime minister twice, the second time for a short period after Rabin was assassinated. He was deeply engaged in peace negotiations with the **Palestinians** and Jordan. Peres, as defense minister, was involved in the **Entebbe** rescue operation and is thought to have been responsible for the development of Israel as a nuclear power. He was elected president of Israel in 2007.

PESACH. *See* PASSOVER (HEBREW PESACH).

PHARISEES. A religious community flourishing in **Palestine** before and just after the Common Era. The Pharisees were the spiritual fathers of Rabbinic Judaism, which produced the **Mishnah** and **Talmuds** in subsequent centuries. They were often in dispute with the priestly groups of **Temple**-based **Sadducees** about control of the **Sanhedrin**. From reports of **Josephus Flavius**, the Pharisees, unlike the Sadducees, believed in life after death, the **Resurrection**, reward and punishment, and the **Messiah**. Although very strict about purity rules, they were not religious conservatives. They developed techniques of biblical interpretation, expressed in the **Oral Torah**, which made them able to survive the destruction of the Second Temple. Reports of the lifestyle, activities, and beliefs of the Pharisees are either biased or were recorded long after they ceased to exist as a separate community. Thus, the Pharisees, often linked with "the Scribes," receive bad press in the New Testament, yet it would seem that Jesus shared many religious assumptions with them. They have been viewed as representing the hopes and aspirations of popular Judaism rather than the extreme asceticism of the **Essenes** or the aristocratic values of the Sadducees.

PICQUART, GEORGE. *See* DREYFUS CASE.

PILGRIMAGE (HEBREW ALIYAH LE-REGEL, "ASCENT BY FOOT"). The ritual of journeying to a holy place, applied most commonly to the journey to **Jerusalem** for the three festivals of **Passover**, **Pentecost**, and **Tabernacles**, or the "three foot festivals." The **Bible** encourages male Jews to appear before the Lord on these three occasions (e.g., Exodus 23:17) and bring sacrifices to the **Temple**. In the past during these times of pilgrimage, the population of the city of Jerusalem used to swell to many times its original size, with pilgrims coming from the **Land of Israel** and from throughout the **Diaspora**.

Even after the destruction of the Second Temple, pilgrims continued to visit holy sites in **Israel**, such as the Cave of Machpelah in **Hebron**, the tomb of the Matriarch Rachel near Bethlehem, and other sites with biblical associations or the graves of saintly individuals. The Western Wall of the Temple Mount was a special focus of pilgrims, and because of the recitation of lamentations there for the destruction of the Temple, it became known as the **Wailing Wall**. Because some of these sites were also holy places for Muslims during the long period of Islamic rule of the **Holy Land**, Jews were barred from approaching too close to the cave in Hebron and to the Temple Mount in Jerusalem.

POGROM. A word of Russian origin meaning a vicious and destructive attack against a certain group. The term has come to be used specifically to refer to **anti-Semitic** attacks against Jews because of the frequency and brutal nature of anti-Jewish attacks. Many of these pogroms took place in Russia, often encouraged by priests, with at least the tacit acquiescence of the Russian authorities. *See also* BLACK DEATH; BLOOD LIBEL; CHMIELNICKI MASSACRES; CRUSADES; DAMASCUS BLOOD LIBEL; DREYFUS CASE; GESTAPO (GEHEIME STAATS-POLIZEI); GHETTO; HAIDAMACKS; HAMAN; HOLOCAUST; HOST DESECRATION; HUSSEINI, HAJ AMIN (1893–1974); IRON GUARD; JEWISH DEFENSE LEAGUE (JDL); KIELCE POGROM; KISHINEV POGROMS; KRISTALLNACHT (GERMAN, "NIGHT OF BROKEN GLASS"); MARTYRDOM (HEBREW KIDDUSH HASHEM, "SANCTIFICATION OF (GOD'S) NAME"); MESHED; PURIM; REVISIONIST ZIONISTS; SHTETL; STERN GANG (HEBREW LOCHAMEI CHERUT YISRAEL OR LECHI).

POLEMICS. *See* GENTILE (HEBREW GOY, PLURAL GOYIM, "NATION" OR "PEOPLE"); KARAITES; ORAL TORAH.

POLL TAX. *See* OMAR, COVENANT OF.

PRAYER SHAWL. *See* TALLIT (ARAMAIC, "PRAYER SHAWL").

PROMISED LAND. The land of Canaan, which according to the **Bible** was promised to **Abraham** and his descendants (Genesis 12:7;

15:18) as part of God's covenant with him. The Israelites journeyed through the desert toward the Promised Land after the **Exodus** from Egypt under the leadership of **Moses**. The land was eventually conquered by Joshua and divided up among the 12 tribes of **Israel**.

Though the people of Israel were exiled from the **Land of Israel**, first by the Assyrians, then by the **Babylonians**, and last by the Romans, it was always the place that they sought to return to, and it figured frequently in their prayers and **Messianic** hopes. After 1967 and the **Six-Day War**, most of the biblical Promised Land, including the holy city of **Jerusalem**, was once again under Jewish control, and this was seen as the renewal and fulfillment of God's covenant, raising Messianic hopes among many religious Jews.

PROSELYTES (HEBREW GERIM, SINGULAR GER). Although **Jews** identify themselves ethnically as the descendants of the **Patriarchs** and Matriarchs, the Jewish religion accepts converts who thus become the spiritual children of **Abraham** and **Sarah**. A proselyte would have to accept the belief in monotheism and that God was the God of **Israel** who revealed His teachings in the Hebrew **Bible**. They would also have to accept the duties and responsibilities of Jewish life and practice.

In traditional conversions, a male ger would be circumcised, and both male and female proselytes would bathe in a **mikveh**. While **Orthodox** conversions usually adhere strictly to the **halakhic** guidelines for conversion, often demanding a long period of study and reflection by the would-be proselyte, **Conservative** and **Reform** conversions make less demands on the ger.

There are major reservations among Orthodox Jews about non-Orthodox conversion procedures and also doubts about the authority and status of the non-Orthodox **rabbis** who implement them. Because conversion has to be supervised by a Beth Din court of rabbis, Orthodoxy does not accept the validity of non-Orthodox conversions. The same problems exist for Conservative Judaism with regard to the validity of Reform conversions. This has led to problems of Jewish identity in the **Diaspora** but even more so in the State of Israel, with some proselytes not recognized as Jews by other Jews.

It is not only individuals who convert to Judaism. At various times, there were large populations of **Gentiles** who became Jews, sometimes through force or under pressure. Thus, the **Hasmonean** rulers of Judea forcibly converted some border tribes, such as the Idumeans from which **Herod**'s family came, to Judaism. At other times, conversion may have been inspired by political considerations as seems to be the case with the **Khazar** conversion in the 8th century to avoid identification with either the Muslim or the Christian worlds.

At other times, groups of proselytes emerged because of their recognition of the religious claims of Judaism or admiration for the unique role of Jews in history. Such a situation is recorded toward the end of the biblical Book of Esther (8:17); many Gentiles in the Persian Empire became proselytes. In the 20th century, a group of peasant villagers from the Italian village of San Nicandro became proselytes after one of the village elders dreamed of the truth of the Old Testament and persuaded some 23 of his fellow villagers to convert. They were accepted as Jews by the Italian Orthodox Rabbinate in Rome in 1944, and many of them made **aliyah** to Israel after the foundation of the State of Israel.

PROTOCOLS OF THE ELDERS OF ZION. A document purporting to show a Jewish conspiracy to take control of the world. The protocols were written in the latter part of the 19th century by an **anti-Semitic** author who sought to shape the policy of Russian czar Nicholas II. Although they have no basis in reality, the protocols were used as anti-Jewish propaganda by various right-wing groups looking for a scapegoat for the world's troubles. They were widely circulated before World War II, even in the United States, and were used as a central part of Nazi propaganda about the threat presented by world Jewry, leading to the **Holocaust**. Today they are mainly produced in Arabic translation and circulated in a number of Arab countries as an anti-**Zionist** tract. They have even been made into a popular television series in Egypt.

PURE SEPHARDI. *See* SEPHARDIM.

PURIFICATION. *See* DAY OF ATONEMENT (HEBREW YOM KIPPUR); DEAD SEA SCROLLS; ESSENES; MIKVEH; MISHNAH; PHARISEES; SHTETL; TEMPLE (HEBREW BET HA-MIKDASH); WAILING WALL (HEBREW KOTEL HA-MAARAVI, "WESTERN WALL").

PURIM. A carnival-like festival falling on the 14th and 15th of Adar that commemorates the salvation of the Jewish people in the Persian Empire as recounted in the biblical Book of Esther. There, we are told of a plot to eradicate the Jews, a policy of genocide instigated by **Haman**, a Persian court official. His plans were thwarted by the Jewish queen of Persia, Esther, and her cousin Mordecai. The Jews were eventually given permission by Ahasuerus, the Persian king, to defend themselves, and they managed to kill Haman and his followers. Though God is nowhere mentioned in the Book of Esther, He is believed to be acting behind the scenes, as it enabled Jewish survival.

During the festival, the Book of Esther is read from a handwritten scroll, megillah, in the evening and the morning. Whenever the name of the villain Haman is mentioned, the congregants make a noise in order to blot out the name of the wicked. It is customary for people to dress up in fancy dress during Purim, the idea behind this being that God works in mysterious ways and things are not what they seem. There is even a tradition for people to get drunk on Purim, for in that condition, the surface appearance of things seems less important. The **halakhah** prescribes the holding of a festive meal, the sending of at least two different food gifts to a friend, and giving charity to more than one poor person.

Ancient walled cities celebrate Purim one day later than elsewhere because the fighting against the followers of Haman in Shushan, the Persian capital, carried on for an extra day. Jews there celebrated their salvation on 15 Adar, and the **rabbis** fixed this day, known as Shushan Purim, for all ancient walled cities that were in existence at the time of Joshua.

Jews regard Purim as a paradigm of persecutions down the ages, so though they may be celebrating events of long ago, they are also remembering persecutions and **pogroms** much closer to home. Haman, the villain of the Purim story, is described in the Book of Esther as a descendant of the tribe of Amalek, which was known for its attacks on the children of **Israel** in the wilderness after the **Exodus**. Purim is thus an affirmation of the belief that the Hamans and **Hitlers** of this world, despite the terrible pogroms they engage in, will ultimately be brought down by God working in the background. *See also* CALENDAR; JEWISH RITUAL YEAR; WOMEN IN JUDAISM.

– Q –

QUMRAN. A region near the Dead Sea where the **Dead Sea Scrolls** were first discovered in caves in 1947. The ruins of a large settlement at Khirbet Qumran have been excavated, which indicate that the area was occupied at different times but almost certainly by the community that produced some, or all, of the scrolls and came to a violent end in 70 CE. A large cemetery containing approximately 1,200 graves, including those of **women**, has also been excavated. It is likely that the Qumran community in the 1st century CE was a subgroup of the **Essenes**.

QUORUM. *See* MINYAN (HEBREW, "NUMBER").

– R –

RABBENU HA-KADOSH. *See* JUDAH THE NASI.

RABBI (HEBREW, "MY MASTER"). Title of the main religious functionary of Judaism. Originally, rabbis were not **synagogue** officials but teachers with students who gathered around them. They were ordained by sages to decide special cases of **halakhah**, the ordination being known as semikhah. In the Middle Ages, rabbis began to be associated with synagogues and communities as spiritual leaders, scholars in residence, and judges that people could turn to to decide disputes. They officiated at weddings and arranged divorces.

Today, the rabbi's role is much broader than in the past. In traditional synagogues, he may still be concerned mostly with teaching **Torah** and preserving halakhic norms, such as supervising **kosher** food—that is, the **dietary laws** of kashrut in the community. In Modern **Orthodox**, **Conservative**, and **Reform** synagogues, he, or in the latter cases she, will be involved in ministerial and pastoral activities as well as purely religious ones, counseling congregants, and liaising with leaders of other religions. *See also* HEBREW UNION COLLEGE (HUC); JEWISH THEOLOGICAL SEMINARY (JTS); SALANTER, ISRAEL (1810–83); YESHIVAH (HEBREW, "PLACE OF SITTING," PLURAL YESHIVOT).

RABBI ISAAC ELHANAN THEOLOGICAL SEMINARY. *See* YESHIVAH (HEBREW, "PLACE OF SITTING," PLURAL YE-SHIVOT).

RABBINICAL ASSEMBLY OF AMERICA. *See* CONSERVATIVE JUDAISM.

RABBINICAL SEMINARIES. *See* YESHIVAH (HEBREW, "PLACE OF SITTING," PLURAL YESHIVOT).

RABIN, YITZCHAK (1922–95). Israeli general and prime minister. Rabin served as a commander in the **Palmach** and became chief of staff of the **Israel Defense Forces** in 1964. In 1967, he was one of the architects of Israeli victory in the **Six-Day War**. After retiring from the army, Rabin went into politics, eventually leading the Labor Party and serving as prime minister on several occasions. During his second term, he was awarded the Nobel Peace Prize, together with **Shimon Peres** and Yasser Arafat, for his efforts to establish peace between Israelis and **Palestinians**. His peacemaking angered certain sections of Israeli society, and during a peace rally in Tel Aviv in 1995, he was assassinated by a young Jewish religious student, Yigal Amir. This left the Israeli nation in shock, and many international dignitaries came to Israel for his funeral.

RACHEL (BIBLICAL FIGURE). *See* JACOB; JOSEPH; PATRI-ARCHS; PILGRIMAGE (HEBREW ALIYAH LE-REGEL, "AS-CENT BY FOOT").

RADZIWIL, PRINCE NICHOLAS. *See* WAHL, SAUL (1541–1617).

REBBE. *See* CHASIDIC MOVEMENT (ALSO HASIDIC); TZAD-DIK (HEBREW, "RIGHTEOUS ONE," PLURAL TZADDIKIM).

REBECCA. *See* PATRIARCHS.

REFORM JUDAISM. The **Enlightenment** had a dramatic effect on the Jews of Western and Central Europe who emerged from their cultural **ghettos** in the 19th century only to find that their religion had stayed behind, enclosed within the mentality of the Middle Ages. Some made their way into forms of Protestant Christianity, but others sought a more relevant Jewish faith. This led to the beginning of Reform Judaism, with shorter services, sermons and prayers in the vernacular, organ music in the **synagogue**, less emphasis on ritual, and the revision of incompatible dogmatic beliefs.

From the first Reform synagogue, the Hamburg **Temple** founded in 1818, German Reform synagogues called themselves temples. The idea that **emancipated** Jews should seek to return to Zion and rebuild the Temple in **Jerusalem** was alien to their outlook. Reform began to produce **rabbis** trained in a university, not merely in a **yeshivah**, who revised the prayer book and adopted a more critical view of Jewish sacred literature. A number of rabbinical conferences took place in Germany in the middle of the 19th century, formulating an ideological outlook for Reform Judaism. Though many changes were approved, there was considerable disagreement as to how far change should go.

The reform of Judaism was vigorously opposed by **Orthodox** traditionalists, but in its different varieties, it gradually spread from Central and Western Europe to the United States, where it founded a major rabbinical seminary, the **Hebrew Union College**. It became a real movement with synagogue organizations, rabbinical training programs, and the appointment of **women** rabbis. Although it was initially antagonistic toward **Zionism** and wary of Jewish national aspirations, it gradually became supportive of both, particularly after the **Holocaust** and the foundation of the State of **Israel**. *See also* BAR MITZVAH/BAT MITZVAH ("COMING OF AGE"); HEAD COVERING; KOSHER ("FIT FOOD," HEBREW KASHER, KASHRUT).

REINCARNATION. *See* FRANK, JACOB (1726–91); KABBALAH; ZOHAR.

REMEMBRANCE DAY. *See* ISRAEL INDEPENDENCE DAY (HEBREW YOM HA-ATZMAUT).

RESH GALUTA (ARAMAIC, "HEAD OF THE EXILE"). *See* EXILARCH (ARAMAIC RESH GALUTA, "HEAD OF THE EXILE").

RESURRECTION. The belief that in the **Messianic** Age the dead will arise in bodily form and be judged. There are passing references to the Resurrection of the dead in some biblical books, particularly in the Book of Daniel, where it is said that many of those "that sleep in the dust will awake" (Daniel ch.12). It was in the **Mishnaic** and **Talmudic** Periods, however, that the Resurrection was considered to be an essential belief of Jewish religion. The Mishnah (Sanhedrin 10:1) lists those who deny the Resurrection of the dead among those who have no portion in the world to come.

Different views were expressed about the timing and nature of the Resurrection, both in the Rabbinic Period and throughout the Middle Ages. Yet, the doctrine in general has continued to be part of **Orthodoxy** until modern times. It is mentioned in the traditional liturgy and influenced the practice of burying the dead. Among Orthodox Jews, cremation of a dead body is disapproved of because it is regarded as negating the fundamental belief in the Resurrection. **Reform** Judaism rejected the belief in the Resurrection of the dead in 19th century, and many Reform communities practice cremation today. *See also* GENTILES (HEBREW GOY, PLURAL GOYIM, "NATION" OR "PEOPLE"); MAIMONIDES, MOSES (1135–1204).

REUVENI, DAVID (15TH–16TH CENTURIES). Mysterious figure claiming to come from the **Ten Lost Tribes**, hence his name from the tribe of Reuben. He claimed that his brother Joseph was king over several tribes and that he was a commander in chief of their armed forces on a mission to the pope. He kept a diary of his adventures relating how he visited Egypt and **Jerusalem** and Damascus. In Venice, he requested help to see the pope, and in Rome, he obtained letters of introduction from the pope, who was looking for potential allies against the Muslims. While in Rome, he was presented with a banner with the **Ten Commandments** on it by a wealthy admirer.

Reuveni caused a stir among the **Marrano**s of Portugal when he visited that country and was received by the Portuguese king in an official capacity. The Marranos regarded him as a **Messianic** figure, and he seems to have encouraged them to reaffirm their Judaism. One Marrano, **Solomon Molcho**, openly proclaimed his Jewish faith. For this, both he and Reuveni were arrested. Molcho was burned at the stake in 1532, while Reuveni was eventually taken to Spain and presumably executed.

REVISIONIST ZIONISTS. The Union of Zionist Revisionists was an organization founded by **Vladimir Jabotinsky** in Paris in 1925. It sought to promote a right-wing version of **Theodor Herzl's Zionism** in opposition to Labor Zionism, which dominated the Zionist Movement. Jabotinsky believed that Zionism should work to establish a Jewish State on both sides of the Jordan in the area of historic **Palestine** as expressed in the **Balfour Declaration** and that the British Mandate authorities should be made to subscribe to the letter and spirit of that declaration. He also believed that Jewish militia, particularly a revised Jewish Legion, should participate with Britain in governing Palestine.

Although for its first 10 years the Revisionist Movement was affiliated to the **World Zionist Organization**, the divisions between them were always likely to cause a rift. In 1933, three Revisionists were accused of murdering a Labor Zionist leader, Chaim Arlosoroff. Though two were acquitted, the third, Abraham Stavsky, was initially found guilty, only to be acquitted by the Supreme Court. The trial split the Jewish community, with Labor Zionists convinced of the guilt of the Revisionists, who had long been seen by them as fascists and reactionaries. Stavsky's supporters, by contrast, regarded the matter as a political show trial. Chief Rabbi **Abraham Isaac Kook** came out publicly in defense of Stavsky, having heard of the confession of an Arab to the murder. For this, Kook was attacked in the left-wing Zionist press but was praised by Jabotinsky as a man of courage who had revived Jabotinsky's belief in religion and in the value of having a "high priest" because Kook was of priestly descent. The trial led to very bad feelings on both sides.

Revisionists also failed to gain acceptance for their demands that millions of Jews should be evacuated to Palestine from dangerous areas of Central and Eastern Europe. Opponents felt this would encourage **anti-Semitism** in countries seeking to get rid of their Jews. Revisionist Zionists seceded from the main Zionist body in 1935 after divisions between them and other Zionists became too wide. They opposed any partition of Palestine as suggested by the Palestine Royal Commission of 1937 and were vehemently against the White Paper of 1939 limiting Jewish immigration.

During World War II, Revisionists, together with the **Irgun Tzevai Leumi**, whom they supported, stopped anti-British activity because they were fighting a common enemy. **David Ben Gurion**, however, was against the return of Revisionists to the World Zionist Organization unless it was unconditional. It was only in 1946 that Revisionists rejoined the World Zionist Organization unconditionally. After the foundation of the State of **Israel**, the Herut Party, headed by **Menachem Begin**, the Irgun leader, continued the Revisionist tradition in the **Knesset**. Herut amalgamated with other parties to form Likkud, which became the largest party in the Knesset after the 1977 elections, when Begin became prime minister. *See also* BETAR (ACRONYM OF BERIT TRUMPELDOR).

ROMANS. *See* BABYLONIA; BAR KOKHBA (d. 135 CE); BETAR (ACRONYM OF BERIT TRUMPELDOR); DIASPORA; EXILARCH (ARAMAIC RESH GALUTA, "HEAD OF THE EXILE"); EXILE (HEBREW GALUT); HEROD; HOLY LAND; JERUSALEM; JOSEPHUS FLAVIUS (1ST CENTURY CE); JUDAH THE NASI; LAND OF ISRAEL (HEBREW ERETZ YISRAEL); MARTYRDOM (HEBREW KIDDUSH HASHEM, "SANCTIFICATION OF (GOD'S) NAME"); NINTH OF AV, FAST OF (HEBREW TISHA B'AV); ORAL TORAH; PALESTINE; PROMISED LAND; SADDUCEES; SANHEDRIN; SEVENTEENTH OF TAMMUZ; TEMPLE (HEBREW BET HA-MIKDASH); WAILING WALL (HEBREW KOTEL HA-MAARAVI, "WESTERN WALL").

ROSH HASHANAH ("HEAD OF THE YEAR"). *See* NEW YEAR FESTIVAL (HEBREW ROSH HASHANAH, LITERALLY "HEAD OF THE YEAR").

ROSH YESHIVAH (HEBREW, "YESHIVAH HEAD"). *See* YESHIVAH (HEBREW, "PLACE OF SITTING," PLURAL YESHIVOT).

ROTHSCHILD, BARON EDMUND JAMES DE. *See* ALLIANCE ISRAÉLITE UNIVERSELLE (AIU); ROTHSCHILD FAMILY.

ROTHSCHILD, LIONEL NATHAN. *See* DISRAELI, BENJAMIN (1804–81); ROTHSCHILD FAMILY.

ROTHSCHILD, LORD LIONEL WALTER. *See* BALFOUR DECLARATION; ROTHSCHILD FAMILY.

ROTHSCHILD, MAYER AMSCHEL. *See* ROTHSCHILD FAMILY.

ROTHSCHILD, MIRIAM. *See* ROTHSCHILD FAMILY.

ROTHSCHILD, LORD NATHANIEL MAYER. *See* ROTHSCHILD FAMILY.

ROTHSCHILD, LORD NATHANIEL MAYER VICTOR. *See* ROTHSCHILD FAMILY.

ROTHSCHILD FAMILY. Ashkenazi dynasty of bankers and financiers. The family originated in Frankfurt on the Main, where a red shield hung above the door of the family home, hence the surname (*Rothschild* means "red shield" in German). The family began to flourish under the leadership of Mayer Amschel Rothschild (1744–1812), who was a successful court agent. One of Mayer Amschel's sons came to London and made a fortune on the stock exchange, while another son set up a powerful French dynasty of Rothschilds in Paris. Branches of the family spread to Italy and Austria, where they were also successful. Napoleonic wars and industrial development in Europe needed cash support, both of which the Rothschilds were able to finance.

Lionel Nathan Rothschild (1808–79) in London, a grandson of Mayer Amschel, became the first professing Jew to enter parliament in 1858 after refusing to take a Christian oath for 11 years, and it was with his help that the Suez Canal was purchased by Prime Minister **Benjamin Disraeli** for Britain in 1875. Many Jewish activities in the 19th and early 20th centuries involved the Rothschilds, who led the United Synagogue in Britain and the **Consistoire** in France. Lionel's son, Nathaniel Mayer (1840–1915), became the first Jewish lord in 1885, and it was to his son, Lionel Walter (1886–1937), the second Lord Rothschild, that the **Balfour Declaration** was addressed.

Settlements in **Palestine** and charitable, educational, and cultural organizations there and subsequently in **Israel** were financed by Rothschilds. The wealth of the Rothschilds was something poor Jews took great pride in, but for **anti-Semites**, it was held up as a symbol of Jewish greed and exploitation. The Nazis confiscated much of the Rothschild wealth and property in Europe, some of which was recovered after World War II. Today many members of the Rothschild family have moved outside the boundaries of the Jewish community through intermarriage and **assimilation**. Yet, the philanthropy of the family has continued and their name is attached to a number of communal institutions.

Members of the family have also branched out into other areas beyond finance. Thus, Lionel Walter Rothschild was a zoologist who at one time had one of the largest natural history collections in the world, and Nathaniel Mayer Victor Rothschild (1910–90), Third Baron Rothschild, was a prominent member of MI5, the British Secret Service, as well as an academic zoologist. Nathaniel Mayer Victor's sister Miriam Rothschild (1908–2005) was also an eminent zoologist and fellow of the Royal Society. *See also* ALLIANCE ISRAÉLITE UNIVERSELLE (AIU); COURT JEWS; SASSOON FAMILY.

RUTH (BIBLICAL FIGURE). *See* DAVID; WOMEN IN JUDAISM.

– S –

SABBATH (HEBREW SHABBAT). Saturday is the Jewish Sabbath, a day of rest based on the biblical story of God creating the world in six days and resting on Saturday, the seventh day (Genesis, chs. 1–2). Jews are asked to practice imitatio dei and to rest on this day just like God, thus acknowledging that the world was created by God. It is the holiest day of the week and has helped shape the nature of Jewish communities because the worries and problems of the weekdays are put aside for the 25 hours of the Sabbath.

Achad Ha-Am, the modern **Zionist** thinker, captured the value of the Sabbath in his much-quoted saying: "More than the Jews have kept the Sabbath, the Sabbath has kept the Jews." Apart from the psychological and spiritual advantages of a day of rest, the prohibition on traveling on the Sabbath has made traditional Jews live in close communities near a **synagogue.**

There is a belief in the **Bible** and postbiblical Rabbinic literature that the Sabbath is not merely a conventional day of rest but is built into nature itself. Thus, the manna that the **Israelites** lived off in the wilderness did not fall on the Sabbath and the legendary river **Sambatyon** is reported to flow differently on Saturdays from the way it flows on weekdays. The Sabbath is thought of as a reflection of the world to come in this life, and if Israel would keep the Sabbath properly, the **Messianic** Age would dawn.

All creative work manifesting man's control over nature is prohibited on the Sabbath. The **Talmudic** rabbis subsumed this under 39 major categories of labor that they derived from the work necessary for the assembling and disassembling of the sanctuary in the wilderness. To this, the Rabbinic tradition added many extra categories of prohibited labor to enhance the special character of the day. Work was prohibited not only for the families of Israelite householders but for their slaves as well, reminding them that they were once slaves in Egypt and redeemed by God.

The importance of the Sabbath is apparent from its appearance as the only ritual element in the **Ten Commandments** and by the penalty of capital punishment in the Bible for breaking the Sabbath. It has influenced the Christian holy day of Sunday and the Muslim holy day of Friday, as well as the seven-day week almost universally found throughout the world. For traditional Jews, the Sabbath is a day of delight, welcomed in by the mother and other **women** of the household kindling two candles to bring extra light into the home. This differs from the **Karaite** approach, which usually involves keeping the house in total darkness for the duration of the Sabbath and prohibiting sexual relations.

The Sabbath is celebrated by the father making blessings over wine, kiddush, at its onset on Friday night and at lunchtime to declare the sanctity of the day. An extra, third, meal is eaten during the afternoon, and two loaves of special bread, challah, are used at each meal to symbolize the extra portion of manna in the wilderness that fell on Fridays. Two angels are pictured as returning home from **synagogue** with the men of the household to see if the house is prepared for this special day, and the family sings a song of greeting, Shalom Aleikhem, to them.

At the conclusion of the Sabbath, a special ceremony, havdalah, involving wine, a double-wicked candle, and some sweet-smelling herbs marks the end of holy time and the beginning of the profane week. The reason given for the sweet-smelling herbs is to revive the soul because it is believed that every Jew has an extra Sabbath soul that leaves at the end of the Sabbath.

The Sabbath is kept strictly by **Orthodox** Jews, except in cases of serious illness or danger to life, when all the Sabbath prohibitions do not apply. Some of the Sabbath restrictions are not part of the **Conservative** Jewish teaching, while **Reform** Judaism has liberalized many of the Sabbath laws in line with patterns of modern life. What all religious Jews have in common is the special nature of the Sabbath day expressed in the liturgy, which is the main service of the week, and involving a long **Torah** reading. Family meals are taken, and traditional Jews sing special Sabbath songs, zemirot, during the meal.

In **Israel**, there have been controversies over the keeping of the Sabbath by state institutions. In most towns, such as **Jerusalem** and Tel Aviv, public transport does not run on the Sabbath and festivals, while in other towns it does. This is because when the State of Israel was founded in 1948, many of the practices were simply frozen rather than raising all the thorny issues of the religious nature of a Jewish state. When it was owned by the state, the Israel national airline, El Al, created problems when it sometimes flew into Israeli airports on the Sabbath, and this led to religious parties resigning from the government coalition. Even today, as a privatized company, El Al has had to respond to threats of an Orthodox boycott by promising not to fly on the Sabbath even outside of Israel. *See also* BAR MITZVAH/ BAT MITZVAH ("COMING OF AGE").

SADDUCEES. An aristocratic, priestly sect that flourished during the Second **Temple** Period. References to them by **Josephus Flavius** and in the New Testament and the **Talmud** do not always agree, but it seems that the Sadducees were more conservative than the larger sect of **Pharisees** and more literal in their interpretation of Scripture. Jewish religion for the Sadducees turned around the sacrificial cult of the Temple, and they rejected Pharisaic innovations associated with the **Oral Torah**. They also did not accept beliefs that were not explicit in Scripture, such as those of life after death and the **Resurrection**. With the destruction of the Temple by the Romans in 70 CE, the Sadducees ceased to exist as a separate religious group because, unlike the Pharisees, they were unable to reinvent Judaism in a post-Temple context. Elements of Sadducean belief may have continued among Jews, however, and resurfaced in more literalist sectarian groups like the **Karaites**.

SALANTER, ISRAEL (1810–83). Founder of the **Musar Movement**, which emphasized the ethical dimension of Judaism. Of independent mind, Salanter believed that **rabbis** should not be merely bookish teachers but should set a moral example. During a cholera epidemic in Vilna in 1848, he insisted that people must eat on the fast of the **Day of Atonement** because fasting would weaken their resistance to disease. To encourage them to do so, he himself stood up in **syna-gogue** and publicly broke the fast in front of the whole congregation. Salanter founded a number of **yeshivot** where ethics, musar, was taught alongside the usual **Talmudic** curriculum. He faced consider-able opposition from leading rabbis for his innovations.

In 1857, Salanter moved to Germany and gave well-attended lectures to community groups promoting his version of ethical **Orthodoxy**. His disciples in Lithuania opened a number of major academies where the emphasis was on musar. Prominent among them were those of Slobodka, Novardok, and Telz. Toward the end of his life, Salanter spent two years in France, continuing the same work as in Germany. His Musar Movement acted as a brake on the seculariza-tion accompanying the Jewish **Enlightenment**, Haskalah.

SAMARITANS. A subgroup of Jews forming their own independent com-munity. According to the biblical account accepted by Rabbinic Judaism, the Samaritans are essentially a mixture of non-**Hebrew** peoples whom the Assyrians brought to Samaria to replace the exiled members of the **Ten Lost Tribes** after the conquest of **Israel** in 722 BCE. These peoples adopted Jewish practices but were regarded with suspicion by other Jews and accused of importing alien practices into Judaism.

According to their own sources, the Samaritans are the descen-dants of the two **Joseph** tribes, Manasseh and Ephraim, of the con-quered northern kingdom of Israel. They believe in the Pentateuch as the main book of revelation but have no other books of Scripture, and their Pentateuch differs somewhat from the official Masoretic text of Judaism. They regard Mt. Gerizim, a mountain near Shechem in modern-day Nablus, as the biblically appointed holy mountain and site for the **Temple**. Samaritans have their own lunar cum solar calendar that determines their festivals, one of the most important of which is the **Passover** celebrated by the Samaritan community with the sacrifice of lambs on Mt. Gerizim.

Samaritans use the ancient Hebrew script for their Pentateuchal scrolls and have one ancient scroll that they claim dates back to biblical times but that seems to be merely of medieval provenance. Over the centuries, Samaritans have been persecuted by Christian and Muslim rulers of the **Holy Land** and have often been in conflict with their fel-low Jews. In the modern State of **Israel**, however, the small commu-nity of Samaritans living in Holon is supported by the Jewish state.

SAMBATYON. A river that, according to Jewish legend, flows wildly during the week, with great stones, and is only quiescent on the **Sabbath**. The **Ten Lost Tribes**, taken into captivity by the Assyrians after the capture of the northern kingdom of **Israel**, are thought to live beyond this river and because they keep the Sabbath are unable to cross. The **Talmud** uses the existence of this legendary river to prove that Saturday, the Jewish Sabbath, was indeed created by God as a day of rest (TB Shabbat 65b). The name *Sambatyon* is thought to derive from the Hebrew word *shabbat*.

According to the medieval traveler **Eldad Ha-Dani**, the river Sambatyon only surrounds one part of the exiled Israelites and flows not with water but with moving sand and stones for six days. Some people believed that the sand from the Sambatyon, even if kept in a jar, would continue to move around for six days and rest on the Sabbath, an example used by **Manasseh Ben Israel**. The followers of **Shabbetai Tzvi** even believed that he had not died but had gone beyond the Sambatyon River to the Ten Lost Tribes only to return eventually to redeem Israel.

Down the ages, there were various reports of the existence of the river in different locations. Obadiah of Bertinoro (15th–16th centuries) reports of hearing from Islamic merchants of the river Sambatyon in the distant desert, beyond which the children of Moses live in holiness, and nearby, the children of Israel live with their own independent kingdom. Although a number of people believed literally in the Sambatyon and even went in search of the river, including the Spanish mystic Abraham Abulafia (13th century), it was never found but remained a legend that appealed to the Jewish imagination.

SAMUEL (PROPHET). *See* DAVID.

SANCTIFICATION OF THE MOON. *See* CALENDAR; DAVID.

SANHEDRIN. The main Jewish law court in **Temple** times. The Great Sanhedrin, consisting of 71 judges, was situated in **Jerusalem**, and there were also smaller Sanhedrin courts consisting of 23 judges in local centers. The Sanhedrin was both a supreme religious court and also seems to have had a major role in political affairs.

There is some dispute among different ancient texts and modern scholars about the actual makeup and function of the Sanhedrin. According to the idealized account of the Rabbinic tradition, the Great Sanhedrin was located in the Chamber of Hewn Stone in the Temple complex and was the ultimate authority for **halakhic** decisions. The members of the Sanhedrin, who were ordained **rabbis**, were responsible for establishing the local smaller Sanhedrins and for the appointment of the high priest. The **Talmud** describes the Sanhedrin as seated in a semicircle and their deliberations as always starting with the most junior judge, dayan, so no judge would be intimidated by having to contradict the views of a more senior colleague.

The Sanhedrin was made up of both **Pharisees** and **Sadducees**, who had serious religious divisions. There were also political elements in the appointment of judges by both the Romans and the Judean secular authorities. After the destruction of the Jerusalem Temple, the Sanhedrin moved out of Jerusalem, and once the **Bar Kokhba** revolt was crushed by the Romans, it relocated to various towns in the Galilee.

The Sanhedrin disappeared as an institution sometime in the 4th century CE. It was revived again when **Napoleon Bonaparte** convened a Sanhedrin of rabbis and laymen to decide issues of integration into French society. There have also been attempts to reconstitute a Sanhedrin in modern **Israel**, but these have been strongly opposed by many leading rabbis.

SAN NICANDRO. *See* PROSELYTES (HEBREW GERIM, SINGULAR GER).

SARAH. Biblical **Matriarch**, wife of **Abraham**, and founding mother of the Jewish people (Isaiah 51:2). According to the biblical account, although she was unable to have children for a long time, she was promised a child by the three angels who visited Abraham and a year later, at an advanced age, gave birth to a son, Isaac. She is seen by the Jewish tradition as a prophetess and a coworker with Abraham in the making of converts to monotheism. All **proselytes** adopt Sarah as their mother. She is buried in the Cave of Machpelah in **Hebron**, the first area of the **Holy Land** acquired by Abraham. *See also* WOMEN IN JUDAISM.

SASSOON, FLORA. *See* SASSOON FAMILY.

SASSOON, SIEGFRIED. *See* SASSOON FAMILY.

SASSOON BEN SALACH. *See* SASSOON FAMILY.

SASSOON FAMILY. Sephardi dynasty of merchants and industrialists. The Sassoon family originated in Baghdad, and its first prominent member was Sassoon ben Salach (1750–1830), who was head of the Jewish community. From Baghdad, the family spread to Bombay in 1832, where, under British influence, they adopted *Sassoon* as a surname, though *Sassoon* is a Sephardi first name (meaning "joy" in **Hebrew**). They set up textile mills and engaged widely in philanthropy, building hospitals, schools, and **synagogues**.

Eventually, members of the family also moved to Britain, where some branches of the family completely **assimilated**. They struck up a friendship with the prince of Wales, intermarried with members of the British aristocracy, converted to Anglicanism, and entered parliament. The best-known member of the assimilated Sassoons was the World War I poet Siegfried Sassoon (1886–1967). Other branches retained their allegiance to Judaism in Bombay, Hong Kong, Shanghai, and England, and among them were noted scholars and bibliophiles. One of these, quite exceptionally, was a **woman**, Flora Sassoon (1859–1936), who won recognition as a **Torah** scholar and was consulted by **rabbis**. *See also* COURT JEWS; ROTHSCHILD FAMILY.

SATMAR CHASIDIM. *See* NETUREI KARTA (ARAMAIC, "GUARDIANS OF THE CITY"); TZADDIK (HEBREW, "RIGHTEOUS ONE," PLURAL TZADDIKIM).

SATURDAY. *See* SABBATH (HEBREW SHABBAT); SAMBATYON; TEN LOST TRIBES.

SAUL, KING. *See* DAVID.

SCAPEGOAT. *See* DAY OF ATONEMENT (HEBREW YOM KIPUR); PROTOCOLS OF THE ELDERS OF ZION.

SCHECHTER, SOLOMON (1847–1915). Judaic scholar who taught at Cambridge University and the University of London before being appointed head of the **Jewish Theological Seminary** in 1902. While at Cambridge, Schechter was involved with the discovery of the manuscripts in the **Cairo Genizah**, which had been known about before but had never been exposed in such large numbers. Schechter was one of the main ideologues of **Conservative Judaism**, putting forward the idea that the experience of Catholic **Israel**, that is, the communal experience of Jews down the ages, determines the traditions that Judaism should preserve.

SCHNEERSON, MENACHEM M. *See* MESSIAH (HEBREW MASHIACH).

SCHNIRER, SARA. *See* YESHIVAH (HEBREW, "PLACE OF SITTING," PLURAL YESHIVOT).

SCOTT, C. P. *See* WEIZMANN, CHAIM (1874–1952).

SCRIBES. *See* PHARISEES.

SEDER MEAL. *See* PASSOVER (HEBREW PESACH).

SEFIROT. *See* KABBALAH; TABERNACLES (HEBREW SUKKOT); ZOHAR.

SELEUCID EMPIRE. *See* CHANUKAH; HASMONEANS; JUDAH MACCABEE, (2ND CENTURY BCE); MACCABEES.

SEMIKHAH (HEBREW, "ORDINATION"). *See* RABBI (HEBREW, "MY MASTER"); YESHIVAH (HEBREW, "PLACE OF SITTING," PLURAL YESHIVOT).

SEPHARDIM. Jews originally of Spanish and Portuguese origin whose ancestors were expelled from the Iberian Peninsula at the end of the 15th century. Jews had flourished under Islam in Spain, but in the middle of the 12th century, the Almohads, a fanatical Muslim sect of Berbers, persecuted and forcibly converted Jews. This led to the migration of Jews both to Christian Spain and North Africa. Once the Christian reconquest of Spain took place under Ferdinand and Isabella, Jews were expelled from the kingdom because they were an encouragement to other Jews who had been forcibly converted to Catholicism to continue to maintain an underground Jewish life as **Marranos**.

The mass expulsion of Sephardim brought Spanish–Jewish culture and practices to the native communities of North Africa and the Levant. Many of the Sephardim continued to speak **Ladino**, a Spanish–Jewish dialect, and set up **synagogues** where the liturgy reflected the particular area of Spain or Portugal they came from.

Disputes arose between the native Jews and the more sophisticated Sephardi émigrés, but in the course of time, the different kinds of neo-Sephardi Judaisms that emerged were often amalgams of the religious culture of the newcomers and that of the established order. Sephardim often looked down on the more primitive practices of the native Jews and would put two Hebrew letters after their name, which stood for the words *pure Sephardi*. See also ASHKENAZIM (SINGULAR ASHKENAZI); CARO, JOSEPH (1488–1575); CONVERSOS; KOSHER ("FIT FOOD," HEBREW KASHER, KASHRUT); SHULCHAN ARUKH (HEBREW, "LAID TABLE").

SETTLER MOVEMENT. *See* MIZRACHI (ABBREVIATION OF MERCAZ RUCHANI, "SPIRITUAL CENTER").

SEVENTEENTH OF TAMMUZ. Fast day remembering the siege of **Jerusalem** both by the **Babylonians** in 586 BCE and by the Romans in 70 CE. This fast day begins the period of three weeks of mourning leading up to the fast day of the **Ninth of Av**, when the First and Second **Temples** were destroyed. *See also* CALENDAR; JEWISH RITUAL YEAR.

SHABBETAI TZVI (1626–76). A **Messianic** figure who was the center of the biggest and most important Messianic movement within Judaism. Shabbetai Tzvi was born in Izmir, in Ottoman Turkey, where he undertook the study of **Kabbalah** and would spend long periods alone in meditation. At times, he felt great ecstasy, and at others, he was tormented by demons. Those who knew him regarded him as mentally unstable, but his strange behavior and claims of a Messianic nature led to his expulsion from Izmir.

He then began a period of wandering and eventually ended up in Gaza to visit a young Kabbalist, **Nathan of Gaza**, who was reputed to be able to prescribe spiritual cures for people. Nathan convinced Shabbetai Tzvi that he was indeed the Messiah and his strange psychological condition could be explained in mystical terms. Shabbetai

Tzvi now adopted an overtly Messianic role, causing great excitement wherever he went. Despite opposition from some leading **rabbis**, the movement spread throughout **Palestinian** communities and throughout the **Diaspora**.

In 1666, the year Shabbetai Tzvi had predicted as the onset of the Messianic Age, he was arrested in Constantinople and brought before the Turkish Sultan, where he was offered the choice of death or conversion to Islam. He chose the latter. The shock of his apostasy caused many people to abandon their belief in him, while others accepted Nathan's explanation that the conversion to Islam made sense in terms of the Kabbalistic teachings of **Isaac Luria**, for the Messiah needed to descend to the depths of evil to free the holy sparks trapped there.

Some faithful Shabbateans followed their master into Islam, constituting a subgroup known as **Doenmeh**, who lived outwardly as devout Muslims but secretly as Shabbatean Jewish Messianists. The majority of believers continued an underground existence within the wider Jewish community, suspected by the Jewish establishment of antinomian practices and occasionally persecuted for them. Shabbateanism in Europe was kept alive by various groups and individuals and resurfaced in the movement surrounding **Jacob Frank**. It also influenced the rise of **Chasidism**.

SHAKESPEARE, WILLIAM. *See* USURY.

"SHALOM ALEIKHEM" (HYMN). *See* SABBATH (HEBREW SHABBAT).

SHAMMASH (BEADLE). *See* SYNAGOGUE (HEBREW BET KNESSET).

SHAVUOT (FESTIVAL). *See* PENTECOST (HEBREW SHAVUOT).

SHEBA, QUEEN OF. *See* ETHIOPIA; FALASHAS (ALSO KNOWN AS BETA ISRAEL); SOLOMON (10TH CENTURY BCE).

SHEKHINAH (DIVINE PRESENCE). *See* KABBALAH; WAILING WALL (HEBREW KOTEL HA-MAARAVI, "WESTERN WALL"); ZOHAR.

SHEMINI ATZERET (FESTIVAL). *See* TABERNACLES (HEBREW SUKKOT).

SHEVAT (MONTH). *See* CALENDAR.

SHIELD OF DAVID. *See* DAVID; MAGEN DAVID (HEBREW, "SHIELD OF DAVID" OR "STAR OF DAVID").

SHIN BET. *See* KASZTNER, RUDOLF (1906–57).

SHIUR (LECTURE). *See* YESHIVAH (HEBREW, "PLACE OF SITTING," PLURAL YESHIVOT).

SHNEUR ZALMAN OF LIADI. *See* EMANCIPATION; MITNAGGEDIC MOVEMENT (HEBREW, "OPPONENTS").

SHOAH (HEBREW, "CATASTROPHE"). *See* HOLOCAUST.

SHOCHET (HEBREW, "RITUAL SLAUGHTERER"). *See* SHTETL.

SHOFAR (HEBREW, "RAM'S HORN"). *See* CHEREM; DAY OF ATONEMENT (HEBREW YOM KIPPUR); NEW YEAR FESTIVAL (HEBREW ROSH HASHANAH, LITERALLY "HEAD OF THE YEAR"); WAILING WALL (HEBREW KOTEL HA-MAARAVI, "WESTERN WALL").

SHOSTAKOVICH, DMITRI. *See* BABI YAR.

SHTETL (YIDDISH, "LITTLE TOWN" OR "VILLAGE"). The term for a town is *shtot*, and the addition of an *l* in **Yiddish** indicates something small. Eastern Europe, particularly Poland, Lithuania, and the **Pale of Settlement**, was dotted with thousands of shtetls in which **Ashkenazi** Jews lived. In many of these, Jews were the majority, and they developed their own Yiddish subculture.

Shtetl society was structured around the **synagogue**, where the males of the family came to pray on a weekly, and often on a daily, basis. The **women** were based in the home looking after the children and preparing the food or in the workplace, which may have been a smallholding with a few animals, mostly cows. The women also ran shops out of their homes or attended the local markets. There would be an educational network, depending on the size of the community, with a cheder for young boys to study the **Bible** and other texts, often run in the home of the teacher. There was little formal education for girls, who would receive religious instruction from their parents and would be expected to marry in their teens soon after puberty.

Authority in the home resided with the father and in the community with the local **rabbi** or community head, parnas, who though elected would often be one of the wealthier members of the shtetl. Most shtetls would have a communal bathhouse attached to which was a **mikveh** for ritual bathing by women after menstruation. There would also be a male who could perform circumcisions, called a mohel, who may well also have acted as a ritual slaughterer, shochet, to whom people would bring their animals to be killed.

Although there was contact between Jew and **Gentile** in the shtetl and its surrounding area, this was less of a social and more of a functional relationship, relating to the division of labor. Jewish males were generally literate; they could read and write **Hebrew** and Yiddish, and their womenfolk though less well educated were able to read prayers and use devotional literature in Yiddish. Their Gentile neighbors, apart from the local priest or members of a higher social class of landowners, were illiterate. For the Gentiles, the Jews were seen through the lens of Christian **anti-Semitism** as Christ-killers and exploiters of the Gentile. Christianity was regarded by Jews as a primitive and often violent religion. At Easter, under the influence of impassioned sermons about the death of Jesus, Christians from the shtetl itself or from outside might initiate a **pogrom** when there was destruction of Jewish-owned property, rape, and bloodshed.

SHTIBL (YIDDISH, "LITTLE ROOM"). *See* SYNAGOGUE (HEBREW BET KNESSET).

SHTOT (YIDDISH, "TOWN"). *See* SHTETL (YIDDISH, "LITTLE TOWN" OR "VILLAGE").

SHULCHAN ARUKH (HEBREW, "LAID TABLE"). The main code of Jewish law written by **Joseph Caro**. The Shulchan Arukh is a collection of decisions about **halakhah** and custom, based on a much longer work of Caro's, the Bet Yosef, which discussed the many different opinions about these issues at great length. Caro summarized his conclusions in the Shulchan Arukh, which was printed in 1565. Because Caro was a **Sephardi** Jew, his code essentially reflects Sephardi practice, particularly as found in the writings of **Moses Maimonides**, but additions were composed by Moses Isserles, an **Ashkenazi rabbi**, which refer to Ashkenazi customs and interpretations of the halakhah. Isserles' notes are known as the "Tablecloth," mappah, of Caro's "Laid Table."

The combined code of Caro and Isserles represented a standardization of halakhah accepted by most Jews. There were some who objected to trying to make all Jewish communities, with their different customs, conform to one model. Others objected to having halakhic rules presented in a simple format because it was believed that they should be derived from the **Talmud** itself. In time, however, major commentaries were composed on the Shulchan Arukh, and it became an authoritative source for all future halakhic decisions. The fact that this code appeared when printed books were becoming common made the text widely available and added to its popularity.

SHUSHAN PURIM (FESTIVAL). *See* PURIM.

SIDDUR (HEBREW, "PRAYER BOOK"). *See* SYNAGOGUE (HEBREW BET KNESSET).

SIMCHAT TORAH (CELEBRATION). *See* TABERNACLES (HEBREW SUKKOT).

SIMEON BAR KOSEBA. *See* BAR KOKHBA (d. 135 CE).

SIMEON BAR YOCHAI. *See* LAG B'OMER; ZOHAR.

SIMON MACCABEUS. *See* HASMONEANS.

SINAI CAMPAIGN. The name given to a war between **Israel** and Egypt that lasted for eight days from October 29 to November 5, 1956. The Israeli reason for the invasion of Egypt was to destroy the bases in Sinai used by fedayeen terrorists to launch attacks into southern Israel and free the Straights of Tiran to Israeli shipping.

The timing of the campaign, however, was undertaken in conjunction with Britain and France after secret negotiations. The latter were annoyed at the nationalization of the Suez Canal by Gamal Abdel Nasser in July 1956 and launched an attack on Egypt ostensibly to protect the canal from Israeli forces, but actually, this was an excuse that they had coordinated with the Israelis. The Israelis conquered Gaza and the majority of the Sinai Peninsula during the campaign, but under pressure from the United States and Soviet Russia, they were forced to withdraw in March 1957, leaving a United Nations peacekeeping force in Sinai to guarantee free movement of Israeli ships in the Red Sea. *See also* BEN GURION, DAVID (1886–1973); DAYAN, MOSHE (1915–81).

SITRA ACHRA (DOMAIN OF EVIL). *See* ARAMAIC.

SIVAN (MONTH). *See* CALENDAR; JEWISH RITUAL YEAR.

SIX-DAY WAR. As its name implies, there was a six-day war between **Israel** and its neighbors, Egypt, Syria, and Jordan, as well as Iraq, which was fought from Monday, June 5, 1967, until Saturday, June 10. The background to the war was the demand by President Nasser of Egypt that United Nations peacekeepers should be withdrawn from Sinai and the movement of seven divisions of Egyptian troops to the Israeli border on May 20. Two days later, Nasser closed the straights of Tiran to Israeli ships. Fearing an immediate attack by overwhelming Arab forces, Israeli Defense Minister **Moshe Dayan** ordered the Israel air force to launch a preemptive strike, destroying the air forces of Egypt, Syria, Jordan, and Iraq.

The Israeli army under the command of **Yitzchak Rabin** then proceeded to invade and conquer the Sinai Peninsula, the Gaza Strip, the Syrian Golan Heights and the West Bank of the Jordan, including **Jerusalem**, which was under Jordanian rule. For the first time for nearly 2,000 years, the **Temple** complex and the **Wailing Wall** were under Jewish control, and the miraculous nature of the war led to a feeling that **Messianic** times had arrived both among religious **Zionists** and others. *See also* ALLON, YIGAL (1918–80); COHEN, ELI (1924–65); MIZRACHI (ABBREVIATION OF MERCAZ RUCHANI, "SPIRITUAL CENTER").

SLOBODKA YESHIVAH. *See* MUSAR MOVEMENT; SALANTER, ISRAEL (1810–83).

SMETANA, BEDRICH. *See* "HA-TIKVAH" (HEBREW, "THE HOPE").

SOLOMON (10TH CENTURY BCE). King of **Israel**, son of **David** and Bath Sheba, and second king of the Davidic line. Little is known about Solomon outside of the biblical narrative, but he plays a prominent role in the Books of Samuel and Kings. Solomon reigned for nearly 40 years and built the First **Temple** in **Jerusalem**, as well as palaces and fortifications.

He had a reputation for great wisdom, and the Jewish tradition regards him as the author of the books of Canticles, Proverbs, and Ecclesiastes. The Bible gives an example of his practical wisdom in the story of the two prostitutes who gave birth at the same time, but one of the babies died. They both claimed the living child, so the case was brought to King Solomon for a decision. Solomon decided that the living child should be split in two and half given to each mother. At that point, one of the prostitutes objected and said that the baby should not be killed but should be given to the other prostitute. Solomon then decided that she was the lawful mother (1Kings, ch. 3). This has become proverbially a "judgment of Solomon."

Another well-known story is of the visit of the queen of Sheba with a great retinue to see Solomon's wisdom for herself and test him with difficult questions (1Kings, ch. 10; 2 Chronicles, ch. 9). According to **Ethiopian** tradition, the queen of Sheba was the queen of Ethiopia, and she became pregnant by Solomon. The son born to them, Menelik, was the ancestor of the Ethiopian kings. The **Falashas** trace themselves back to the Jews who returned to Ethiopia with the queen of Sheba.

Solomon's reign was a relatively peaceful one, unlike that of his father, David, and Solomon forged relationships with neighboring countries by marrying **women** from their royal families, including Pharaoh's daughter. He had hundreds of wives and hundreds of concubines, and the Bible describes how his foreign wives "turned his heart after foreign gods" (1Kings 11:4) The extravagance of Solomon's reign, with its high taxation and demand on its citizens, led to a revolt on his death. The northern tribes, led by the **Joseph** tribes, broke away from **Judah**, which was the center of the Davidic kingdom, and formed an independent kingdom of Israel.

SOLOVEITCHIK, JOSEPH DOV. *See* YESHIVAH (HEBREW, "PLACE OF SITTING," PLURAL YESHIVOT).

SONGS. *See* "HA-TIKVAH" (HEBREW, "THE HOPE"); PALMACH; PARTISANS; SABBATH (HEBREW SHABBAT); SYNAGOGUE (HEBREW BET KNESSET); SZENES, HANNAH (1921–44); TEMPLE (HEBREW BET HA-MIKDASH); TRUMPELDOR, JOSEPH (1880–1920); TZADDIK (HEBREW, "RIGHTEOUS ONE,"PLURAL TZADDIKIM).

SONS OF THE COVENANT. *See* BNAI B'RITH (HEBREW, "SONS OF THE COVENANT").

SS. *See* KAPO.

STAR OF DAVID. *See* DAVID; MAGEN DAVID (HEBREW, "SHIELD OF DAVID" OR "STAR OF DAVID").

STAVSKY, ABRAHAM. *See* REVISIONIST ZIONISTS.

STERN, ABRAHAM. *See* STERN GANG (HEBREW LOCHAMEI CHERUT YISRAEL OR LECHI).

STERN COLLEGE. *See* YESHIVAH (HEBREW, "PLACE OF SITTING," PLURAL YESHIVOT).

STERN GANG (HEBREW LOCHAMEI CHERUT YISRAEL OR LECHI). An underground militia founded by Abraham Stern in 1940 when the main anti-British militia, the **Irgun**, decided not to attack the British while they fought the Germans in World War II. Stern was originally a member of the Irgun but disagreed with their policy of collaborating with the British, insisting that the White Paper of 1939 restricting Jewish immigration left Jewish refugees from Europe with nowhere to flee. He therefore founded a new right-wing militia. The Stern Gang was regarded by the British as a terrorist organization, and it is said that they killed its members when they were arrested, including Abraham Stern himself. After his death, the organization continued its activities of attacking members of the British army, police force, and politicians until the new Jewish state came into being. The Stern Gang was eventually banned by the **Israeli** government. *See also* KASZTNER, RUDOLF (1906–57); WAR OF INDEPENDENCE (HEBREW MILCHEMET HA-ATZMAUT).

STROOP, GENERAL JÜRGEN. *See* WARSAW GHETTO UPRISING.

SUEZ CANAL. *See* DISRAELI, BENJAMIN (1804–81); ROTHSCHILD FAMILY; SINAI CAMPAIGN.

SUKKAH (HEBREW, "BOOTH"). *See* TABERNACLES (HEBREW SUKKOT).

SUKKOT (FESTIVAL). *See* TABERNACLES (HEBREW SUKKOT).

SYNAGOGUE (HEBREW BET KNESSET). The main sacred space of Judaism that came into its own after the destruction of the **Temple** in 70 CE. Little is known about the true origins of the synagogue as an institution, but most scholars trace it back to the **Babylonian** captivity when Jews met together informally. Those Jews who returned from **exile** in the Babylonian **Diaspora** to rebuild the Second Temple brought the primitive synagogue idea back with them.

Although the synagogue may have started as a meeting place for community discussion, it developed into a place of prayer and Scripture reading. Eventually, it became an established institution with a standardized internal structure consisting of an ark containing the **Torah** scrolls; a platform, bimah, from which prayers are conducted and the Torah is read; and, in traditional synagogues, a separate section for **women** behind a partition, mechitzah.

Synagogues also developed a professional staff, such as the **rabbi**, who was originally a teacher of Torah but in modern times delivers sermons and has taken on many pastoral duties; the cantor, chazzan, who leads the prayers on **Sabbaths** and festivals; the beadle, shammash, who ensures that every worshipper has a prayer shawl, tallit, and a prayer book, siddur; and the Torah reader, baal keriah, who chants the text from a Torah scroll. There are also lay leaders led by the warden, gabbai, who are responsible for the efficient running of the synagogue.

The remains of early synagogues, from the 3rd century BCE onward, have been excavated, showing considerable variety and differing from the later type of synagogue that became standard from the Middle Ages. There is a description in both Philo and the **Talmud** of the great synagogue in Alexandria, Egypt, in the 1st century CE, which was so big that the congregation could not hear the prayer leader and so someone had to wave a flag so the congregants could answer "amen" at the end of each blessing.

The synagogue was in many ways the model for Christian churches and Muslim mosques. Yet, within Judaism, the synagogue took a variety of forms. One of the most common was the synagogue cum study hall, bet hamidrash, where regular prayers were held but was primarily used for Torah lessons and private study. This study hall has less sanctity than a synagogue, and people are permitted to eat in its confines, which they should not do in a synagogue proper. Among **Chasidim**, the preferred type of synagogue is one with a very informal setting, often a small and intimate building known as a stibl, or "little room," where there is less decorum than in the synagogue proper, and prayers are conducted with song and dance.

Although **Sephardi** and **Ashkenazi** synagogues have somewhat different arrangements of their internal furniture, the actual prayers tend to follow similar lines laid down in Talmudic literature. The designs of Ashkenazi synagogues were influenced by the architecture of churches, while those of Sephardim living in Islamic countries were influenced by the architecture of mosques. In the 19th and 20th centuries, **Reform** synagogues in the Western world were overtly modeled after churches so that **emancipated** Jews should feel at home. They had mixed seating, with organs and choirs, and decorum was strictly maintained during services. Many Reform synagogues were called temples to indicate that they, and not some future Temple to be rebuilt in the **Holy Land**, were the ultimate sacred space of Judaism.

A synagogue is known as a "little sanctuary," a term already found in the **Bible** (Ezekiel 11:16), and some of the Temple rituals were transferred from the **Jerusalem** sanctuary to it, prayer substituting for sacrifices. The rabbis insisted that items specific to the Temple, such as the seven-branched candelabrum, should not be reduplicated in the synagogue. Unlike the Temple, which was run by priests and Levites, the synagogue is almost entirely a lay institution because neither rabbis nor prayer leaders need to be priests.

According to the **halakhah**, a synagogue should be the tallest building in the area. This was not always possible in Christian and Muslim countries, where restrictions were often placed on the building of synagogues, and they were certainly not allowed to be higher than the local church or mosque. Wherever there was a Jewish community, there would be a synagogue of one type or another, where the community would gather at least on Sabbaths and festivals and which would be crowded on the Jewish **New Year** and **Day of Atonement**.

When Jewish communities were exiled or destroyed, synagogues were taken over and turned into churches or mosques or were burned to the ground. In 1938, at the beginning of the Nazi era, the **pogrom** of **Kristallnacht** led to the complete destruction of hundreds of synagogues in Germany and Austria, most of which were burned to the ground. According to the Jewish tradition, all synagogues in the Diaspora will be uprooted and transferred to the **Land of Israel** in the **Messianic** Age. *See also* TEN COMMANDMENTS (OR DECALOGUE).

SZENES, HANNAH (1921–44). Resistance operative killed by the Hungarian Fascist regime after she parachuted into occupied Europe. Hannah was born in Hungary and made **aliyah** to **Palestine** in 1939. There, she was recruited by the **Haganah**, and working for the British army, she was parachuted into Yugoslavia, joining the **partisans**. When she crossed into Hungary, she was arrested but refused to divulge any information even though she was tortured. She was subsequently shot in a Budapest prison. Hannah is regarded as a heroine in **Israel**, and her remains were transferred to there in 1950 and reburied on Mt. Herzl. A **kibbutz**, Yad Hannah, was founded in her memory. Plays and documentaries have been written about Hannah Szenes, and her poetry, songs, and diary have been published. One of her best-known songs, written just before she set off on her mission, begins "Blessed is the match consumed in kindling flame." *See also* HOLOCAUST.

– T –

TABERNACLES (HEBREW SUKKOT). A festival commemorating the end of the harvest season, particularly of the grape harvest, and remembering the travels of the **Israelites** in the desert after the **Exodus**. The festival begins on 15 Tishri and lasts for seven days in Israel and eight in the **Diaspora**. The day after Tabernacles is a concluding festival known as Shemini Atzeret.

There are two main rituals associated with Tabernacles. The first, after which the festival is named, is a boothlike structure, sukkah, which traditional Jews live in for the duration of the festival. The second is the taking of four species from nature, making a blessing over them, and shaking them together during the prayers.

Dwelling in a temporary tabernacle or booth is to remind Jews that they were protected by God in the desert when they dwelled in temporary structures, so the booth has to be erected under the sky with a roof made out of vegetation not substantial enough to prevent rain from seeping through. Some **Reform** communities erect a booth inside the **synagogue** building so that congregants can symbolically experience dwelling in a booth. Because such a booth is not exposed to the heavens, it is not considered a real sukkah by the **Orthodox**.

The taking of the four species represents thanksgiving for God's bounty in nature, and they are usually shaken in the four directions of the compass as well as up and down to signify God's rule throughout the physical world. The four species consist of a long palm branch, lulav; a yellow citrus fruit, etrog; three branches of myrtle; and two branches of willow.

Tabernacles is the most joyous of the festivals and is referred to in the liturgy as the "period of our rejoicing." The **Kabbalists** introduced a custom of inviting seven guests from the biblical past to the sukkah each evening. **Abraham** is the main guest on the first night, then Isaac, **Jacob, Moses**, Aaron, **Joseph**, and finally **David**. They are meant to represent the seven lower Sefirot through which God created the world and interacts with it.

The seventh day of Tabernacles is known as Hoshana Rabba, the day of the Great Hosanna. Each day of Tabernacles, people circumambulate the synagogue with their four species, but on this day, they circumambulate seven times chanting Hosannas and then take bundles of willow and beat them until the leaves fall off. This is partly because the willow is a tree that grows by the riverside and is associated with water. At the end of Tabernacles, on Shemini Atzeret, the rainy season begins in the **Holy Land**, and prayers for rain are added to the liturgy. Hoshana Rabba is also the conclusion of the period of repentance for sins that began with the **New Year Festival** and reached its peak on the **Day of Atonement**. There is a folk belief that if a person does not see his shadow on the evening before Hoshana Rabba, it means that judgment is against him and he will not live out the year.

On the concluding festival of Shemini Atzeret, the **Torah** reading is finished at the end of Deuteronomy and begun again at the beginning of Genesis. This is accompanied by dancing in the synagogue and great celebration, known as Simchat Torah, "Rejoicing over the Torah." There is a biblical teaching that in **Messianic** times, all **Gentile** nations will come to **Jerusalem** to join in the festival of Tabernacles (Zechariah 14:16). *See also* CALENDAR; JEWISH RITUAL YEAR; PILGRIMAGE (HEBREW ALIYAH LE-REGEL, "ASCENT BY FOOT").

TALLIT (ARAMAIC, "PRAYER SHAWL"). A four-cornered garment with fringes, tzitzit, known in English as a prayer shawl because it is worn during morning prayers and by the cantor, chazzan, when leading the prayer services. The practice of wearing a fringed garment is in fulfillment of the biblical injunction (Numbers 15:38-41) that **Israelites** should put fringes on the corners of their garments to remind them that they are subject to God's commands.

Originally, all clothes had corners, and Jews were able to attach these fringes to their everyday garments. With the change of clothing style, the fringes came to be worn on a tallit used during morning prayers or on a smaller four-cornered garment, a "little tallit," tallit katan, which **Orthodox** Jews wear under their clothes often with only the fringes showing. Although **women** do not have to wear a tallit, they do so in some **Conservative** and Modern Orthodox communities because of the desire of modern women for religious equality with men. *See also* DAY OF ATONEMENT (HEBREW YOM KIPPUR); SYNAGOGUE (HEBREW BET KNESSET).

TALLIT KATAN ("LITTLE TALLIT"). *See* TALLIT (ARAMAIC, "PRAYER SHAWL").

TALMUD. The most authoritative text of the **Oral Torah**, which appears in two versions. The **Palestinian** Talmud, also known as the **Jerusalem** Talmud, although it was not edited in Jerusalem, was redacted around 400 CE, and the **Babylonian** Talmud was redacted around 500 CE. The Talmud is based on the **Mishnah** and represents a wide-ranging commentary on large parts, though not all, of the Mishnaic text. Both versions of the Talmud are written mostly in **Aramaic**, the Palestinian in a Western dialect and the Babylonian in an Eastern dialect.

Because the Babylonian **Diaspora** contained the main centers of Jewish intellectual life and the biggest concentration of Jews, it was the Babylonian Talmud, rather than the earlier and smaller Palestinian one, that became the basis for all subsequent developments in Rabbinic Judaism. The determination of **halakhah** invariably goes back to precedents set in the Babylonian Talmud, and much of the Jewish theology and philosophy of the Middle Ages bases itself, if somewhat loosely, on the homiletical material (aggadah) of this Talmud. All **yeshivot** have the Babylonian Talmud and its classical commentaries as the main items of their curriculum, and it is said somewhat sarcastically that the students of a yeshivah know the text of Scripture because they know on which page in the Talmud a particular verse of the **Bible** is mentioned and commented on.

The Talmud was censored by the Catholic Church because it was regarded as anti-Christian, and many manuscript volumes were burned so that only one complete manuscript of the whole Talmud, the Munich codex of 1334, actually survived into modern times. Jewish apostates were the ones who originally brought the Talmud to the notice of the Church authorities, claiming that it contained profane teachings about Jesus. These accusations became one of the subject matters of medieval **disputations**, which were often followed by the public burning of Talmudic texts. Even when the Talmud was allowed to be printed, all references to whatever the Christian censor assumed were overt, or covert, allusions to Jesus or Christians were deleted. Ironically enough, books were printed with all the seemingly blasphemous passages to show what needed to be deleted from printed editions of the Talmud.

The destruction of the Talmud by the Church continued until the mid-18th century, when members of the **Frankist** Movement converted to Catholicism in Poland and denigrated the Talmud and its teachings.

The local bishop, Nicholas Dembowski, took the side of the Frankist and ordered the burning of the Talmud and other Jewish books. *See also* SHULCHAN ARUKH (HEBREW, "LAID TABLE").

TALMUD TORAH (RELIGIOUS SCHOOL). *See* YESHIVAH (HEBREW, "PLACE OF SITTING," PLURAL YESHIVOT).

TAMMUZ (MONTH). *See* CALENDAR; JEWISH RITUAL YEAR.

TANNA (ARAMAIC, "SAGE," PLURAL TANNAIM). *See* MISHNAH.

TARGUM (ARAMAIC, "TRANSLATION"). *See* ARAMAIC.

TARGUM ONKELOS ("BIBLE TRANSLATION"). *See* ARAMAIC.

TARTAR LANGUAGE. *See* KRIMCHAKS.

TAT (LANGUAGE). *See* MOUNTAIN JEWS.

TEITELBAUM, JOEL. *See* TZADDIK (HEBREW, "RIGHTEOUS ONE," PLURAL TZADDIKIM).

TELZ YESHIVAH. *See* SALANTER, ISRAEL (1810–83).

TEMPLE (HEBREW BET HA-MIKDASH). The main sanctuary of Judaism that was built on the Temple Mount in Jerusalem, known as Mt. Moriah, on a site associated by Jewish tradition with **Abraham**'s attempt to sacrifice his son Isaac to God. The First Temple was erected by King **Solomon** in the 10th century BCE, modeled on the small sanctuary, mishkan, that, according to the **Bible**, accompanied the **Israelites** in the wilderness after the **Exodus** from Egypt. The Solomonic Temple was destroyed by the **Babylonians** in 586 BCE and was rebuilt some 70 years later when Jewish exiles returned from Babylonian captivity after the Persians conquered the Babylonian Empire. The Second Temple was destroyed by the Romans in 70 CE after a revolt by the Jews in Judea was crushed.

The daily worship of God in the Temple was through the offering of sacrifices by the priests, kohanim, and by the singing of psalms by the Levites accompanied by musical instruments. Jews and **Gentiles** would make contributions to the upkeep of the Temple, and every Jew was meant to donate at least half a shekel each year to the Temple treasury. The Temple treasury was thus well endowed with precious metals and money. This made it a prime target for invading armies from outside the **Holy Land**, and it was sacked a number of times. The Temple was a place of **pilgrimage**, particularly on festivals, and people would also bring private offerings there. The pilgrims included both Jews and Gentiles, and there were special regulations for the sacrifices brought by the latter.

The most sacred part of the Temple was the Holy of Holies, a separate room containing the Ark of the Covenant, which was only entered by the high priest on the **Day of Atonement** to offer up incense to God. Above the Ark were two angelic golden cherubim with wings outstretched. The Temple contained various altars used for sacrifices and a seven-branched gold candelabrum that was refilled with olive oil each day and kindled by a priest. The priests in general had to keep strict rules of purity in order to perform any of the Temple rituals, and even ordinary Israelites could not enter the Temple area unless they, too, were in a state of ritual purity, which often necessitated bathing in a **mikveh**.

The Temple was the focus of Jewish worship, and though for the last 2,000 years it has been replaced by the **synagogue, Orthodox** Jews still pray daily for it to be rebuilt. It is believed that this will come about in the **Messianic** Age when the Third Temple will descend bodily from heaven where it is currently situated. *See also* TEN COMMANDMENTS (OR DECALOGUE).

TEN COMMANDMENTS (OR DECALOGUE). Two sections of the Pentateuch (Exodus 20:2–14 and Deuteronomy 5:6–18) that describe the revelation of God to **Moses** and the **Israelites** at Mt. Sinai after the **Exodus** from Egypt. Although these sections are generally known as the Ten Commandments, the Jewish tradition refers to them as the aseret ha-dibrot, the "Ten Sayings," because the introductory verse, "I am the Lord your God who brought you out of the land of Egypt, out of the house of bondage," is regarded as the first of these sayings and it itself is not a commandment. The Greek word *decalogue* used of the Ten Commandments is a literal translation of "Ten Sayings."

According to the biblical account, the Ten Sayings were carved on two stone tablets. When Moses descended from Mt. Sinai with the tablets, which were written "by the finger of God" (Exodus 31:18), he found the Israelites worshipping a golden calf. Angered by this idolatry, Moses smashed the tablets. He subsequently ascended Mt. Sinai once more and brought down a new set of tablets with the Ten Sayings on them. The tablets and the broken tablet pieces were both kept in the Ark of the Covenant during the time of the First **Temple**. The Jewish tradition sees the variations in text between the version of the Ten Sayings in Exodus and that in Deuteronomy as reflecting this incident because Deuteronomy has the slightly different text inscribed on the second set of tablets.

The Ten Sayings portray God as an active, redemptive force in history (1). They prohibit the worship of other gods or the making and worship of idolatrous images (2) and the taking of God's name in vain (3). They demand that the **Sabbath** day be preserved as a day of rest (4) and that children should honor their parents (5). They also prohibit murder (6), adultery (7), theft (8), bearing false witness against one's neighbor (9), and coveting the belongings of others (10).

Apart from the command to keep the Sabbath, there is nothing of a ritual nature in the Ten Sayings. At various times, Jewish sects maintained that only the Ten Sayings represented divine revelation, and all of the many laws and rituals found in the Bible were not essential to Jewish religion. This was also one of the claims of the early Christian Church. To counter this, the Jewish tradition did not allow the recitation of the Ten Sayings to be included in the liturgy as part of the daily prayer service, although they had been recited in the Temple prayers. They could only be read as part of the regular Bible reading from a scroll when the Exodus or Deuteronomy sections were reached and on the festival of **Pentecost**, which commemorates the revelation at Mt. Sinai.

Nevertheless, the Ten Sayings retained a special sanctity for Jews. Though the whole of the Bible was regarded as divine revelation, the Ten Sayings alone were uttered directly by God to the Israelites during the theophany at Mt. Sinai. It is still customary today for the whole congregation to stand during the reading of the Ten Sayings from a **Torah** scroll in the **synagogue** and for the text to be chanted to a special tune. *See also* JEWISH RITUAL YEAR; REUVENI, DAVID (15TH–16TH CENTURIES).

TEN DAYS OF PENITENCE. *See* JEWISH RITUAL YEAR.

TEN LOST TRIBES. When the northern kingdom of **Israel**, which had broken away from the southern kingdom of **Judah** after the death of King **Solomon**, was conquered by the Assyrians in 722 BCE, many of its inhabitants were taken away into captivity (2Kings 17:5–6). The fate of these captives is unknown, and because 10 of the 12 Hebrew tribes lived in the Kingdom of Israel, they are known as the Ten Lost Tribes.

   Early Jewish sources in the Apocrypha and Rabbinic literature expressed the belief that they did not merely vanish but continue to exist, and there are many legends indicating their whereabouts. One persistent theme is that they are trapped behind the river **Sambatyon**, which is impassable on weekdays and is only quiescent on Saturdays, the Jewish **Sabbath**, when members of the lost tribes cannot travel. **Eldad ha-Dani** claimed to be from the lost tribe of Dan and told stories about the other tribes. **David Reuveni** claimed association with the tribes of Reuben and Gad, which were settled in Arabia. Others claimed the tribes were in areas of Persia, Afghanistan, **Ethiopia**, Japan, Britain (as believed by **British Israelites**), or South America. *See also* CROMWELL, OLIVER (1599–1658); DIASPORA; FALASHAS (ALSO KNOWN AS BETA ISRAEL); HOLY LAND; JACOB; MANASSEH BEN ISRAEL (1604–57); MOUNTAIN JEWS; SAMARITANS.

TEN PLAGUES. *See* MOSES.

TEN SAYINGS. *See* TEN COMMANDMENTS (OR DECA-LOGUE).

TENTH OF TEVET, FAST OF. *See* JEWISH RITUAL YEAR.

TEVET (MONTH). *See* CALENDAR; JEWISH RITUAL YEAR.

THIRTEEN PRINCIPLES OF JEWISH FAITH (MAIMONIDES). *See* GENTILE (HEBREW GOY, PLURAL GOYIM, "NATION" OR "PEOPLE"); MAIMONIDES, MOSES (1135–1204).

THE THIRTEENTH TRIBE **(BOOK).** *See* KHAZARS.

THREE FOOT FESTIVALS. *See* PILGRIMAGE (HEBREW ALI-YAH LE-REGEL, "ASCENT BY FOOT").

TISHRI (MONTH). *See* CALENDAR; DAY OF ATONEMENT (HE-BREW YOM KIPPUR); JEWISH RITUAL YEAR; NEW YEAR FESTIVAL (HEBREW ROSH HASHANAH, LITERALLY "HEAD OF THE YEAR"); TABERNACLES (HEBREW SUKKOT).

TORAH (HEBREW, "TEACHING"). A term used of the Pentateuch, the "teaching" of God and by extension of the whole of Scripture. Often the Jewish tradition in its widest sense is also referred to as Torah because it is based on Scripture. The implication of this wide-ranging term is that the Jewish religion must be studied and the main purveyor of religion in the post-**Temple** period was not the prophet or priest but the **rabbi**, whose primary role was as a teacher. *See also* BAR MITZVAH/BAT MITZVAH ("COMING OF AGE"); BIBLE.

TORQUEMADA, TOMAS DE (1420–98). Infamous head of the Spanish **Inquisition**. Torquemada was an influential father confessor to Queen Isabella and King Ferdinand of Spain and encouraged them to complete the Christian reconquest of Spain by defeating the king-dom of Granada, the last remaining bastion of Islam on the peninsula. It was at his instigation that the pope set up the Inquisition for all of Spain in 1478, and he became its first head.

Torquemada set about investigating whether any Jews who had converted to Catholicism, particularly those forcibly converted in 1391, still maintained secret Jewish practices as **Marranos**. Those suspected of Judaizing were tortured until they confessed and were cruelly punished. In order to pursue these ends, he needed to remove those Jews who were still allowed to practice their faith openly, so he persuaded the king and queen to expel all Jews from Spain in 1492. Torquemada, in Jewish consciousness, is thought of as an exemplar of the merciless and intolerant face of Catholic Christianity. *See also* CONVERSOS; NEW CHRISTIANS; SEPHARDIM.

TRANSMIGRATION OF SOULS. *See* FRANK, JACOB (1726–91); KABBALAH; ZOHAR.

TRANSUBSTANTIATION. *See* HOST DESECRATION.

TREBLINKA. *See* KORCZAK, JANUSZ (PSEUDONYM OF HENRYK GOLDSZMIDT, 1878–1942); WARSAW GHETTO UPRISING.

TRIBES OF ISRAEL. *See* BRITISH ISRAELITES; DAVID; DIASPORA; ELDAD HA-DANI (9TH CENTURY); EXODUS; FALASHAS (ALSO KNOWN AS BETA ISRAEL); HOLY LAND; JACOB; JERUSALEM; JOSEPH; JUDAH (HEBREW YEHUDAH); KHAZARS; MANASSEH BEN ISRAEL (1604–57); MOUNTAIN JEWS; PROMISED LAND; REUVENI, DAVID (15TH–16TH CENTURIES); SAMARITANS; SAMBATYON; SOLOMON (10TH CENTURY BCE); TEN LOST TRIBES.

TRUMPELDOR, JOSEPH (1880–1920). Zionist pioneer and soldier. After having served with distinction in the Russian army, where he lost his left arm, Trumpeldor made **aliyah** with a group of pioneers in 1912 to work the **Land of Israel**. As a non-Ottoman citizen, he was deported from **Palestine** to Egypt and there helped found the Zion Mule Corps for the British army to liberate Palestine from the Turks. After spending some time back in Russia during the Revolution where he engaged in Zionist activities, he returned to Palestine in 1919 and helped organize the defense of Jewish settlements against Arab bands. He was killed when the settlement of Tel Chai came under fierce attack and is reputed to have said as he died, "It is good to die for the sake of our country." He soon came to be regarded as a Zionist hero, and his life and death an example of a true pioneer, celebrated in song and poetry. The **Betar** Movement was named after him as was a settlement in northern **Israel** near Mt. Gilboa.

TZADDIK (HEBREW, "RIGHTEOUS ONE," PLURAL TZAD-DIKIM). A term used to characterize someone who lives by God's commandments and is thought of as a true partner of God in the maintenance of the world. The title of tzaddik has come to be used in the **Chasidic** Movement for a spiritual leader, otherwise referred to as a rebbe. Chasidic communities were able to organize themselves around a specific charismatic tzaddik because they believed that their leader was a great-souled individual of a different spiritual level from his Chasidic followers and as a mystic able to help their prayers ascend to God. This special status gave tzaddikim unrivalled authority over their communities, and often the eldest son of a tzaddik inherited his father's mantle on the latter's death, forming family dynasties of tzaddikim.

Chasidim support their tzaddik with financial gifts, and those who lived far from the court of their tzaddik remained loyal to their particular rebbe and would go on **pilgrimage** to visit him at certain festivals. Each Chasidic dynasty would have its own songs, customs, and distinctive style of dress, although in many cases the dress of the tzaddik marked him off as a leader.

During the **Holocaust**, many of the East European tzaddikim were killed with their Chasidim. Some were saved by their followers and escaped in disguise. The tzaddik of the Satmar Chasidim, Joel Teitelbaum, was rescued from Hungary on the train that **Rudolf Kasztner** arranged with **Adolph Eichmann** to save Jews. When, at Kasztner's trial, he asked the Satmar leader to testify that he had saved him, Teitelbaum refused and replied, "You did not save me; God saved me."

A few tzaddikim survived the Nazi persecution and after World War II set up their courts in the United States, **Israel**, and Europe. Much of the opposition to modernity, the **Enlightenment**, and **Zionism** has come from Chasidic tzaddikim.

TZITZIT (HEBREW, "FRINGES"). *See* TALLIT (ARAMAIC, "PRAYER SHAWL").

– U –

UGANDA. *See* ZIONISM.

ULTRA-ORTHODOX JUDAISM. *See* AGUDAT ISRAEL (ALSO KNOWN AS AGUDAH); BNAI B'RITH (HEBREW, "SONS OF THE COVENANT"); BOARD OF DEPUTIES OF BRITISH JEWS; DAY OF ATONEMENT (HEBREW YOM KIPPUR); EMANCIPATION; ENLIGHTENMENT (HEBREW HASKALAH); "HA-TIKVAH" (HEBREW, "THE HOPE"); HEBREW UNIVERSITY OF JERUSALEM; HERTZ, JOSEPH HERMAN (1872–1946); HOLY LAND; KOOK, ABRAHAM ISAAC (1865–1935); NAPOLEON BONAPARTE (1769–1821); NETUREI KARTA (ARAMAIC, "GUARDIANS OF THE CITY"); ORTHODOX JUDAISM; RE-

FORM JUDAISM; SABBATH (HEBREW SHABBAT); WAILING WALL (HEBREW KOTEL HA-MAARAVI, "WESTERN WALL"); YESHIVAH (HEBREW, "PLACE OF SITTING," PLURAL YESHI-VOT); YIDDISH; ZIONISM; ZOHAR.

UNION FOR TRADITIONAL JUDAISM. *See* JEWISH THEO-LOGICAL SEMINARY (JTS).

UNITED SYNAGOGUE (LONDON). *See* CONSERVATIVE JUDA-ISM; HERTZ, JOSEPH HERMAN (1872–1946); JEWISH THEO-LOGICAL SEMINARY (JTS); ROTHSCHILD FAMILY.

UNITED SYNAGOGUE OF AMERICA. *See* CONSERVATIVE JU-DAISM; JEWISH THEOLOGICAL SEMINARY (JTS).

UNIVERSITY OF JUDAISM. *See* JEWISH THEOLOGICAL SEMI-NARY (JTS).

USURY. Jews are prohibited from lending money to each other or bor-rowing money from each other on interest but are allowed to do so to those outside the community. During the Middle Ages, many occupa-tions were closed to Jews; they were not allowed to join professional guilds or own land. The one activity open to them was lending money on interest, which Jews were heavily engaged in when Christianity did not approve of Christians becoming moneylenders. Usury by Jews added to already-existing theological prejudice against them, thus increasing **anti-Semitic** feelings, and in general, it made Jews even more disliked by Christians. Shylock in William Shakespeare's play *The Merchant of Venice* was the most famous Jewish usurer.

Jews were a very highly taxed minority and thus of considerable value to the state. Yet, it was Jewish moneylending that often con-tributed to expulsions because debts owed to them would be annulled if they were expelled from the country. According to the **Sanhedrin** convened by **Napoleon** that raised the question of usury to non-Jewish Frenchman, French **Gentiles** were to be considered "brothers," and no discrimination should be shown to them in the practice of usury.

UTOPIA. *See* KIBBUTZ (HEBREW, "COLLECTIVE," PLURAL KIBBUTZIM).

– V –

VAAD HA-LASHON HA-IVRIT. *See* ACADEMY OF THE HEBREW LANGUAGE (HEBREW VAAD HA-LASHON HA-IVRIT).

VICHY FRANCE. *See* PALMACH.

VICTORIA, QUEEN. *See* DISRAELI, BENJAMIN (1804–81); MONTEFIORE, SIR MOSES (1784–1885).

VILNA GAON. *See* ELIJAH OF VILNA (1720–97).

VITAL, CHAIM. *See* LURIA, ISAAC (1534–72).

VOLOZHIN YESHIVAH. *See* CHAIM OF VOLOZHIN (1749–1821); YESHIVAH (HEBREW, "PLACE OF SITTING," PLURAL YESHIVOT).

VON RATH, ERNEST. *See* GRYNSZPAN, HERSCHEL (1921–?); KRISTALLNACHT (GERMAN, "NIGHT OF BROKEN GLASS").

– W –

WAHL, SAUL (1541–1617). Polish merchant and leading figure of Polish Jewry. Wahl was born in Padua, Italy, where his father, Samuel Judah Katzenellenbogen, was the **rabbi**. He arrived in Brest Litovsk in the Duchy of Lithuania to study and eventually became a successful merchant with contacts at the Polish court. According to a widespread but unsubstantiated legend, when there was a council of Polish nobles in 1587 to decide who should succeed to the Polish throne after the death of King Stefan Batory, opinions were divided. Rather than allow an interregnum, they appointed Saul Wahl, whose patron was the Lithuanian Prince Nicholas Radziwil, as temporary king of Poland because he was neutral between the two parties to the dispute. The next day, the council elected Sigismund III as Polish king. Thus, Saul Wahl was king of Poland for a day.

The Jews of Poland and Lithuania remembered his efforts to ameliorate Jewish life, and the town of Brest Litovsk owed some of

its **synagogue** buildings, **yeshivah**, and **mikveh** to his largesse. He
made it a condition when endowing the mikveh that his descendants
should be able to use it without paying, and this was still the practice
until the **Holocaust**, when the community of Brest Litovsk was destroyed by the Nazis. *See also* COURT JEWS.

**WAILING WALL (HEBREW KOTEL HA-MAARAVI, "WEST-
ERN WALL").** The wall around the **Temple** Mount on the Western
side, which is the only remnant of the original Temple. Although
not actually part of the Temple complex, the wall is one of the
holiest sites of Judaism because **Orthodox** Jews do not enter the
Temple area proper due to their state of ritual impurity. The wall
itself is closest to where the Holy of Holies was situated in the
Temple, and there is a Rabbinic tradition that the Divine Presence,
Shekhinah, having withdrawn from the destroyed Temple, remains
over the Wailing Wall. It is known as the Wailing Wall because
Jewish pilgrims down the ages would come there to cry and mourn
for the destruction of the Temple, though Jews prefer to call it the
Western Wall.

The large exposed stones at the bottom of the wall are from the
period of **Herod**, and there are many layers of similar stones underground. The smaller stones above are from the Roman period,
and the stones at the very top were added by the Muslim rulers of
Jerusalem. Until modern times, Jewish access to the Wailing Wall
was restricted because of objections by the Muslim authorities, the
Waqf, responsible for Muslim holy sites. Indeed, the mufti of Jerusalem, **Haj Amin Husseini**, claimed that the Wailing Wall was really a
Muslim holy site after the **Balfour Declaration** had raised Arab opposition to **Zionist** aspirations. It was associated with Mohammed's
night journey to Jerusalem, and thus, further restrictions were placed
on Jewish prayers there.

In order not to upset Muslim sensitivities, the British Mandate police in 1928 removed a division that Jews had erected between men
and **women** for prayers on the **Day of Atonement**. In 1929, Arabs
attacked Jews praying at Wailing Wall, and this led in 1930 to an
International Committee that decided that the Wailing Wall belonged
to Muslims but Jews had the right to pray there though not to blow
the ram's horn, shofar. After 1948, Jews were completely banned
from visiting the Wailing Wall, which was under Jordanian control,

although according to the cease-fire agreement with Jordan, Jews should have had access to their holy places.

Since the reconquest of Jerusalem in the **Six-Day War** of 1967, a large area has been cleared in front of the Wailing Wall so that a plaza has been created that can contain thousands of visitors. Many tourists come there to pray, to celebrate a **bar mitzvah**, or to place a written prayer in the cracks of the wall. Indeed, services are provided for people from abroad to fax prayers to **Israel** to be placed in the wall.

Feminists who come to pray at the wall have been involved in disputes with some of the ultra-Orthodox by trying to hold their own public prayer services in the women's section. They have even petitioned the Israeli Supreme Court for the right to hold such public prayers, which are not approved by Orthodoxy.

WANDERING JEW. A legendary figure, often called Ahasuerus, who, according to Christian folklore, mocked Jesus as he was being led to the cross. As a punishment, he is condemned to wander around the world unable to find rest until Jesus returns at the Second Coming. The legend has evolved since its first literary appearance in Italy in the 13th century, with Ahasuerus depicted as a cobbler who cursed Jesus but afterward repented of his act and can only rest for a few moments before having to wander on.

Claims were made by people who believed they had actually met this hoary figure, and he has appeared in the literature of many European languages, even figuring in a **Yiddish** poem. Most of the accounts of the Wandering Jew are simply an **anti-Semitic** personification of the Jews of Europe. His legend is a popular reflection on Christian teaching about Jewish responsibility for the crucifixion of Jesus and the deserved punishment suffered by Jews ever since, though some versions are more positive in their depiction of him than others.

WANNSEE CONFERENCE (1942). *See* EICHMANN, ADOLPH (1906–62); FINAL SOLUTION; HITLER, ADOLPH (1889–1945).

WAQF (MUSLIM AUTHORITY). *See* WAILING WALL (HEBREW KOTEL HA-MAARAVI, "WESTERN WALL").

WAR OF INDEPENDENCE (HEBREW MILCHEMET HA-ATZ-MAUT). The war between the newly born state of **Israel** and the armies of surrounding Arab states, as well as **Palestinian** militia groups, that lasted from May 15, 1948, until July 20, 1949. The British pulled out the last of their troops, having controlled Mandate Palestine for 31 years, on May 14, and **David Ben Gurion** declared the establishment of Israel at the same time. Although the United Nations had voted for the partition of Palestine into a Jewish and an Arab state, which the **Jewish Agency** had reluctantly accepted, the Palestinians and Arab states refused to accept this.

The **Israel Defense Forces** (IDF), which emerged from the **Haganah** and incorporated members of the Jewish underground, the **Irgun** and the **Stern Gang**, had to defend the Jewish towns, settlements, **kibbutzim**, and Jewish minorities in Arab towns in Palestine. They were badly armed compared to the invading armies from Egypt, Syria, Iraq, Jordan, and Lebanon, which had tanks, heavy arms, and three separate air forces. The invading Egyptian army made considerable progress toward Tel Aviv but was held up by kibbutzim and the destruction of a main bridge just north of Ashdod by the IDF.

In the center of the country, the Jewish quarter of the Old City of **Jerusalem** fell to the Jordanian Arab Legion, but though West Jerusalem was surrounded and the 100,000 Jews there were living on a starvation diet, it held out. A relief road to West Jerusalem, nicknamed the Burma Road, was built by mostly elderly Jews to lift the siege.

The Syrian army invaded from the north and intended to drive all the way to Haifa, but it, too, was held up by kibbutzim en route. The first kibbutz in Israel, Deganiah, which was founded in 1909, repelled a Syrian tank attack mainly by using Molotov cocktails.

A temporary truce lasting one month was arranged on June 11, 1948, organized by UN mediator for Palestine Count Folke Bernadotte. It was during this period that Ben Gurion ordered the blowing up of an arms ship, the *Altalena*, which had been brought to the shores of Tel Aviv by the Irgun, who refused to surrender it to the Israeli army. The IDF bolstered its military capabilities by using this break in the fighting to give military training to the new immigrants who swelled its ranks from Displaced Person camps in Europe and to the volunteers from abroad known as machal.

When fighting resumed, the IDF managed to hold the Egyptian army attacks and break through to the Negev Desert. In the center of the country, the IDF captured the main airport at Lydda and a number of towns and villages between Tel Aviv and Jerusalem. They also captured some of the surrounding areas of Jerusalem but were unable to recapture the Old City. In the north of the country, the Arab town of Nazareth was captured, as well as other sections of the Galilee, and the Syrian army, though not pushed back, was held.

A second truce came into being on July 18, but with sporadic shelling and fighting still continuing, the IDF responded against the Egyptian and Jordanian forces. This fighting continued for several months, during which the Negev town of Beer Sheba was captured by the IDF, and eventually all Egyptian forces were cleared from Israel, and the IDF crossed into the Sinai Desert.

Eventually a ceasefire came into being on January 7, 1949, and armistice agreements were signed on February 24 at Rhodes between Israel and Egypt and on April 3 between Israel and Jordan. On July 20, an armistice agreement was signed with Syria. *See also* ARAB REFUGEES.

WARSAW GHETTO UPRISING. The Nazis formed the Warsaw **Ghetto** surrounded by a large wall in October 1940, into which the Jews of Warsaw and its surroundings were brought. Aryans living in the ghetto area were moved out, and over 400,000 Jews were moved in. Deportations of Jews to the Treblinka concentration camp began in July 1942, when thousands each day were rounded up, and continued for two months. Eventually, more than three quarters of the Jews in the ghetto were deported.

The Jewish resistance in the ghetto was divided into various groups: **Zionist, Revisionist Zionist, Bundist**, and communist. They decided to engage in active resistance and managed to obtain some arms from various Polish underground militia. They also manufactured homemade bombs and built underground bunkers.

The head of the Jewish Fighting Organization, known in Polish as the ZOB (Żydowska Organizacja Bojowa), was Mordecai Anielewicz, and the organization was based at 18 Mila Street. When German soldiers entered the ghetto on April 19, 1943, they were attacked by fighters of the ZOB and driven out. They returned under General Jürgen Stroop but were unable to penetrate the ghetto because of fierce resistance, despite their much greater firepower. To overcome this resistance, the German troops started destroying the ghetto, house by house, dropping hand grenades into the bunkers. The battles continued for about three weeks until May 8, when the ZOB headquarters were captured. After that, sporadic resistance continued for several more weeks, and some resistance fighters escaped to the nearby forest with the help of Polish **partisans**.

After the end of the war, a memorial was erected on the site of the ghetto showing the resistance fighters, and in **Israel, Holocaust Memorial Day**, Yom Hashoah, was established close to the time that the Warsaw Ghetto Uprising began. A **kibbutz** in Israel, Yad Mordekhai, was named after Mordecai Anielewicz. The uprising became an icon of Jewish resistance, particularly because it contrasted with the fate of most Jews who were said to have gone "like sheep to the slaughter." The Warsaw Ghetto Uprising helped to restore the Jewish self-image.

WEIZMANN, CHAIM (1874–1952). Charismatic **Zionist** leader and first president of the State of **Israel**. Weizmann was born near Pinsk, Russia, and in later life referred to himself as the "Yid from Pinsk." He moved as a student to Germany and then to Switzerland to obtain a scientific education and became a prominent chemist. Later, while working in England, he developed a method for producing acetone that helped the British government in making explosives during World War I.

As a student, Weizmann developed his interest in Zionism, influenced by the Zionist thinker **Achad Ha-Am**, and was a delegate to the second **Zionist Congress** in 1898. Though impressed by **Theodor Herzl**, he differed from him by emphasizing cultural Zionist needs and criticized Herzl for high-flown talk rather than for practical action on the ground. Weizmann was instrumental in the founding of the **Hebrew University of Jerusalem** in 1918, and later on, while living in Rechovot in **Palestine**, he set up a scientific institute that eventually became the Weizmann Institute of Science.

In 1904, Weizmann moved to Britain and taught at Manchester University, where he eventually became reader in biochemistry. Together with the historian Lewis Namier, on whom Weizmann had a powerful influence, he convinced Arthur James Balfour of the validity of the Zionist ideal, and Weizmann, with the help of his friend C. P. Scott, editor of the *Manchester Guardian*, was one of the main instigators of the **Balfour Declaration** on November 2, 1917, despite the opposition of some leading British Jews.

In 1918, Weizmann was head of the Zionist Commission to Palestine, where he met Emir Feisal in Akaba, and in 1920, he became president of the **World Zionist Organization**. At the 1931 Zionist Congress, he was deposed from his leadership because of his pro-British attitudes, though he strongly opposed British pro-Arab sentiments and limitations on immigration that failed to save many Jews from the **Holocaust**.

When out of office, he devoted himself to spreading Zionist propaganda, particularly in the United States, which led to the **Biltmore Program**. He also helped Jewish scientist refugees escaping Nazi persecution in the 1930s so that they could contribute to the development of the Jewish community in Palestine and strongly advocated the use of **Hebrew** as a national language there.

After **David Ben Gurion** declared the State of Israel on May 14, 1948, Weizmann, the elder statesman of Zionism, was the most obvious candidate for president, and he was duly elected by the **Knesset** in February 1949.

WEIZMANN INSTITUTE OF SCIENCE. *See* WEIZMANN, CHAIM (1874–1952).

WESTERN WALL. *See* PILGRIMAGE (HEBREW ALIYAH LE-REGEL, "ASCENT BY FOOT"); WAILING WALL (HEBREW KOTEL HA-MAAVRAVI, "WESTERN WALL").

WILHELM II, KAISER. *See* ALLIANCE ISRAÉLITE UNIVERSELLE (AIU); HERZL, THEODOR (1860–1904).

WILLIAM OF NORWICH. *See* BLOOD LIBEL.

WINE. *See* DIETARY LAWS; GENTILE (HEBREW GOY, PLURAL GOYIM, "NATION" OR "PEOPLE"); PASSOVER (HEBREW PE-SACH); PURIM; SABBATH (HEBREW SHABBAT).

WINGATE, ORDE. *See* DAYAN, MOSHE (1915–81).

WISE, ISAAC MAYER. *See* HEBREW UNION COLLEGE (HUC).

WOMEN IN JUDAISM. Though there are a number of outstanding women in the Bible, such as the Matriarch **Sarah**; Miriam, prophetess and sister of **Moses**; Deborah, prophetess and judge; Ruth, the ancestress of King **David**; and Queen Esther, the heroine of the **Purim** story, it is clear that women play secondary roles to those of men. The religion of the Bible is decidedly **patriarchal**, and this has set the pattern for all of later Judaism. It is true that occasionally we find women who were the equals of their male colleagues in Rabbinic literature, such as Beruriah, a 2nd-century **Palestinian** scholar, but they were clearly the exceptions.

The primary roles of women throughout the premodern period were as wives and mothers, instilling the spirit of Judaism in the home. Most of the positive commandments that have to be performed in a limited time were thought not to apply to women, who were excused because of their other responsibilities. Some specific commandments were regarded as their special responsibility, namely bathing in the **mikveh** after menstruation, separating off a tithe from the bread they baked in **Temple** times to give to the priests, and kindling the **Sabbath** and festival lights in the home just before twilight on Friday and on the eve of festivals to bring light and joy into a Jewish house.

With the changing nature of Jewish life after the **Enlightenment** in the 18th century, women began to play more public roles both within the Jewish community and also in wider social circles. **Reform Judaism** was the first to provide religious **emancipation** for women, allowing women equal roles inside the **synagogue** and eventually ordaining female **rabbi**s. This precedent has been followed more recently by **Conservative Judaism**, and Modern **Orthodoxy** has allowed girls to have a bat mitzvah ceremony in synagogue when they come of age modeled on the **bar mitzvah** ceremony for a boy. Traditional groups within Judaism, such as the members of **Agudat Israel** and the **Neturei Karta**, still do not permit their womenfolk any public roles, although the Agudah does provide education for girls up to a high standard in their Beis Yaakov schools and seminaries.

Among secular Jews, there is considerable animosity to the subservient position of women within Orthodoxy, and secular **Zionists** are proud of the fact that **Golda Meir** was able to become prime minister of **Israel**, even though her appointment was opposed by leading rabbis. Some of this secular feminism has spilled over onto religious groups among Modern Orthodox women, who are trying to push back the boundaries of the Rabbinic authorities with regard to restrictions on women. Some synagogues on the fringes of Orthodoxy do indeed allow women to take part in leading the services, and some more mainstream Orthodox synagogues allow women to become lay leaders of the community. The religious glass ceiling that women confront, however, is still very apparent in every traditional Jewish organization and environment. *See also* HEAD COVERING; TALLIT (ARAMAIC, "PRAYER SHAWL").

WORLD HEBREW COVENANT. *See* BRIT IVRIT OLAMIT (HEBREW, "WORLD HEBREW COVENANT").

WORLD TO COME. *See* RESURRECTION; SABBATH (HEBREW SHABBAT).

WORLD ZIONIST ORGANIZATION (WZO). An organization established at the first **Zionist Congress** held in 1897 in Basel. **Theodor Herzl**, who convened the congress to unite various **Zionist** bodies throughout the world, was elected president of the WZO and retained this position until his death in 1904. In Herzl's view, the purpose of the organization was to have a body that could engage in political negotiations about settling Jews in the **Land of Israel** and building financial institutions that would support such settlement. *See also* JEWISH AGENCY; JEWISH NATIONAL FUND (HEBREW KEREN KAYEMET LEYISRAEL, JNF); REVISIONIST ZIONISTS; WEIZMANN, CHAIM (1874–1952).

WÜRTTEMBERG, KARL ALEXANDER, DUKE OF. *See* COURT JEWS; OPPENHEIMER, JOSEPH (1698–1738, KNOWN AS JEW SUESS).

– Y –

YADIN, YIGAL (1917–84). Israeli general and archaeologist. Yadin was a distinguished soldier, a leading figure in the prestate **Haganah**, and subsequently chief of staff of the Israeli army. His father, Professor E. L. Sukenik, was an eminent archaeologist, and Yadin followed in his father's footsteps. He is best known for his work on the **Dead Sea Scrolls** and his discovery of remains of the **Bar Kokhba** revolt in the Judean desert. Yadin trained a whole generation of young Israeli archaeologists and popularized Jewish history. He was elected to the **Knesset** in the 1970s and served for a short period as deputy prime minister.

YAD VASHEM. A **Holocaust** memorial institution in **Jerusalem** whose name is taken from the prophet Isaiah (56:4–5): "For thus says the Lord . . . to them will I give in my house and within my walls a memorial and a name (Hebrew yad vashem) better than sons and daughters. I will give them an eternal name, that will not be cut off." Given the importance that Jews attach to remembering the Holocaust, Yad Vashem has become a **pilgrimage** center for Jews throughout the **Diaspora** and for visiting dignitaries to **Israel**. It is a large complex containing museums, monuments, halls of remembrance, and records of those who perished as well as a tree-lined avenue of the righteous **Gentiles**, where trees with attached plaques are planted in honor of those Gentiles who risked their own lives to save Jews from Nazi persecution. *See also* KASZTNER, RUDOLF (1906–57).

YALE UNIVERSITY. *See* NUMERUS CLAUSUS (LATIN, "CLOSED NUMBER").

YARMULKA. *See* HEAD COVERING.

YEHUDAH. *See* BABYLONIA; JUDAH (HEBREW YEHUDAH).

YEHUDI. *See* BABYLONIA; JEW (HEBREW YEHUDI); JUDAH (HEBREW YEHUDAH).

YESHIVAH (HEBREW, "PLACE OF SITTING," PLURAL YE-SHIVOT). The main academy for Jewish studies, the curriculum of which involves intense study of the **Babylonian Talmud** and its commentaries. It was in the yeshivot of **Palestine** and Babylonia that the **Oral Torah** was redacted first in the **Mishnah** and then in the Palestinian and Babylonian Talmuds. Yeshivot were established in all the main areas of Jewish life in the **Diaspora**, throughout the Middle East, from North Africa to Spain and Portugal, in Italy, France, Germany, and Austria, and from there to Eastern Europe.

A student would graduate to a yeshivah in his early teens from an elementary religious school, known as a cheder or talmud torah. The principal of a yeshivah, known as a rosh yeshivah, is often an eminent **rabbi** and usually gives a text-based lecture, shiur, at regular intervals. Much of the learning, however, is done by the students themselves in small groups, often by two learning partners, chavruta, who prepare the material for the lecture and then go over the lecture after it has been delivered. While **Ashkenazi** yeshivot concentrate on Talmudic studies, **Sephardi** yeshivot include some **Bible** studies and **halakhic** topics as well, and the modern **Musar Movement** introduced the study of ethical texts, though this was not approved of by many of the Ashkenazi yeshivah heads.

In the premodern **Orthodox** world, all rabbis were graduates of yeshivot, where they devoted part of their studies to the curriculum for ordination, semikhah, though many yeshivot did not encourage their students to undergo ordination, preferring them to study **Torah** for its own sake. In the 19th and 20th centuries, a number of rabbinical seminaries were opened in Central Europe, Western Europe, and then the United States with the express purpose of training rabbis, some Orthodox but mainly **Conservative** and **Reform**. There was considerable opposition even to the most Orthodox of these from the established yeshivot. An Italian seminary was opened in Padua in 1829 and a French one in Metz in 1830; a major center for training rabbis, called the **Jewish Theological Seminary**, was opened in Breslau in 1854. Jews College was opened in London in 1855, the Jüdische Hochschule in Berlin in 1872, the Orthodox Hildesheimer Seminary also in Berlin in 1873, a Hungarian seminary in Budapest in 1877, an Austrian seminary in Vienna in 1862, the Reform **Hebrew Union College** in Cincinnati in 1875, the Conservative Jewish Theological Seminary in New York in 1887, and the Orthodox Rabbi Isaac Elhanan Theological Seminary in New York in 1897.

The model for all Ashkenazi yeshivot was set in the early 19th century by the founding of the Volozhin Yeshivah by **Chaim of Volozhin**, the main disciple of **Elijah of Vilna**. Volozhin was headed by a series of gifted rabbis, and at its height, hundreds of students flocked there from all over Eastern Europe and beyond. Many of the leading rabbis in the 19th century were graduates of Volozhin. A whole series of Lithuanian yeshivot on the Volozhin model came to dominate Ashkenazi Jewish education throughout the 19th and 20th centuries.

Originally, the **Chasidic Movement** was against students studying in yeshivot because such study encouraged intellectual arrogance;

rather, Chasidic students studied either in a local **synagogue** cum study hall, bet hamidrash, or in the court of their **tzaddik**. In the course of time, faced by problems of the **Enlightenment**, Chasidim began to model their educational systems on the established yeshivot of the **Mitnaggedim**, except that they focused on teaching Chasidic ideas as well as the Talmud. In Germany, the **Neo-Orthodoxy** of **Samson Raphael Hirsch** was originally against studying in yeshivot, preferring a more well-rounded education. Eventually, however, the pressure from students led to it relenting.

Although the **Holocaust** destroyed many of the great yeshivah centers in Europe, survivors reconstituted these academies in the United States, Western Europe, and **Israel** in the second half of the 20th century, in many cases continuing the tradition of teaching in **Yiddish**.

Some modern Israeli yeshivot have grown up with **Hebrew** as the language of instruction, a wider curriculum, and a **Zionist** ideology. This more modern outlook, associated specifically with Chief Rabbi **Abraham Isaac Kook**, has also been the approach of Yeshiva University in the United States, which was originally founded as a rabbinical seminary, the Rabbi Isaac Elhanan Theological Seminary, in 1897. Yeshiva University, as its name implies, teaches a variety of secular studies as well as Jewish studies, with a college for **women**, known as Stern College. One of the leading thinkers of Modern Orthodoxy, Rabbi Joseph Dov Soloveitchik (1903–93), taught at Yeshiva University during the second half of the 20th century and was the mentor of several generations of Orthodox rabbis. The Orthodox Bar Ilan University in Israel has also combined secular and Jewish studies in all of its programs.

In Israel, yeshivot have sprouted since the foundation of the state, and many of them also have a yeshivah for married students, known as a kolel. One of the reasons students continue to study in a yeshivah or kolel is that Israeli law excuses a rabbinical student from army service. This has caused a backlash of criticism from more secular Israelis who have to serve regularly as reserves in the **Israel Defense Force**, particularly since the traditional yeshivot, whether Mitnaggedic or Chasidic, are bastions of anti-Zionism.

Traditional yeshivot were only for male students, yet under the inspiration of the Beis Yaakov educational network founded by Sara Schnirer in Krakow in 1917 and with the desire of women for greater educational opportunities, many women's seminaries have been opened even for ultra-Orthodox women. They generally provide a much wider curriculum for female students than the classical yeshivot.

YESHIVA UNIVERSITY. *See* YESHIVAH (HEBREW, "PLACE OF SITTING," PLURAL YESHIVOT).

YESHIVAH WORLD. *See* MITNAGGEDIC MOVEMENT (HEBREW, "OPPONENTS"); ORTHODOX JUDAISM.

YEVSEKTSIYA. The Communist Party of Soviet Russia had a special section dealing with Jewish issues known as Yevsektsiya. Its main purpose was to integrate Jews into Soviet society and to secularize and **assimilate** them. Because there were millions of Jews in the Russian Empire with their own subculture, **Yiddish** language, and beliefs, this was a mammoth task. Judaism, **Zionism**, and the general bourgeois attitudes of Jews were the main targets of the local Yevsektsiya, who used the force of the state to close down **synagogues, yeshivot,** and organizations inimical to communism. Many Jewish groups went underground, but their leaders were arrested, sent to Siberia, or simply killed.

YEVTUSHENKO, YEVGENI. *See* BABI YAR.

YIDDISH. A variety of Jewish dialects of German spoken by **Ashkenazi** Jews throughout Europe from the Middle Ages until modern times and written in **Hebrew** characters. The widespread use of the language was caused by the expulsion of Jews from German-speaking lands and their migration to Eastern Europe, taking with them their lingua franca. In the new host countries, Yiddish underwent development, where its vocabulary and certain structural features were influenced not merely by Hebrew and **Aramaic** but by Slavic and Romance languages. Yiddish was, and still is in many cases, the language of instruction in Ashkenazi **yeshivot** but is only spoken as a living language by **Chasidim** and ultra-**Orthodox** Jews who reject modernity.

YISHUV (PRE-ZIONIST JEWS IN PALESTINE). *See* ASHKENAZIM (SINGULAR ASHKENAZI).

YOM HA-ATZMAUT. *See* ISRAEL INDEPENDENCE DAY (HEBREW YOM HA-ATZMAUT).

YOM HASHOAH. *See* HOLOCAUST REMEMBRANCE DAY (HEBREW YOM HASHOAH); WARSAW GHETTO UPRISING.

YOM KIPPUR. *See* DAY OF ATONEMENT (HEBREW YOM KIPPUR).

YOM KIPPUR WAR. *See* MEIR, GOLDA (ORIGINALLY MYERSON, 1898–1978).

YORK MARTYRS. *See* CRUSADES.

YOUNG TURK MOVEMENT. *See* DOENMEH.

– Z –

ZANGWILL, ISRAEL. *See* ZIONIST CONGRESS.

ZEMIROT (HEBREW, "RELIGIOUS SONGS"). *See* SABBATH (HEBREW SHABBAT).

ZION. *See* CHIBBAT TZION (HEBREW, "LOVE OF ZION"); "HATIKVAH" (HEBREW, "THE HOPE"); HEBREW UNIVERSITY OF JERUSALEM; HOLY LAND; MESSIAH (HEBREW MASHIACH); MIZRACHI (ABBREVIATION OF MERCAZ RUCHANI, "SPIRITUAL CENTER"); PROTOCOLS OF THE ELDERS OF ZION; REFORM JUDAISM; ZIONISM; ZIONIST CONGRESS.

ZIONISM. Zion was an alternative name for **Jerusalem**, and the term *Zionism* was coined in the late 19th century for the movement advocating the return of the Jewish people to the **Land of Israel**. The name was adopted by various groups who differed ideologically but shared the hope of a return to Zion. **Theodor Herzl**, by convening the first **Zionist Congress** in Basel in 1897, gave the movement a focus and provided an international identity for the name *Zionism*. There were disagreements between the practical Zionists, that is, those who were practically oriented and wanted a program of immediate settlement of the Land of Israel, and those aiming for a more political solution to Jewish homelessness—the political Zionists like Herzl—who wanted the nations of the world to agree about the founding of a Jewish state.

Unlike those Zionists who were rooted in traditional Judaism, Herzl was primarily interested in finding a land for Jews, and he was not necessarily committed to a **Palestinian** Zion. When his efforts to persuade the Ottoman sultan to assign a charter for Jews to settle in the **Holy Land** were unsuccessful, he was tempted by a British offer in 1903 to set aside land in Uganda for Jewish settlement. The Uganda option was strongly opposed by a majority of members of the **World Zionist Organization** of all persuasions, and Herzl was forced to abandon it.

The **Balfour Declaration** issued by Arthur James Balfour, the British foreign secretary to Lord **Rothschild**, in 1917 was seen as a major coup within the political Zionist camp, particularly because the British government was given control of Mandate Palestine by the League of Nations after World War I. Unlike the Uganda option, it was also welcomed by the practical Zionists and religious Zionist groups.

An escape from **anti-Semitism** was one of the main elements that had inspired Herzl and a number of the early Zionist thinkers. It resurfaced strongly in the immediate pre- and post-**Holocaust** era and turned many anti-Zionists, both religious and secular, into supporters of statehood who subscribed to the **Biltmore Program** of a Jewish state in Palestine. The vote of the United Nations on November 29, 1947, in favor of the partition of Palestine, the subsequent withdrawal of the British from Mandate Palestine, and the declaration of Israeli statehood on May 14, 1948, changed the Zionist dream into a reality.

There was opposition from various Jewish groups to Zionism. **Assimilated** Jews could not identify with the separate Jewish ethnicity implied by Zionism. **Reform** Jews originally believed that Judaism could, and should, exist merely as a religion rather than as the mark of a distinctive nationality. Many **Orthodox** Jews believed that any return to Zion should be the prerogative of God in the **Messianic Age**, not of secular nationalists. Though in the early days of Zionism the opponents of the movement were found throughout **Diaspora** Jewry, the establishment of a Jewish state, the State of **Israel**, meant that the opposition shrank to a small, if highly vocal, minority in such groups as the **American Council for Judaism** or the **Neturei Karta**. *See also* ACHAD HA-AM (HEBREW, "ONE OF THE PEOPLE"); AGUDAT ISRAEL (ALSO KNOWN AS AGUDAH); ALIYAH (HEBREW, "GOING UP," PLURAL ALIYOT); *ALTNEULAND*

(NOVEL); ARAB REFUGEES; BASEL PROGRAM; BETAR (ACRONYM OF BERIT TRUMPELDOR); CHIBBAT TZION (HEBREW, "LOVE OF ZION"); CONSERVATIVE JUDAISM; "HA-TIKVAH" (HEBREW, "THE HOPE"); HEAD COVERING; HOLY LAND; IRGUN TZEVAI LEUMI (HEBREW, "NATIONAL ARMY ORGANIZATION," KNOWN AS THE IRGUN); ISRAEL INDEPENDENCE DAY (HEBREW YOM HA-ATZMAUT); JEWISH NATIONAL FUND (HEBREW KEREN KAYEMET LEYISRAEL, JNF); KIBBUTZ (HEBREW, "COLLECTIVE," PLURAL KIBBUTZIM); KOOK, ABRAHAM ISAAC (1865–1935); LAW OF RETURN; MIZRACHI (ABBREVIATION OF MERCAZ RUCHANI, "SPIRITUAL CENTER"); PROMISED LAND; REVISIONIST ZIONISTS; STERN GANG (HEBREW LOCHAMEI CHERUT YISRAEL OR LECHI); WAR OF INDEPENDENCE (HEBREW MILCHEMET HA-ATZMAUT).

ZIONIST CONGRESS. The first Zionist Congress was called together by **Theodor Herzl** in August 1897 in Basel to create a movement of political **Zionism**, to unify the various Zionist groups, and to formulate Zionist policy. It was a massive undertaking, and it began a process that gathered momentum and raised expectations of Jews throughout the world. Herzl's book, *Der Judenstaat* (1896), had depicted the possibility of a Jewish state, and the Zionist Congress seemed the first step to its realization in setting up the **World Zionist Organization**.

Israel Zangwill, the British novelist, wrote after the first congress "By the waters of Basel there we sat down but we did not weep." This was a play on the words of Psalm 137, composed by **Babylonian** Jews **exiled** in the **Diaspora**: "By the waters of Babylon there we sat down and we wept when we remembered Zion."

Thereafter, Zionist congresses met almost every year, the first six of which Herzl was the chairman. The congresses were sometimes very stormy with the different factions divided over central issues, the early ones concerned with **Palestine** or other options for a Jewish national home. *See also* BASEL PROGRAM; BILTMORE PROGRAM.

ZION MULE CORPS. *See* TRUMPELDOR, JOSEPH (1880–1920).

ZOB (ŻYDOWSKA ORGANIZACJA BOJOWA). *See* WARSAW GHETTO UPRISING.

ZOHAR. One of main texts of Jewish mysticism, **Kabbalah**, that appeared in uncertain circumstances at the end of the 13th century CE. Copies of what was claimed to be an ancient text were circulated piecemeal by Moses de Leon (d. 1305), a member of a Spanish mystical fellowship. The Zohar is set in 2nd-century **Palestine** and deals with the teachings of the sage Simeon bar Yochai. Kabbalists believe that the Zohar text is a true account of the events surrounding bar Yochai and not a fictitious recreation written a millennium later. Today, among **Orthodox** Jews, the Zohar ranks with Scripture and the **Talmud** as a divinely inspired interpretation of Judaism and is known as the "**Bible** of the Kabbalists."

The influence of the Zohar on Jews and Judaism has been considerable. It has made teachings about the 10 Sefirot, which are the structures through which God creates and interacts with the world; about the feminine side of God, Shekhinah; about the reality of the powers of evil; and about the transmigration of souls, gilgul, all part of the common background of pre-**Enlightenment** Judaism. *See also* FRANK, JACOB (1726–91); LAG B'OMER; LURIA, ISAAC (1534–72).

ZOLA, EMILE. *See* DREYFUS CASE.

ZYKLON B (GAS). *See* AUSCHWITZ.

Bibliography

CONTENTS

INTRODUCTION

The reason that the bibliography is divided into subject areas is to enable those interested in different aspects of Jewish history to locate books reflecting their particular interest. Apart from general works of Jewish history or of Jewish culture, like the *Encyclopaedia Judaica*, Salo Baron's monumental *A Social and Religious History of the Jews*, or *The Blackwell Companion to Jewish Culture*, which cover a large span of material, there are also many more focused studies that deal with limited subjects in greater detail.

Only books in English are included in this bibliography, though obviously many of the works on Jewish history and Judaism are in other languages, particularly Hebrew. Some of the English books that have been included contain substantial selections of original texts, while others are themselves translations of these texts. This should enable the reader to become acquainted with a range of source material as well as with the particular interpretations given by different authors to that material. Older works have also been included because of their importance, some of them having become minor classics.

In the dictionary, the history of the Jews and their religion is presented in a way that Jews today would recognize as depicting their past and their faith. We may call this a mainstream view of the history of the Jews. It is apparent from some of the entries in the dictionary that there are alternative views of Jewish history because it has been surrounded by controversy over the past two millennia due to the bitter conflict with Christianity and to a lesser extent with Islam. The bibliographical references under "Christianity and Islam" cover much of the negative and positive side of the relationship with these two faiths and deal with future prospects perhaps of less antagonism and greater cooperation.

Anti-Semites, and latterly virulent anti-Zionists, obviously proffer a series of very different perspectives on Jews and Judaism, and some of their views are described in those bibliographical references under "Anti-Semitism and the Holocaust" and "Zionism," which seek to refute their opinions. The bibliography has avoided referring the reader directly to these more radical views, which have little historical merit, even though it is a salutary experience to discover the extent of prejudice still current in the 21st century in anti-Semitic and anti-Zionist books and Web sites.

Much space has been devoted in the bibliography to the Holocaust because of its uniqueness as a historical phenomenon. The Holocaust/ Shoah is still a live issue in the consciousness of most Jews, not merely in the minds of the diminishing number of survivors. It has also stirred the conscience of many Gentiles, who find it difficult to understand why and how it was allowed to occur. Despite the vast amount of historical data, there are still a number of people, including some historians, who deny it ever happened.

Though Jewish versions of their "salvation history," particularly as found in the Hebrew Bible and Rabbinic literature, have long been questioned by academic scholars, the dictionary does not present the range of scholarly theories about the ancient Hebrews or early Rabbinic Judaism. Some of these can be found in the references under "Bible," "Rabbinic Lore and Literature," and "History." Many Jews today identify with the images, stories, and practices of that "salvation history," whether they take them all literally or not, and the different theories usually remain the preserve of specialists.

Although there is obviously much material about the Jewish past in the bibliography, references to some of the ongoing issues that affect the Jewish present and will shape the Jewish future have also been included. Those issues relating to the State of Israel, Jewish identity, and the future of the Diaspora can be found under "Ashkenazim and Sephardim," "Communities and Jewish Identity," "Israel," and "Zionism."

The ideologies and practices of the main subgroups within Judaism appear under "Halakhah, Ritual, and the Synagogue"; "Kabbalah and Chasidism"; "Philosophy"; "Religion"; and "Sects," as do the relationship between Jewish tradition and modernity. Some of the more contentious issues in contemporary Jewish life are dealt with in references under "Homosexuality" and "Women in Judaism."

It is often important to read more than one account of a subject to gain perspective and realize that one does not have to accept a particular view merely because it is found in a book, even one with footnotes and references.

ANTI-SEMITISM AND THE HOLOCAUST

Bauer, Yehuda. *A History of the Holocaust*. New York: Watts, 1982.

Beck, Gad. *An Underground Life: Memoirs of a Gay Jew in Nazi Berlin*. Written with Frank Heibert, translated by Allison Brown. Madison: University of Wisconsin Press, 1999.

Berkovits, Eliezer. *Faith after the Holocaust*. New York: Ktav, 1973.

Birnbaum, Pierre. *Anti-Semitism in France* (Studies in Social Discontinuity). Oxford: Blackwell, 1992.

Braham, Randolph. *The Politics of Genocide: The Holocaust in Hungary*. 2 vols. New York: Columbia University Press, 1981; revised edition, 1994.

Browning, Christopher R. *Collected Memories: Holocaust History and Post-War Testimony* (George L. Mosse Series in Modern European Culture and Intellectual History). Madison: University of Wisconsin Press, 2003.

Carmichael, Joel. *The Satanizing of the Jews: Origin and Development of Mystical Anti-Semitism*. New York: Fromm International, 1992.

Chazan, Robert. *Medieval Stereotypes and Modern Antisemitism*. Berkeley: University of California Press, 1997.

Cohen, Jeremy. *The Friars and the Jews: The Evolution of Medieval Anti-Judaism*. Ithaca, N.Y.: Cornell University Press, 1982.

Cohn, Norman. *Warrant for Genocide: The Myth of the Jewish World Conspiracy and the Protocols of the Elders of Zion*. New York: Harper and Row, 1967; London: Eyre and Spottiswoode, 1967; new ed., London: Serif, 1996.

Davies, Alan T., ed. *Antisemitism and the Foundations of Christianity*. New York: Paulist, 1979.

Dawidowicz, Lucy S. *The Holocaust and the Historians*. Cambridge, Mass.: Harvard University Press, 1997.

———. *The War against the Jews 1933–1945*. New York: Holt, Rinehart, and Winston, 1975.

Edelstein, Alan. *An Unacknowledged Harmony: Philo-Semitism and the Survival of European Jewry* (Contributions in Ethnic Studies, no. 4). Westport, Conn.: Greenwood, 1982.

Eliach, Yaffa. *Hasidic Tales of the Holocaust*. New York: Avon Books, 1982.

Evans, Richard J. *Lying about Hitler: History, Holocaust, and the David Irving Trial*. New York: Basic Books, 2002.

Fackenheim, Emil. *An Epitaph for German Judaism: From Halle to Jerusalem* (Modern Jewish Philosophy and Religion). Madison: University of Wisconsin Press, 2007.

Flannery, Edward H. *The Anguish of the Jews: Twenty-Three Centuries of Anti-Semitism*. New York: Macmillan, 1965; rev. and updated ed., New York: Paulist 1985.

Frank, Anne. *The Diary of a Young Girl: The Definitive Edition*. Ed. Otto Frank and Mirjam Pressler, trans. Susan Massotty. New York: Doubleday, 1995; London: Viking, 1997.

Frankel, Jonathan. *The Damascus Affair: "Ritual Murder," Politics, and the Jews in 1840*. Cambridge: Cambridge University Press, 1997.

Gaon, Solomon, and M. Mitchell Serels, eds. *Sephardim and the Holocaust*. New York: Yeshiva University, 1987.

Gilbert, Martin. *Atlas of the Holocaust*. London: Joseph, 1982; as *The Macmillan Atlas of the Holocaust*. New York: Macmillan, 1982; 2nd ed., as *The Dent Atlas of the Holocaust*. London: Dent, 1993; as *Atlas of the Holocaust*. New York: Morrow, 1993.

————. *The Holocaust: A History of the Jews during the Second World War*. New York: Holt, Rinehart, and Winston, 1975; London: Weidenfeld and Nicolson, 1975; 10th anniversary ed., 1985, with new intro. and bib., New York: Seth, and Harmondsworth; Penguin, 1986.

Goldhagen, Daniel Jonah. *Hitler's Willing Executioners: Ordinary Germans and the Holocaust*. New York: Knopf, 1996; London: Little, Brown, 1996.

Hartman, Geoffrey, ed. *Holocaust Remembrance: The Shapes of Memory*. Oxford: Blackwell, 1994.

Hilberg, Raul. *The Destruction of the European Jews*. New York: Harper and Row, 1961; London: Allen, 1961; rev. and definitive ed., 3 vols. New York: Holmes and Meier, 1985.

Katz, Jacob. *From Prejudice to Destruction: Antisemitism 1700–1933*. Cambridge, Mass.: Harvard University Press, 1980.

Langmuir, Gavin I. *Towards a Definition of Antisemitism*. Berkeley: University of California Press, 1990.

Lipstadt, Deborah. *Denying the Holocaust: The Growing Assault on Truth and Memory*. New York: Free Press, 1993; London: Penguin Books, 1994.

Ogilvie, Sarah A., and Scott Miller. *Refuge Denied: The St. Louis Passengers and the Holocaust*. Madison: University of Wisconsin Press, 2006.

Parkes, James. *The Conflict of the Church and the Synagogue: A Study in the Origins of Antisemitism*. London: Soncino, 1934; Philadelphia: Jewish Publication Society, 1961.

Peck, Abraham J. *Jews and Christians after the Holocaust*. Philadelphia: Fortress, 1982.

Roskies, David G. *Against the Apocalypse: Responses to Catastrophe in Modern Jewish Culture*. Cambridge, Mass.: Harvard University Press, 1984.

Rubinstein, William D., and Hilary L. Rubinstein. *Philosemitism: Admiration and Support in the English-Speaking World for Jews, 1840–1939*. London: Macmillan, 1999.

Ruether, Rosemary Radford. *Faith and Fratricide: The Theological Roots of Anti-Semitism*. New York: Seabury, 1974; London: Search, 1975.

Trachtenberg, Joshua. *The Devil and the Jews: The Medieval Conception of the Jew and Its Relation to Modern Antisemitism*. New Haven, Conn.: Yale University Press; and London: Oxford University Press, 1943; new ed., Philadelphia: Jewish Publication Society, 2002.

Vago, Bela, and George Lachmann Mosse. *Jews and Non-Jews in Eastern Europe, 1918–1945*. New York: Wiley, 1974.

Weiss, John. *Ideology of Death: Why the Holocaust Happened in Germany*. Chicago: Dee, 1996.

Wiesel, Elie. *Night*. New York: Hill and Wang, 1958.

Wiesenthal, Simon. *The Sunflower*. London: Allen, 1970; New York: Schocken, 1976, rev. ed., 1997.

Wistrich, Robert. *Antisemitism: The Longest Hatred*. New York: Pantheon, 1991; London: Thames Methuen, 1991.

ASHKENAZIM AND SEPHARDIM

Angel, Marc D. *Voices in Exile: A Study in Sephardic Intellectual History* (Library of Sephardic History and Thought). Hoboken, N.J.: Ktav, 1991.
Barnett, R. D., ed. *The Sephardi Heritage*. New York: Ktav, 1971.
Beinart, Haim. *The Expulsion of the Jews from Spain*. Trans. Jeffrey M. Green. Oxford: Littman Library of Jewish Civilization, 2002.
Biale, David, ed. *Cultures of the Jews: A New History*. 3 vols. New York: Schocken Books, 2006.
Dawidowicz, Lucy S., ed. *The Golden Tradition: Jewish Life and Thought in Eastern Europe*. Boston: Beacon Press, 1968.
Elazar, Daniel J. *The Other Jews: The Sephardim Today*. New York: Basic Books, 1989.
Haumann, Heiko. *A History of East European Jews*. Trans. James Patterson. Budapest, Hungary: Central European University Press, 2001.
Kedourie, Elie, ed. *Spain and the Jews: The Sephardi Experience in 1492 and After*. London: Thames and Hudson, 1992.
Levy, A., ed. *The Jews of the Ottoman Empire*. Princeton, N.J.: Darwin Press, 1994.
———. *The Sephardim in the Ottoman Empire*. Princeton, N.J.: Darwin Press, 1999.
Raphael, Chaim. *The Road from Babylon: The Story of Sephardi and Oriental Jews*. London: Weidenfeld and Nicolson, 1985.
Roth, Norman. *Conversos, Inquisition, and the Expulsion of the Jews from Spain*. Madison: University of Wisconsin Press, 2002.
Vital, David. *A People Apart: the Jews in Europe, 1789–1939*. Oxford: Oxford University Press, 1998.
Zimmels, H. J. *Ashkenazim and Sephardim: Their Relations, Differences, and Problems as Reflected in the Rabbinical Responsa* (Jews' College Publications, new series, no. 2). London: Oxford University Press, 1958; rev. ed., Hoboken, N.J.: Ktav, 1996.

BIBLE

Brookes, Roger. *The Spirit of the Ten Commandments: Shattering the Myth of Rabbinic Legalism*. San Francisco: Harper and Row, 1990.
Cherry, Shai. *Torah through Time: Understanding Bible Commentary, from Rabbinic Times to Modern Day*. Philadelphia: Jewish Publication Society, 2007.

Cohn, Haim H. *Human Rights in the Bible and Talmud*. Tel Aviv: MOD, 1989.

Goldman, Solomon. *The Ten Commandments*. Chicago: University of Chicago Press, 1956.

Greenberg, Moshe. *Studies in the Bible and Jewish Thought* (JPS Scholar of Distinction Series). Philadelphia: Jewish Publication Society, 1995.

Hertz, J. H. *The Pentateuch and Haftorahs: Hebrew Text English Translation and Commentary*. 2nd ed. London: Soncino Press, 1960.

Heschel, Abraham J. *Prophetic Inspiration after the Prophets: Maimonides and Other Medieval Authorities*. Ed. Morris Faierstein. Hoboken, N.J.: Ktav, 1996.

————. *The Prophets*. 2 vols. New York: Harper and Row, 1962.

Levenson, Jon D. *Sinai and Zion: An Entry into the Jewish Bible* (New Voices in Biblical Studies). Minneapolis, Minn.: Winston, 1985.

Sarna, Nahum M., ed. *The JPS Torah Commentary*. 5 vols. Philadelphia: Jewish Publication Society, 1989-96.

Segal, Ben-Zion, ed. *The Ten Commandments in History and Tradition* (Publications of the Perry Foundation for Biblical Research). English edition ed. Gershon Levi. Jerusalem: Magnes Press of the Hebrew University of Jerusalem, 1990.

Stein, David E. S. *The Contemporary Torah: A Gender-Sensitive Adaption of the JPS Translation*. Philadelphia: Jewish Publication Society, 2006.

Tanakh: The Holy Scriptures: The New JPS Translation According to the Traditional Hebrew Text. Philadelphia: Jewish Publication Society, 1985.

Thompson, Henry O. *Biblical Archaeology: The World, the Mediterranean, the Bible*. New York: Paragon, 1987.

BIOGRAPHIES OF INDIVIDUALS AND FAMILIES

Agus, Jacob B. *Banner of Jerusalem: The Life, Times, and Thought of Abraham Isaac Kuk, the Late Chief Rabbi of Palestine*. New York: Bloch, 1946.

Bar-Zohar, Michael. *Ben Gurion: A Biography*. London: Weidenfeld and Nicholson, 1978; New York: Delacorte, 1979.

Bentwich, Norman De Mattos. *Solomon Schechter: A Biography*. Cambridge: Cambridge University Press; Philadelphia: Jewish Publication Society, 1938.

Ferguson, Niall. *The House of Rothschild*. vol. 1, *Money's Prophets, 1798–1848.*; vol. 2, *The World's Banker 1849–1998*. New York: Penguin Books, 1999–2000.

Friedman, Maurice. *Encounter on the Narrow Ridge: A Life of Martin Buber*. New York: Paragon House, 1991.

Jackson, Stanley. *The Sassoons*. New York: Dutton, 1968; London: Heinemann, 1968; new ed., London: Heinemann, 1989.

Kaplan, Lawrence, and David Shatz, eds. *Rabbi Abraham Isaac Kook and Jewish Spirituality* (Reappraisals in Jewish Social and Intellectual History). New York: New York University Press, 1995.

Mendes-Flohr, Paul, ed. *Gershom Scholem: The Man and His Work*. Albany: State University of New York Press, 1994.

Morton, Frederic. *The Rothschilds: Portrait of a Dynasty*. Tokyo: Kodansha Globe, 1962; new ed., 1998.

Rose, Norman. *Chaim Weizmann: A Biography*. New York: Viking, 1986; London: Weidenfeld and Nicolson, 1987.

Rosenblum, Yonason. *The Vilna Gaon*. Brooklyn, N.Y.: Mesorah, 1994.

Roth, Cecil. *The Sassoon Dynasty*. London: Hale, 1941; New York: Arno, 1977.

Weizmann, Chaim. *Trial and Error: The Autobiography of Chaim Weizmann*. Philadelphia: Jewish Publication Society, 1949; London: Hamilton, 1949.

Zweig, Ronald W., ed. *David Ben Gurion: Politics and Leadership in Israel*. London: Cass, 1991.

CHRISTIANITY AND ISLAM

Ashtor, Eliyahu. *The Jews of Moslem Spain*. 3 vols., Philadelphia: Jewish Publication Society, 1973–1984.

Baer, Yitzchak F. *A History of the Jews in Christian Spain*. Trans. L. Schoffman. 2 vols. Philadelphia: Jewish Publication Society, 1961–1966.

Bat Ye'or. *The Dhimmi: Jews and Christians under Islam*. Trans. David Maisel, Paul Fenton, and David Littman. Rutherford, N.J.: Fairleigh Dickinson University Press, 1985; London: Associated University Presses, 1985.

Bowker, John. *Jesus and the Pharisees*. Cambridge: Cambridge University Press, 1973.

Boys, Mary C., Sara S. Lee, and Dorothy C. Bass. *Christians and Jews in Dialogue: Learning in the Presence of the Other*. Woodstock, Vt.: Jewish Lights Press, 2006.

Chazan, Robert. *European Jewry and the First Crusade*. Berkeley: University of California Press, 1987.

Cohen, Mark R. *Under Crescent and Cross: The Jews in the Middle Ages*. Princeton, N.J.: Princeton University Press, 1994.

Gilbert, Arthur. *The Vatican Council and the Jews*. Cleveland, Ohio: World, 1968.

Goitein, S. D. *Jews and Arabs: Their Contacts through the Ages*. New York: Schocken, 1955; rev. ed., 1974.

Greenberg, Irving. *For the Sake of Heaven and Earth: The New Encounter between Judaism and Christianity*. Philadelphia: Jewish Publication Society, 2004.

Kamen, Henry Arthur Francis. *The Spanish Inquisition*. New York: New American Library, 1956; London: Weidenfeld and Nicholson, 1965; rev. as *The Spanish Inquisition: An Historical Revision*. London: Weidenfeld and Nicholson, 1997; New Haven, Conn.: Yale University Press, 1998.

Katz, Jacob. *Exclusiveness and Tolerance: Studies in Jewish–Gentile Relations in Medieval and Modern Times* (Scripta Judaica, vol. 3). Oxford: Oxford University Press, 1961; New York: Behrman, 1961.

Lasker, Daniel J. *Jewish Philosophical Polemics against Christianity in the Middle Ages*. New York: Ktav, 1977.

Lewis, Bernard. *The Jews of Islam*. Princeton, N.J.: Princeton University Press, 1984; London: Routledge and Kegan Paul, 1984.

Maccoby, Hyam. *Judaism on Trial: Jewish–Christian Disputations in the Middle Ages*. (Littman Library of Jewish Civilization). Rutherford, N.J.: Fairleigh Dickinson University Press, 1982; London: Associated University Presses, 1982.

Netanyahu, Benzion. *The Origins of the Inquisition in Fifteenth Century Spain*. New York: Random House, 1995.

———. *Toward the Inquisition: Essays on Jewish and Converso History in Late Medieval Spain*. Ithaca, N.Y.: Cornell University Press, 1997.

Novak, David. *Jewish–Christian Dialogue: A Jewish Justification*. New York: Oxford University Press, 1989.

Patai, Raphael. *Jadid al-Islam. The Jewish "New Muslims" of Meshed* (Jewish Folklore and Anthropology Series). Detroit, Mich.: Wayne State University Press, 1997.

———. *The Seed of Abraham: Jews and Arabs in Contact and Conflict*. Salt Lake City: University of Utah Press, 1986.

Rappaport, Solomon. *Jew and Gentile: The Philo-Semitic Aspect*. New York: The Philosophical Library, 1980.

Rosenthal, E. I. J. *Judaism and Islam* (Popular Jewish Library). New York: Yoseloff, 1961.

Roth, Cecil. *A History of the Marranos*. Philadelphia: Jewish Publication Society, 1932; 3rd ed., New York: Harper and Row, 1966.

———. *The Spanish Inquisition*. London: Hale, 1937; New York: Norton, 1964.

Roth, Norman. *Conversos, Inquisition, and the Expulsion of the Jews from Spain*. Madison: University of Wisconsin Press, 1995.

Shermis, Michael, and Arthur E. Zannoni, ed. *Introduction to Jewish Christian Relations*. New York: Paulist, 1991.

Stillman, Norman. *The Jews of Arab Lands: A History and Source Book*. Philadelphia: Jewish Publication Society, 1979.

Wasserstrom, Steven. *Between Muslim and Jew: The Problem of Symbiosis under Early Islam*. Princeton, N.J.: Princeton University Press, 1995.

COMMUNITIES AND JEWISH IDENTITY

Arendt, Hannah. *The Jew as Pariah: Jewish Identity and Politics in the Modern Age.* New York: Grove, 1978.

Baer, Yitzhak F. *Galut.* New York: Schocken Books, 1947.

Baron, Salo. *The Jewish Community.* 3 vols., Philadelphia: Jewish Publication Society, 1942.

Beker, Avi. *Jewish Communities of the World.* Jerusalem: Institute of the World Jewish Congress, 1996; Minneapolis, Minn.: Lerner, 1998.

Ben-Zvi, Itzhak. *The Exiled and the Redeemed.* Philadelphia: Jewish Publication Society, 1957; 2nd ed., Jerusalem: Ben-Zvi Institute, 1976.

Brook, Kevin Alan. *The Jews of Khazaria.* 2nd ed. Lanham, Md.: Rowman and Littlefield, 2009.

Dawidowicz, Lucy S. *The Jewish Presence: Essays on Identity and History.* New York: Holt, Rinehart, and Winston, 1977.

Dubnow, S. M. *History of the Jews in Russia and Poland from the Earliest Times until the Present Day.* 3 vols. Trans. I. Friedlaender. Philadelphia: Jewish Publication Society, 1916.

Dunlop, D. M. *The History of the Jewish Khazars.* Princeton, N.J.: Princeton University Press, 1954.

Eisen, Arnold M. *Galut: Modern Jewish Reflections on Homelessness and Homecoming* (Modern Jewish Experience). Bloomington: Indiana University Press, 1986.

Finkelstein, Louis. *Jewish Self-Government in the Middle Ages.* New York: Jewish Theological Seminary, 1924.

Gay, Ruth. *The Jews of Germany: A Historical Portrait.* New Haven, Conn.: Yale University Press, 1992.

Gitelman, Zvi, ed. *The Quest for Utopia: Jewish Political Ideas and Institutions through the Ages.* Armonk, N.Y.: Sharpe, 1992.

Golden, Peter B. *Khazar Studies: An Historico-Philological Inquiry into the Origins of the Khazars.* 2 vols. Budapest, Hungary: Akadémiai Kiadó, 1980.

———. *Nomads and Their Neighbours in the Russian Steppe: Turks, Khazars and Qipchaqs* (Variorum Collected Studies Series). Aldershot, U.K.: Ashgate, 2003.

Hertzberg, Arthur. *The Jews in America: Four Centuries of an Uneasy Encounter: A History.* New York: Simon and Schuster, 1989; Chichester, West Sussex: Columbia University Press, 1997.

Himmelfarb, Milton. *The Jews of Modernity.* New York: Basic Books, 1973.

Hundert, Gershon David, and Gershon C. Bacon. *The Jews in Poland and Russia: Bibliographical Essays* (The Modern Jewish Experience). Bloomington: Indiana University Press, 1984.

Isenberg, Shirley Berry. *India's Bene Israel: A Comprehensive Inquiry and Sourcebook*. Berkeley, Calif.: J.L. Magnes Museum, 1988.

Kaplan, Steven. *The Beta Israel (Falasha) in Ethiopia: From Earliest Times to the Twentieth Century*. New York: New York University Press, 1992.

Katz, Jacob. *Tradition and Crisis*. New York: Free Press of Glencoe, 1961; new trans. Bernard Cooperman, New York: New York University Press, 1993.

Katz, Nathan, ed. *Studies of Indian Jewish Identity*. New Delhi: Manohar, 1995.

Koestler, Arthur. *The Thirteenth Tribe: The Khazar Empire and Its Heritage*. New York: Random House, 1976.

Leslie, Donald Daniel. *The Survival of the Chinese Jews: The Jewish Community of Kaifeng* (T'oung Pao Monographie, no. 10). Leiden, Netherlands: Brill, 1972.

Lyons, Len. *The Ethiopian Jews of Israel: Personal Stories of Life in the Promised Land*. Woodstock, Vt.: Jewish Lights Press, 2007.

Novack, David. *The Election of Israel: The Idea of the Chosen People.* Cambridge: Cambridge University Press, 1995.

Parfitt, Tudor. *Journey to the Vanished City: The Search for a Lost Tribe of Israel*. London: Hodder and Stoughton, 1992; New York: St. Martin's Press, 1993.

———. *The Lost Tribes of Israel: The History of a Myth*. London: Weidenfeld and Nicolson, 2002.

Parfitt, Tudor, and Emanuela Trevisan Sevi, eds. *The Beta Israel in Ethiopia and Israel: Studies on Ethiopian Jews*. Surrey, U.K.: Curzon, 1999.

Patai, Raphael. *Tents of Jacob: The Diaspora, Yesterday and Today*. Englewood Cliffs, N.J.: Prentice-Hall, 1971.

Patai, Raphael, and Jennifer Patai. *The Myth of the Jewish Race*. New York: Scribner, 1974; rev. ed., Detroit, Mich.: Wayne State University Press, 1989.

Pollak, Michael. *Mandarins, Jews and Missionaries: The Jewish Experience in the Chinese Empire*. Philadelphia: Jewish Publication Society, 1980.

Rejwan, Nissim. *The Jews of Iraq: 3000 Years of History and Culture*. London: Weidenfeld and Nicolson, 1985; Boulder, Colo.: Westview, 1985.

Rubin, Barry. *Assimilation and Its Discontents*. New York: Times/Random House, 1995.

Sachar, Howard M. *A History of the Jews in America*. New York: Knopf, 1992.

Sassoon, David Solomon. *A History of the Jews in Baghdad*. Letchworth, U.K.: S. D. Sassoon, 1949.

Schechtman, Joseph B. *On Wings of Eagles: The Plight, Exodus, and Homecoming of Oriental Jewry*. New York: Yoseloff, 1961.

Scholem, Gershom. *On Jews and Judaism in Crisis: Selected Essays*. New York: Schocken, 1976.

Shaw, Stanford J. *The Jews of the Ottoman Empire and the Turkish Republic*. New York: New York University Press, 1991; London: Macmillan, 1991.

Slapak, Orpa, ed. *The Jews of India: A Story of Three Communities*. Jerusalem: Israel Museum, 1995.

Sorin, Gerald. *Tradition Transformed: The Jewish Experience in America* (The American Moment). Baltimore, Md.: John Hopkins University Press, 1997.

Strizower, Schifra. *The Bene Israel of Bombay: A Study of a Jewish Community*. New York: Schocken, 1971; as *The Children of Israel: The Bene Israel of Bombay*. Oxford: Blackwell, 1971.

Weil, Shalva, et al., eds. *Beyond the Sambatyon: The Myth of the Ten Lost Tribes*. Tel Aviv: Beth Hatefutsoth, The Nahum Goldman Museum of the Jewish Diaspora, 1991.

Wertheimer, Jack. *A People Divided: Judaism in Contemporary America*. Hanover, N.H.: Brandeis University Press, 1997.

Zborowski, Mark, and Elizabeth Herzog. *Life Is with People: The Culture of the Shtetl*. New York: Schocken, 1962.

HALAKHAH, RITUAL, AND THE SYNAGOGUE

Birnbaum, Philip. *Encyclopedia of Jewish Concepts*. New York: Hebrew Publishing, 1977; rev. ed., 1979.

Bloch, Abraham P. *The Biblical and Historical Background of Jewish Customs and Ceremonies*. New York: Ktav, 1980.

De Breffny, Brian. *The Synagogue*. New York: Macmillan, 1978; London: Weidenfeld and Nicholson, 1978.

Diamant, Anita. *Saying Kaddish: How to Comfort the Dying, Bury the Dead, and Mourn as a Jew*. New York: Schocken, 1998.

Dorfman, Rivka, and Ben-Zion Dorfman. *Synagogues without Jews: And the Communities That Built and Used Them*. Philadelphia: Jewish Publication Society, 2000.

Elper, Ora Wiskind. *Traditions and Celebrations for the Bat Mitzvah*. Jerusalem and New York: Urim, 2003.

Fine, Steven. *Sacred Realm: The Emergence of the Synagogue in the Ancient World*. New York: Oxford University Press and Yeshiva University Museum, 1996.

Forst, Binyomin. *The Laws of Kashrus: A Comprehensive Exposition of Their Underlying Concepts and Applications*. New York: Mesorah, 1993.

Ganzfried, Solomon. *Code of Jewish Law/Kitzur Schulchan Aruch: A Compilation of Jewish Laws and Customs*. Trans. Hyman E. Goldin. New York: Hebrew Publishing, 1927; annotated rev. ed., 1963.

Gaster, Theodor H. *Passover: Its History and Traditions*. Boston, Beacon Press, 1962.

Geffen, Rela M. *Celebration and Renewal: Rites of Passage in Judaism*. Philadelphia: Jewish Publication Society, 1993.

Greenberg, Irving. *The Jewish Way: Living the Holidays*. New York: Summit, 1988.

Grossman, Susan, and Rivka Haut, eds. *Daughters of the King: Women and the Synagogue: A Survey of History, Halakhah, and Contemporary Realities*. Philadelphia: Jewish Publication Society, 1992.

Grunfeld, Isidor. *The Jewish Dietary Laws*. 2 vols., London: Soncino, 1972; 3rd ed., 1982.

Heilman, Samuel C. *Synagogue Life: A Study in Symbolic Interaction*. Chicago: University of Chicago Press, 1976.

Heschel, Abraham Joshua. *The Sabbath: Its Meaning for Modern Man*. New York: Farrar, Straus, and Young, 1951.

Jakobovits, Immanuel. *Jewish Medical Ethics*. New York: Bloch, 1959.

Kaplan, Aryeh. *Waters of Eden: An Exploration of the Concept of Mikveh: Renewal and Rebirth*. New York: National Conference of Synagogue Youth of the Union of Orthodox Jewish Congregations, 1976; 2nd ed., 1982.

Klein, Isaac. *A Guide to Jewish Religious Practice* (Moreshet Series, vol. 6). New York: Jewish Theological Seminary, 1979.

Lamm, Maurice. *The Jewish Way in Death and Mourning*. New York: David, 1969; rev. ed., 1972.

———. *The Jewish Way in Love and Marriage*. San Francisco: Harper and Row, 1980; London: Harper and Row, 1982.

Levine, Lee I., ed. *Ancient Synagogues Revealed*. Jerusalem: Israel Exploration Society, 1981; Detroit, Mich.: Wayne State University Press, 1982.

———, ed. *The Synagogue in Late Antiquity*. New York: Jewish Theological Seminary, 1987; Philadelphia: American Schools of Oriental Research, 1987.

Novak, David. *Jewish Social Ethics*. New York: Oxford University Press, 1992.

Reif, Stefan C. *Judaism and Hebrew Prayer: New Perspectives on Jewish Liturgical History*. Cambridge: Cambridge University Press, 1993.

Riemer, Jack, ed. *Jewish Reflections on Death*. New York: Schocken, 1975.

Rosner, Fred. *Modern Medicine and Jewish Law*. New York: Yeshiva University, Department of Special Publications, 1972.

Salkin, Jeffrey K. *Putting God on the Guest List: How to Reclaim the Spiritual Meaning of Your Child's Bar or Bat Mitzvah*. Woodstock, Vt.: Jewish Lights, 1992; 2nd ed., 1996.

Schauss, Hayyim. *The Jewish Festivals: From Their Beginnings to Our Own Day*. New York: Union of American Hebrew Congregations, 1938.

Shear, Eli M., and Chaim Miller. *The Rich Go to Heaven: Giving Charity in Jewish Thought*. Northvale, N.J.: Aronson, 1998.

Unterman, Alan. *Dictionary of Jewish Lore and Legend*. London: Thames and Hudson, 1991.

Waskow, Arthur. *Seasons of Our Joy: A Handbook of Jewish Festivals*. New York: Bantam, 1982.

Wigoder, Geoffrey. *The Story of the Synagogue: A Diaspora Museum Book*. London: Weidenfeld and Nicholson, 1986; San Francisco: Harper and Row, 1986.

Winkler, Gershon. *Sacred Secrets: The Sanctity of Sex in Jewish Law and Lore*. Northvale, N.J.: Aronson, 1998.

Zahavy, Tzvee. *Studies in Jewish Prayer* (Studies in Judaism). Lanham, Md.: University Press of America, 1990.

HISTORY

General

Baron, Salo Wittmayer. *History and Jewish Historians: Essays and Addresses*. Ed. Arthur Hertzberg and Leon A. Feldman. Philadelphia: Jewish Publication Society, 1964.

———. *A Social and Religious History of the Jews*. New York: Columbia University Press, 1937; 2nd ed., 18 vols., 1952–1983.

Ben-Sasson, Haim Hillel. *A History of the Jewish People*. Cambridge, Mass.: Harvard University Press, 1976; London: Weidenfeld and Nicolson, 1976.

Carmilly-Weinberger, Moshe. *Censorship and Freedom of Expression in Jewish History: Great Ideological and Literary Conflicts in Judaism from Antiquity to Modern Times*. New York: Sepher-Hermon Press with Yeshiva University Press, 1977.

Encyclopaedia Judaica. Jerusalem: Keter, 1971/72; rev. ed., 2006.

Finkelstein, Louis, ed. *The Jews: Their History, Culture and Religion*. 2 vols., New York: Harper, 1949; 3rd ed., 1960; repr., 3 vols. as 4th edition, New York: Schocken, 1970.

Funkenstein, Amos. *Perceptions of Jewish History*. Berkeley: University of California Press, 1993.

Gilbert, Martin. *Jewish History Atlas*. New York: Macmillan, 1969; London: Weidenfeld and Nicolson, 1969; 4th ed., London: Weidenfeld and Nicolson, 1992; as *The Atlas of Jewish History*. New York: Morrow, 1993.

Graetz, Heinrich. *History of the Jews*. 6 vols., Philadelphia: Jewish Publication Society, 1891; London: Nutt, 1891.

Kobler, Franz, ed. *Letters of Jews through the Ages*. New York: East and West Library, 1978.

Meyer, Michael A., comp. *Ideas of Jewish History*. New York: Behrman House, 1974.

Rapoport-Albert, Ada, ed. *Essays in Jewish Historiography* (History and Theory, Beiheft 27). Middletown, Conn.: Wesleyan University, 1988.

Rubens, Alfred. *A History of Jewish Costume.* New York: Funk and Wagnalls, 1967; London: Valentine Mitchell, 1967; rev. ed., London: Owen, 1981.

Schorsch, Ismar. *From Text to Context: The Turn to History in Modern Judaism* (Tauber Institute for the Study of European Jewry Series, 19). Hanover, N.H.: University Press of New England, 1994.

Seltzer, Robert. *Jewish People, Jewish Thought: The Jewish Experience in History.* New York: Macmillan, 1980.

Yerushalmi, Yosef Hayim. *Zakhor: Jewish History and Jewish Memory* (Samuel and Althea Stroum Lectures in Jewish Studies). Seattle: University of Washington Press, 1982.

Ancient

Alon, Gedalia. *Jews, Judaism, and the Classical World: Studies in Jewish History in the Times of the Second Temple and Talmud.* Trans. Israel Abrahams. Jerusalem: Magnes Press of Hebrew University, 1977.

Cohen, Shaye J. D. *From the Maccabees to the Mishnah* (Library of Early Christianity, 7). Philadelphia: Westminster, 1987.

———. *Josephus in Galilee and Rome: His Vita and Development as a Historian* (Columbia Studies in the Classical Tradition, vol. 8). Leiden, Netherlands: Brill, 1979.

Gruen, Erich S. *Heritage and Hellenism: The Reinvention of Jewish Tradition.* Berkeley: University of California Press, 1998.

Hengel, Martin. *Judaism and Hellenism: Studies in Their Encounter in Palestine during the Early Hellenistic Period.* 2 vols. Philadelphia: Fortress, 1974; London: SCM, 1974.

Marks, Richard G. *The Image of Bar Kokhba in Traditional Jewish Literature: False Messiah and National Hero* (Hermeneutics, Studies in the History of Religions). University Park: Pennsylvania State University Press, 1994.

Moore, George Foot. *Judaism in the First Centuries of the Christian Era: The Age of the Tannaim.* Cambridge, Mass.: Harvard University Press, 1954.

Neusner, Jacob. *First Century Judaism in Crisis: Yohanan ben Zakkai and the Renaissance of Torah.* Nashville, Tenn.: Abingdon, 1975.

Rajak, Tessa. *Josephus, the Historian and His Society.* London: Duckworth, 1983; Philadelphia: Fortress, 1984.

Sanders, E. P. *Judaism: Practice and Belief, 63 BCE–66 CE.* Philadelphia: Trinity Press International, 1992; London: SCM, 1992; 2nd impr. with corrections, 1994.

Schiffman, Lawrence H. *From Text to Tradition: A History of Second Temple and Rabbinic Judaism.* Hoboken, N.J.: Ktav, 1991.

———. *Reclaiming the Dead Sea Scrolls: The History of Judaism, the Background of Christianity, the Lost Library of Qumran.* Philadelphia: Jewish Publication Society, 1994.

Schürer, Emil: *The History of the Jewish People in the Age of Jesus Christ (175 B.C.–A.D. 135).* Rev. and ed. Geza Vermes and Fergus Millar. 3 vols. Edinburgh: T. and T. Clark, 1973–1986.

Schwartz, Seth. *Josephus and Judean Politics* (Columbia Studies in the Classical Tradition, 18). New York: Brill, 1990.

Shanks, Hershel, ed. *Understanding the Dead Sea Scrolls: A Reader from the Biblical Archaeology Review.* New York: Random House, 1992.

Stemberger, Günter. *Jewish Contemporaries of Jesus: Pharisees, Sadducees, Essenes.* Minneapolis, Minn.: Fortress, 1995.

Tcherikover, Avigdor. *Hellenistic Civilization and the Jews.* Philadelphia: Jewish Publication Society, 1959.

VanderKam, James C. *The Dead Sea Scrolls Today.* Grand Rapids, Mich.: Eerdmans, 1994.

Vermes, Geza. *The Complete Dead Sea Scrolls in English.* New York: Lane/ Penguin, 1997; London: Lane, 1997.

Yadin, Yigael. *Bar-Kokhba: The Rediscovery of the Legendary Hero of the Last Jewish Revolt against Imperial Rome.* New York: Random House, 1971; London: Weidenfeld and Nicholson, 1971.

Medieval

Abrahams, Israel. *Jewish Life in the Middle Ages.* New York: Macmillan, 1896; new ed., London: Goldston, 1932.

Benjamin of Tudela. *The Itinerary of Benjamin of Tudela.* Critical text, trans., and commentary by Marcus Nathan Adler. New York: Philipp Feldheim, 1907.

Chazan, Robert. *European Jewry and the First Crusade.* Berkeley: University of California Press, 1987.

Eidelberg, Shlomo. *The Jews and the Crusades: The Hebrew Chronicles of the First and Second Crusades.* Madison: University of Wisconsin Press, 1977.

Gitlitz, David M. *Secrecy and Deceit: The Religion of the Crypto-Jews.* Philadelphia: Jewish Publication Society, 1996.

Kaplan, Yosef, Henry Méchoulan, and Richard Popkin, eds. *Menasseh ben Israel and His World* (Brill's Studies in Intellectual History, vol. 15). New York: Brill, 1989.

Marcus, Jacob R., ed. *The Jew in the Medieval World: A Source Book.* Westport, Conn.: Greenwood Press, 1975.

Roth, Cecil. *A Life of Menasseh ben Israel: Rabbi, Printer, and Diplomat.* Philadelphia: Jewish Publication Society, 1934.

Spiegel, Shalom. *The Last Trial: On the Legends and Lore of the Command to Abraham to Offer Isaac as a Sacrifice: The Akedah.* Trans. Judah Golden. New York: Pantheon, 1967.

Modern

Abramson, Glenda. *The Blackwell Companion to Jewish Culture: From the Eighteenth Century to the Present.* Oxford: Basil Blackwell, 1989.

Altmann, Alexander. *Moses Mendelssohn: A Biographical Study.* London: Routledge and Kegan Paul, 1973; Philadelphia: Jewish Publication Society, 1973.

Arkush, Allan. *Moses Mendelssohn and the Enlightenment* (SUNY Series in Judaica). Albany: State University of New York Press, 1994.

Bacon, Gershon C. *The Politics of Tradition: Agudat Yisrael in Poland, 1916–1939.* Jerusalem: Magnes Press of Hebrew University, 1996.

Birnbaum, Pierre, and Ira Katznelson, eds. *Paths of Emancipation: Jews, States, and Citizenship.* Princeton, N.J.: Princeton University Press, 1995.

Blau, Joseph L. *Modern Varieties of Judaism* (Lectures on the History of Religions Sponsored by the American Council of Learned Societies, New Series, no. 8). New York: Columbia University Press, 1966.

Burns, Michael. *Dreyfus: A Family Affair, 1789–1945.* New York: HarperCollins, 1991; London: Chatto and Windus, 1992.

Eckman, Lester. *The History of the Musar Movement: 1840–1945.* New York: Shengold, 1975.

Etkes, Immanuel. *Rabbi Israel Salanter and the Mussar Movement: Seeking the Torah of Truth.* Philadelphia: Jewish Publication Society, 1993.

Fishman, David. *Russia's First Modern Jews.* New York: New York University Press, 1995.

Florence, Ronald. *Blood Libel: The Damascus Affair of 1840.* Madison: University of Wisconsin Press, 2004.

Friesel, Evyatar. *Atlas of Modern Jewish History.* Oxford: Oxford University Press, 1990.

Goldstein, Joseph. *Jewish History in Modern Times.* Brighton, U.K.: Sussex Academic Press, 1995.

Goodman, Saul, ed. *The Faith of Secular Jews* (Library of Judaic Learning). New York: Ktav, 1976.

Hertzberg, Arthur. *The French Enlightenment and the Jews.* New York: Columbia University Press, 1968.

Katz, Jacob. *Out of the Ghetto: The Social Background of Jewish Emancipation 1770–1870.* Cambridge, Mass.: Harvard University Press, 1973.

Lamm, Norman. *Torah Lishmah: Torah for Torah's Sake in the Works of Rabbi Hayyim of Volozhin and His Contemporaries.* Hoboken, N.J.: Ktav, 1989.

Laskier, Michael M. *The Alliance Israélite Universelle and the Jewish Communities of Morocco 1862–1962* (SUNY Series in Modern Jewish History). Albany: State University of New York Press, 1983.

Mendelssohn, Moses. *Jerusalem, or, On Religious Power and Judaism.* Hanover, N.H.: University Press of New England, 1983.

Mendes-Flohr, Paul, and Jehuda Reinharz, eds. *The Jew in the Modern World: A Documentary History.* New York: Oxford University Press, 1980; 2nd ed., 1995.

Nadler, Allan. *The Faith of the Mithnagdim: Rabbinic Responses to Hasidic Rapture.* Baltimore, Md.: John Hopkins University Press, 1997.

Rodrigue, A. *French Jews, Turkish Jews: The Alliance Israélite Universelle and the Politics of the Jewish Schooling in Turkey, 1860–1925.* Bloomington: Indiana University Press, 1990.

Rosenbloom, Noah H. *Tradition in an Age of Reform: The Religious Philosophy of Samson Raphael Hirsch.* Philadelphia: Jewish Publication Society, 1976.

Sachar, Howard. *The Course of Modern Jewish History.* Cleveland, Ohio: World, 1958; London: Weidenfeld, 1958; new rev. ed., New York: Vintage, 1990.

Schwarzfuchs, Simon. *Napoleon, the Jews, and the Sanhedrin* (Littman Library of Jewish Civilization). London: Routledge and Kegan Paul, 1979.

Sharot, Stephen. *Judaism: A Sociology.* Newton Abbot, Devon: David and Charles, 1976; New York: Holmes and Meier, 1976.

Sorkin, David. *Moses Mendelssohn and the Religious Enlightenment.* Berkeley: University of California Press, 1996; London: Halban, 1996.

Zimmerman, Joshua D. *Poles, Jews, and the Politics of Nationality: The Bund and the Polish Socialist Party in Late Czarist Russia, 1892–1914.* Madison: University of Wisconsin Press, 2003.

HOMOSEXUALITY

Alpert, Rebecca. *Like Bread on the Seder Plate: Jewish Lesbians and the Transformation of Tradition* (Between Men–Between Women). New York: Columbia University Press, 1997.

Balka, Christie, and Andy Rose. *Twice Blessed: On Being Lesbian, Gay, and Jewish.* Boston: Beacon, 1989.

Brod, Harry, ed. *A Mensch among Men: Explorations in Jewish Masculinity.* Freedom, Calif.: The Crossing Press, 1988.

Dorff, Elliot. *"This Is My Beloved, This Is My Friend": A Rabbinic Letter on Intimate Relations.* New York: Rabbinical Assembly, 1996.

Greenberg, Steven. *Wrestling with God and Men: Homosexuality in the Jewish Tradition*. Updated ed. Madison: University of Wisconsin Press, 2005.

Magonet, Jonathan, ed. *Jewish Explorations of Sexuality*. Providence, R.I.: Berghahn Books, 1995.

Moore, Tracy, ed. *Lesbiot: Israeli Lesbians Talk about Sexuality, Feminism, Judaism and Their Lives*. London: Cassell, 1995.

Raphael, Lev. *Journeys and Arrivals: On Being Gay and Jewish*. Boston: Faber, 1996.

ISRAEL

Aviad, Janet. *Return to Judaism: Religious Renewal in Israel*. Chicago: University of Chicago Press, 1983.

Barak-Erez, Daphne. *Outlawed Pigs: Law, Religion, and Culture in Israel*. Madison: University of Wisconsin Press, 2007.

Ben-Dov, M., Mordechay Naor, and Zeev Anner, eds. *The Western Wall*. Trans. Raphael Posner. New York: Adama, 1983.

Benvenisti, Meron. *City of Stone: The Hidden History of Jerusalem*. Berkeley: University of California Press, 1996.

Buber, Martin. *On Zion: The History of an Idea*. New York: Schocken, 1973; London: Horovitz, 1973.

Cohen-Almagor, Raphael. *The Boundaries of Liberty and Tolerance: The Struggle against Kahanism in Israel*. Gainesville: University Press of Florida, 1994.

Davies, W. D. *The Territorial Dimension of Judaism*. Berkeley: University of California Press, 1982.

Dinur, Ben Zion. *Israel and the Diaspora*. Philadelphia: Jewish Publication Society, 1969.

Gilbert, Martin. *The Arab–Israeli Conflict: Its History in Maps*. 4th ed., London: Weidenfeld and Nicolson, 1993.

———. *Jerusalem: Rebirth of a City*. New York: Viking, 1985; London: Chatto and Windus, 1985.

———. *Jerusalem in the Twentieth Century*. New York: Wiley, 1996; London: Chatto and Windus, 1996.

Heschel, Abraham Joshua. *Israel: An Echo of Eternity*. New York: Farrar, Straus and Giroux, 1969.

Hoffman, Lawrence, ed. *The Land of Israel: Jewish Perspectives* (University of Notre Dame Center for the Study of Judaism and Christianity in Antiquity, no. 6). Notre Dame, Ind.: University of Notre Dame Press, 1986.

Kasher, Menahem M. *The Western Wall: Its Meaning in the Thought of the Sages*. Trans. Charles Wengrov. New York: Judaica Press, 1972.

Korn, Eugene. *The Jewish Connection to Israel, the Promised Land: A Brief Introduction for Christians.* Woodstock, Vt.: Jewish Lights Press, 2007.

Kushner, Gilbert. *Immigrants from India in Israel: Planned Change in an Administered Community.* Tucson: University of Arizona Press, 1973.

Leon, Dan. *The Kibbutz: A New Way of Life* (The Commonwealth and International Library). New York: Pergamon, 1969.

Levine, Lee I., ed. *Jerusalem: Its Sanctity and Centrality to Judaism, Christianity, and Islam.* New York: Continuum, 1999.

Liebman, Charles S., and Eliezer Don-Yehiya. *Religion and Politics in Israel* (Jewish Political and Social Studies). Bloomington: Indiana University Press, 1984.

Near, Henry. *The Kibbutz Movement: A History* (Littman Library of Jewish Civilization). 2 vols. Oxford: Oxford University Press, 1992–1997.

Newman, David, ed. *The Impact of Gush Emunim: Politics and Settlement in the West Bank.* London: Croom Helm, 1985.

Parkes, James. *A History of Palestine from 135 AD to Modern Times.* New York: Oxford University Press, 1949.

Smith, Charles. *Palestine and the Arab–Israeli Conflict.* New York: St. Martin's, 1988; 3rd ed., 1995.

Sprinzak, Ehud. *The Ascendance of Israel's Radical Right.* New York: Oxford University Press, 1991.

————. *Brother against Brother: Violence and Extremism in Israeli Politics from Altalena to the Rabin Assassination.* New York: Free Press, 1999.

Wigoder, Geoffrey, editor-in-chief. *New Encyclopedia of Zionism and Israel.* Rev. ed., Madison, N.J.: Farleigh Dickinson University Press, 1994.

Zerubavel, Yael. *Recovered Roots: Collective Memory and the Making of Israeli National Tradition.* Chicago: University of Chicago Press, 1995.

KABBALAH AND CHASIDISM

Buber, Martin. *The Origin and Meaning of Hasidism.* New York: Horizon, 1960.

Cooper, David A. *God Is a Verb: Kabbalah and the Practice of Mystical Judaism.* New York: Riverhead, 1997.

Dan, Joseph. *Jewish Mysticism and Jewish Ethics.* Seattle: University of Washington Press, 1986; 2nd ed., Northvale, N.J.: Aronson, 1996.

Fine, Lawrence, ed. *Essential Papers on Kabbalah* (Essential Papers on Jewish Studies). New York: New York University Press, 1995.

Green, Arthur. *Tormented Master: A Life of Rabbi Nahman of Bratslav* (Judaic Studies Series). University: University of Alabama Press, 1979.

Halamish, Mosheh. *An Introduction to the Kabbalah* (SUNY Series in Judaica). Albany: State University of New York Press, 1989.

Hundert, Gershon D., ed. *Essential Papers on Hasidism: Origins to Present* (Essential Papers on Jewish Studies). New York: New York University Press, 1991.

Idel, Moshe. *Hasidism: Between Ecstasy and Magic* (SUNY Series in Judaica). Albany: State University of New York Press, 1995.

———. *Kabbalah: New Perspectives*. New Haven, Conn.: Yale University Press, 1988.

Jacobs, Louis. *Hasidic Prayer* (Littman Library of Jewish Civilization). London: Routledge and Kegan Paul, 1972; New York: Schocken, 1973.

Kaplan, Aryeh. *The Light Beyond: Adventures in Hassidic Thought*. New York: Maznaim, 1981.

Lamm, Norman. *The Religious Thought of Hasidism: Text and Commentary*. New York: Yeshiva University Press, 1999.

Loewenthal, Naftali. *Communicating the Infinite: The Emergence of the Habad School*. Chicago: University of Chicago Press, 1990.

Mahler, Raphael. *Hasidism and the Jewish Enlightenment: Their Confrontation in Galicia and Poland in the First Half of the Nineteenth Century*. Philadelphia: Jewish Publication Society, 1985.

Matt, Daniel Chanan. *The Essential Kabbalah: The Heart of Jewish Mysticism*. San Francisco: HarperSanFrancisco, 1995.

Rose, Or N., ed. and trans., with Ebn D. Leader. *God in All Moments: Mystical and Practical Spiritual Wisdom from Hasidic Masters*. Woodstock, Vt.: Jewish Lights Press, 2003.

Rosman, Murray J. *Founder of Hasidism: A Quest for the Historical Ba'al Shem Tov* (Contraversions, 5). Berkeley: University of California Press, 1996.

Schochet, Elijah J. *The Hasidic Movement and the Gaon of Vilna*. Northvale, N.J.: Aronson, 1994.

Scholem, Gershom. *Jewish Gnosticism, Merkabah Mysticism, and Talmudic Tradition*. New York: Jewish Theological Seminary, 1960; 2nd ed., 1965.

———. *Kabbalah*. New York: New American Library, 1974.

———. *Major Trends in Jewish Mysticism*. New York: Schocken, 1941; 3rd ed., New York: Schocken, 1954; London: Thames and Hudson, 1955.

———. *On the Kabbalah and Its Symbolism* Trans. Ralph Manheim. New York: Schocken, 1965; London: Routledge and Kegan Paul, 1965.

———. *Origins of the Kabbalah*. Ed. R. J. Zwi Werblowsky. Philadelphia: Jewish Publication Society, 1987.

Sears, Dovid. *The Path of the Baal Shem Tov: Early Chasidic Teachings and Customs*. Northvale, N.J.: Aronson, 1997.

Tishby, Isaiah, and Yeruham Fishel Lachower. *The Wisdom of the Zohar* (Littman Library of Jewish Civilization). Trans. David Goldstein. 3 vols. Oxford: Oxford University Press, 1989.

Unterman, Alan, ed. and trans. *The Kabbalistic Tradition: An Anthology of Jewish Mysticism* (Penguin Classics). London: Penguin Books, 2008.

Werblowsky, R. J. Zwi. *Joseph Karo, Lawyer and Mystic* (Scripta Judaica, 4). London: Oxford University Press, 1962; 2nd ed., Philadelphia: Jewish Publication Society, 1977.

Wolfson, Elliot. *Through a Speculum That Shines: Vision and Imagination in Medieval Jewish Mysticism.* Princeton, N.J.: Princeton University Press, 1994.

LANGUAGES

Fellman, Jack. *The Revival of a Classical Tongue: Eliezer ben Yehuda and the Modern Hebrew Language* (Contributions to the Sociology of Language, 6). The Hague: Mouton, 1973.

Fishman, Joshua A., ed. *Never Say Die! A Thousand Years of Yiddish in Jewish Life and Letters.* New York: Mouton, 1981.

Harris, Tracy K. *Death of a Language: The History of Judeo–Spanish.* Newark: University of Delaware Press, 1994; London: Associated University Presses, 1994.

Spiegel, Shalom. *Hebrew Reborn.* Philadelphia: Jewish Publication Society, 1930; London: Benn, 1931.

Weinreich, Max. *History of the Yiddish Language.* Trans. Shlomo Noble with the assistance of Joshua A. Fishman. Chicago: University of Chicago Press, 1980.

MESSIANISM

Kochan, Lionel. *Jews, Idols and Messiahs: The Challenge from History.* Oxford: Blackwell, 1990.

Lenowitz, Harris. *The Jewish Messiahs: From the Galilee to Crown Heights.* New York: Oxford University Press, 1998.

Liebes, Yehuda. *Studies in Jewish Myth and Jewish Messianism* (SUNY Series in Judaica). Albany: State University of New York Press, 1993.

Magid, Shaul. *Hasidism on the Margin: Reconciliation, Antinomianism, and Messianism in Izbica and Radzin Hasidism* (Modern Jewish Philosophy and Religion). Madison: University of Wisconsin Press, 2004.

Mandel, Arthur. *The Militant Messiah; or The Flight from the Ghetto: The Story of Jacob Frank and the Frankist Movement.* Atlantic Highlands, N.J.: Humanities Press, 1979.

Ravitzky, Aviezer. *Messianism, Zionism, and Jewish Religious Radicalism* (Chicago Studies in the History of Judaism). Trans. M. Zwirsky and J. Chipman. Chicago: University of Chicago Press, 1996.

Saperstein, Mark, ed. *Essential Papers on Messianic Movements and Person-alities in Jewish History* (Essential Papers in Jewish Studies Series). New York: New York University Press, 1992.

Scholem, Gershom. *The Messianic Idea in Judaism and Other Essays on Jewish Spirituality*. New York: Schocken, 1971; London: Allen and Unwin, 1971.

———. *Sabbatai Sevi: The Mystical Messiah, 1626–1676* (Bollingen Series, 93). Princeton, N.J.: Princeton University Press, 1973; London: Routledge and Kegan Paul, 1973.

Sharot, Steven. *Messianism, Mysticism, and Magic: A Sociological Analysis of Jewish Religious Movements*. Chapel Hill: University of North Carolina Press, 1982.

PHILOSOPHY

Bleich, J. David. *With Perfect Faith: The Foundations of Jewish Belief*. New York: Ktav, 1983.

Buber, Martin. *I and Thou*. Trans. Walter Kaufmann. New York: Scribner, 1970; Edinburgh: Clark, 1970.

Cohen, Arthur A., and Paul Mendes-Flohr, eds. *20th Century Jewish Religious Thought*. Philadelphia: Jewish Publication Society, 2009.

Cohn-Sherbock, Dan. *Fifty Key Jewish Thinkers* (Key Concepts Series). London: Routledge, 1997.

Fox, Marvin. *Interpreting Maimonides: Studies in Methodology, Metaphysics, and Moral Philosophy*. Philadelphia: Jewish Publication Society, 1989; London: University of Chicago Press, 1994.

Guttmann, Julius. *Philosophies of Judaism: The History of Jewish Philosophy from Biblical Times to Franz Rosenzweig*. Trans. David W. Silverman. New York: Holt, Rinehart and Winston, 1964; London: Routledge, 1964.

Hartman, David. *Maimonides: Torah and Philosophic Quest*. Philadelphia: Jewish Publication Society, 1976.

Heschel, Abraham Joshua. *God in Search of Man*. Philadelphia: Jewish Publication Society, 1956.

Husik, Isaac. *A History of Medieval Jewish Philosophy*. New York: Macmillan, 1916; new ed., 1930.

Jacobs, Louis. *Principles of the Jewish Faith: An Analytical Study*. New York: Basic Books, 1964; London: Valentine Mitchell, 1964; repr. with a new preface, Northvale, N.J.: Aronson, 1988.

Kellner, Menachem. *Dogma in Medieval Jewish Thought: From Maimonides to Abravanel* (Littman Library of Jewish Civilization). Oxford: Oxford University Press, 1986.

Lamm, Norman. *Faith and Doubt: Studies in Traditional Jewish Thought*. New York: Ktav, 1971; 2nd ed., 1986.

Leaman, Oliver. *Moses Maimonides*. London: Routledge, 1990; rev. ed., Richmond, North Yorkshire: Curzon, 1997.

Maimonides, Moses. *The Guide of the Perplexed*. Trans. with an introduction and notes by Shlomo Pines. 2 vols. Chicago: University of Chicago Press, 1963.

Rosenberg, Shalom. *Good and Evil in Jewish Thought*. Tel Aviv: MOD, 1989.

Sarachek, Joseph. *Faith and Reason: The Conflict over the Rationalism of Maimonides*. Williamsport, Penn.: Bayard, 1935.

Sherwin, Byron. *In Partnership with God: Contemporary Jewish Law and Ethics*. Syracuse, N.Y.: Syracuse University Press, 1990.

Silver, Daniel. *Maimonidean Criticism and the Maimonidean Controversy, 1180–1240*. Leiden, The Netherlands: Brill, 1965.

Sirat, Colette. *A History of Jewish Philosophy in the Middle Ages*. Cambridge: Cambridge University Press, 1985.

Tamari, Meir. *The Challenge of Wealth: A Jewish Perspective on Earning and Spending Money*. Northvale, N.J.: Aronson, 1995.

Unterman, Alan. *The Jews: Their Religious Beliefs and Practices* (Library of Religious Beliefs and Practices). London: Routledge and Kegan Paul, 1981; 2nd rev. ed., Brighton, U.K.: Sussex Academic Press, 1999.

RABBINIC LORE AND LITERATURE

Bowker, John. *The Targums and Rabbinic Literature*. Cambridge: Cambridge University Press, 1969.

Ehrlich, Avrum M. *Sanhedrin Studies*. Cambridge: Cambridge University Press, 2000.

Epstein, Isidore, ed. *The Talmud*. 18 vols. London: Soncino Press, 1961.

Freehof, Solomon B. *The Responsa Literature*. Philadelphia: Jewish Publication Society, 1955.

Ginzberg, Louis. *The Legends of the Jews*. 7 vols. Philadelphia: Jewish Publication Society, 1909.

Jacobs, Louis. *Theology in the Responsa*. London: Routledge and Kegan Paul, 1975.

Kadushin, Max. *The Rabbinic Mind*. 3rd ed., Binghamton, N.Y.: Global Publications, 2001.

Peskowitz, Miriam B. *Spinning Fantasies: Rabbis, Gender and History*. Berkeley: University of California Press, 1997.

Schechter, Solomon. *Some Aspects of Rabbinic Theology*. New York: Macmillan, 1909; as *Aspects of Rabbinic Theology*. New York: Schocken, 1961.

Schofer, Jonathan Wyn. *The Making of a Sage: A Study in Rabbinic Ethics*. Madison: University of Wisconsin Press, 2005.

Steinsaltz, Adin. *The Essential Talmud*. New York: Basic Books, 1976; London: Weidenfeld and Nicolson, 1976.

Waxman, Meyer. *A History of Jewish Literature*. 5 vols. New York: Yoseloff, 1960.

RELIGION

Bayme, Steven, and Gladys Rosen, eds. *The Jewish Family and Jewish Continuity*. Hoboken, N.J.: Ktav, 1994.

Berman, Louis A. *Vegetarianism and the Jewish Tradition*. New York: Ktav, 1982.

Borowitz, Eugene B. *Reform Judaism Today*. 3 vols. New York: Behrman House, 1977.

———. *Studies in the Meaning of Judaism*. Philadelphia: Jewish Publication Society, 2002.

Bulka, Reuven P., ed. *Dimensions of Orthodox Judaism*. New York: Ktav, 1983.

Cohen, Steven M., and Paula Hyman, eds. *The Jewish Family: Myth and Reality*. New York: Holmes and Meier, 1986.

Danzger, M. Herbert. *Returning to Tradition: The Contemporary Revival of Orthodox Judaism*. New Haven, Conn.: Yale University Press, 1989.

Dorff, Elliot. *Conservative Judaism: Our Ancestors to Our Descendants*. New York: Youth Commission, United Synagogue of America, 1977.

———. *Knowing God: Jewish Journeys to the Unknowable*. Northvale, N.J.: Aronson, 1992.

Fackenheim, Emil L. *To Mend the World: Foundations of Future Jewish Thought*. New York: Schocken, 1982; as *To Mend the World: Foundations of Post-Holocaust Jewish Thought*. New York: Schocken, 1989.

———. *What Is Judaism? An Interpretation for the Present Age*. New York: Summit, 1987.

Gordis, Robert, ed. *Emet Ve-Emunah: Statement of Principles of Conservative Judaism*. New York: Jewish Theological Seminary, 1988.

Green, Arthur, ed. *Jewish Spirituality: From the Sixteenth Century Revival to the Present* (World Spirituality, vol. 14). New York: Crossroad, 1987; London: Routledge and Kegan Paul, 1988.

Heilman, Samuel C. *Defenders of the Faith: Inside Ultra-Orthodox Jewry*. New York: Schocken, 1992.

Heilman, Samuel C., and Steven M. Cohen. *Cosmopolitans and Parochials: Modern Orthodox Jews in America*. Chicago: University of Chicago Press, 1989.

Helmreich, William. *The World of the Yeshiva: An Intimate Portrait of Orthodox Jewry.* New York: Free Press, 1982; London: Collier Macmillan, 1982.

Hirsch, Samson Raphael. *The Nineteen Letters on Judaism.* New York: Feldheim, 1969.

Jacobs, Louis. *Holy Living: Saints and Saintliness in Judaism.* Northvale, N.J.: Aronson, 1990.

———. *The Jewish Religion: A Companion.* Oxford: Oxford University Press, 1995.

———. *A Tree of Life: Diversity, Flexibility, and Creativity in Jewish Law* (Littman Library of Jewish Civilization). Rutherford, N.J.: Fairleigh Dickinson University Press, 1983; London: Associated University Presses, 1983.

Kellner, Menachem Marc, ed. *Contemporary Jewish Ethics.* New York: Sanhedrin Press, 1978.

Landau, David. *Piety and Power: The World of Jewish Fundamentalism.* New York: Hill and Wang, 1993; London: Secker and Warburg, 1993.

Meyer, Michael. *Response to Modernity: A History of the Reform Movement in Judaism* (Studies in Jewish History). New York: Oxford University Press, 1988.

Novak, David. *The Image of the Non-Jew in Judaism: An Historical and Constructive Study of the Noahide Laws* (Toronto Studies in Theology, vol. 14). New York: Mellen, 1983.

Patai, Raphael. *On Jewish Folklore.* Detroit, Mich.: Wayne State University Press, 1983.

———. *The Vanished World of Judaism.* New York: Macmillan, 1980; London: Weidenfeld and Nicolson, 1981.

Plaut, W. Gunther. *The Rise of Reform Judaism: A Sourcebook of Its European Origins.* New York: World Union for Progressive Judaism, 1963.

Rosenbloom, Joseph R. *Conversion to Judaism: From the Biblical Period to the Present.* Cincinnati, Ohio: Hebrew Union College Press, 1978.

Roth, Leon. *Judaism: A Portrait.* New York: Viking, 1960; London: Faber, 1960.

Rudavsky, David. *Emancipation and Adjustment: Contemporary Jewish Religious Movements, Their History and Thought.* New York: Diplomatic Press, 1967; as *Modern Jewish Religious Movements: A History of Emancipation and Adjustment.* New York: Behrman House, 1979.

Sacks, Jonathan, ed. *Orthodoxy Confronts Modernity.* Hoboken, N.J.: Ktav in association with Jews' College, London, 1991.

Siegel, Seymour, and Elliot Gertel, eds. *God in the Teachings of Conservative Judaism* (Emet Ve'emunah: Studies in Conservative Jewish Thought, vol. 3). New York: Rabbinical Assembly, 1985.

Silver, Abba Hillel. *Where Judaism Differed: An Inquiry into the Distinctiveness of Judaism.* New York: Collier Books, 1989.

Sklare, Marshall. *Conservative Judaism: An American Religious Movement.* Glencoe, Ill.: Free Press, 1955; new augmented ed., New York: Schocken, 1972.

Soloveitchik, Joseph. *The Lonely Man of Faith.* New York: Doubleday, 1992.

Sonsino, Rifat, and Daniel B. Syme. *Finding God: Ten Jewish Responses.* New York: Union of American Hebrew Congregations, 1986.

Trachtenberg, Joshua. *Jewish Magic and Superstition: A Study in Folk Religion.* New York: Behrman, 1939.

SECTS

Birnbaum, Philip, comp. *Karaite Studies.* New York: Hermon, 1971.

Crown, Alan D., ed. *The Samaritans.* Tübingen, Germany: Mohr (Siebeck), 1989.

Crown, Alan D., Reinhard Pummer, and Abraham Tal, eds. *A Companion to Samaritan Studies.* Tübingen, Germany: Mohr (Siebeck), 1993.

Gaster, Moses. *The Samaritans: Their History, Doctrines and Literature* (Schweich Lectures, 1923). London: Oxford University Press for the British Academy, 1925.

Nemoy, Leon. *Karaite Anthology.* New Haven, Conn.: Yale University Press, 1952.

Saldarini, Anthony J. *Pharisees, Scribes and Sadducees in Palestinian Society: A Sociological Approach.* Wilmington, Del.: Glazier, 1988.

WOMEN IN JUDAISM

Adler, Rachel. *Engendering Judaism: An Inclusive Theology and Ethics.* Philadelphia: Jewish Publication Society, 1998.

Baskin, Judith R. *Jewish Women in Historical Perspective.* 2nd ed., Detroit, Mich.: Wayne State University Press, 1998.

Biale, Rachel. *Women and Jewish Law: An Exploration of Women's Issues in Halakhic Sources.* New York: Schocken, 1984.

Cantor, Aviva. *Jewish Women/Jewish Men: The Legacy of Patriarchy in Jewish Life.* San Francisco: HarperSanFrancisco, 1995.

Davidman, Lynn. *Tradition in a Rootless World: Women Turn to Orthodox Judaism.* Berkeley: University of California Press, 1991.

Davis, Natalie Z. *Women on the Margins: Three Seventeenth-Century Lives.* Cambridge, Mass.: Harvard University Press, 1995.

Feld, Merle. *A Spiritual Life: A Jewish Feminist Journey* (SUNY Series in Modern Jewish Literature and Culture). Albany: State University of New York Press, 1998.

Firestone, Tirzah. *With Roots in Heaven: One Woman's Passionate Journey into the Heart of Her Faith.* New York: Dutton, 1998.

Fishman, Sylvia Barack. *A Breath of Life: Feminism in the American Jewish Community.* New York: Free Press, 1993.

Frankel, Ellen. *The Five Books of Miriam: A Woman's Commentary on the Torah.* New York: Putnam, 1996.

Frankiel, Tamar. *The Voice of Sarah: Feminine Spirituality and Traditional Judaism.* New York: Biblio Press, 1990.

Greenberg, Blu. *On Women and Judaism: A View from Tradition.* Philadelphia: Jewish Publication Society, 1981.

Greenberg, Simon, ed. *On the Ordination of Women as Rabbis.* New York: Jewish Theological Seminary, 1988.

Hauptman, Judith. *Rereading the Rabbis: A Woman's Voice.* Boulder, Colo.: Westview, 1997; Oxford: Westview, 1998.

Heschel, Susannah, ed. *On Being a Jewish Feminist: A Reader.* New York: Schocken, 1983.

Hoffman, Lawrence A. *Covenant of Blood: Circumcision and Gender in Rabbinic Judaism* (Chicago Studies in the History of Judaism). Chicago: University of Chicago Press, 1996.

Hyman, Paula E. *Gender and Assimilation in Modern Jewish History: The Roles and Representation of Women* (Samuel and Althea Stroum Lectures in Jewish Studies). Seattle: University of Washington Press, 1995.

Koltun, Elizabeth. *The Jewish Woman: New Perspectives.* New York: Schocken, 1976.

Kuzmack, Linda Gordon. *Woman's Cause: The Jewish Woman's Movement in England and the United States, 1881–1933.* Columbus: Ohio State University Press, 1990.

Levitt, Laura. *Jews and Feminism: The Ambivalent Search for Home.* New York: Routledge, 1997.

Nussbaum Cohen, Debra. *Celebrating Your New Jewish Daughter: Creating Jewish Ways to Welcome Baby Girls into the Covenant.* Woodstock, Vt.: Jewish Lights Press, 2001.

Plaskow, Judith. *Standing Again at Sinai: Judaism from a Feminist Perspective.* San Francisco: Harper and Row, 1990.

Rudavsky, T. M., ed. *Gender and Judaism: The Transformation of Tradition.* New York: New York University Press, 1995.

Sacks, Maurie. *Active Voices: Women in Jewish Culture.* Urbana: University of Illinois Press, 1995.

Saidel, Rochelle G. *The Jewish Women of Ravensbrück Concentration Camp.* Madison: University of Wisconsin Press, 2004.

Tallan, Cheryl, Sondra Henry, and Emily Taitz. *JPS Guide to Jewish Women 600 B.C.E.–1900C.E.* Philadelphia: Jewish Publication Society, 2003.

Umansky, Ellen, and Dianne Ashton. *Four Centuries of Jewish Women's Spirituality: A Sourcebook*. Boston: Beacon, 1992.

Wolfson, Elliot R. *Circle in the Square: Studies in the Use of Gender in Kabbalistic Symbolism*. Albany: State University of New York Press, 1995.

ZIONISM

Avineri, Shlomo. *The Making of Modern Zionism: Intellectual Origins of the Jewish State*. New York: Basic Books, 1981; as *The Making of Modern Zionism: The Intellectual Origins of the Jewish State*. London: Weidenfeld and Nicholson, 1981.

Bein, Alex. *Theodore Herzl: A Biography*. Trans. Maurice Samuel. Philadelphia: Jewish Publication Society, 1941; new ed., London: East and West Library, 1956; Philadelphia: Jewish Publication Society, 1956.

Hertzberg, Arthur, ed. *The Zionist Idea: A Historical Analysis and Reader*. Garden City, N.Y.: Doubleday, 1959.

Herzl, Theodor. *The Jewish State*. London: Nutt, 1896: New York: Maccabaean, 1904.

———. *Old–New Land*. Trans. Lotta Levensohn. New York: Bloch, 1941.

Kaplan, Eran. *The Jewish Radical Right: Revisionist Zionism and Its Ideological Legacy*. Madison: University of Wisconsin Press, 2004.

Kobler, Franz. *The Vision Was There: A History of the British Movement for the Restoration of the Jews to Palestine*. London: Lincolns-Prager, 1956.

Kornberg, Jacques. *Theodor Herzl: From Assimilation to Zionism* (Jewish Literature and Culture). Bloomington: Indiana University Press, 1993.

Laqueur, Walter. *A History of Zionism*. New York: Holt, Rinehart and Winston, 1972; London: Weidenfeld and Nicolson, 1972.

Reinharz, Jehuda, and Anita Shapira, eds. *Essential Papers on Zionism* (Essential Papers on Jewish Studies). New York: New York University Press, 1996.

Selzer, Michael, ed. *Zionism Reconsidered: The Rejection of Jewish Normalcy*. New York: Macmillan, 1970.

Vital, David. *The Future of the Jews: A People at the Crossroads*. Cambridge, Mass.: Harvard University Press, 1990.

———. *The Origins of Zionism*. Oxford: Clarendon, 1975.

Zipperstein, Steven J. *Elusive Prophet: Ahad Ha'am and the Origins of Zionism*. Berkeley: University of California Press, 1993; London, Halban, 1993.

About the Author

Dr. **Alan Unterman** was born in Hertfordshire, England, in 1942. His father, of Lithuanian origin, came to Great Britain just before World War II via Belgium and Ireland and was a rabbi in London. His mother, born in the East End of London, was evacuated with her family to the countryside to avoid the worst excesses of the blitz.

He grew up in Stamford Hill in the north of London, where many Jewish refugees both from the shattered East End and from the ruins of Nazi Europe had relocated after the war. He was educated at a local cheder, a Jewish grammar school, various yeshivot, and the Regent's Street Polytechnic. He went to Birmingham University for his first degree in philosophy, did a postgraduate degree at Wadham College, Oxford, and was awarded a commonwealth scholarship to Delhi University, India, where he did research for his Ph.D. in comparative religion. He has taught religious studies at universities in Israel, Australia, and England, and among his publications are *The Wisdom of the Jewish Mystics*, *The Jews: Their Religious Beliefs and Practices*, *A Dictionary of Jewish Lore and Legend*, and *The Kabbalistic Tradition*. Dr. Unterman has also written articles on comparisons between Judaism and Hinduism, human rights in the Jewish tradition, religious experience, the Salman Rushdie controversy, rites of passage, censorship and heresy, and Orthodox Jewish perspectives on sexuality.

He met his wife, Nechama, a Palestinian Jewess, while working for the *Encyclopedia Judaica* in Israel. They have three children, Yael, Joseph Dov, and Abraham Isaac, each born on a different continent. He is now living in Jerusalem, having served as the minister of an Orthodox synagogue in Manchester, England, for 26 years before his retirement.

Breinigsville, PA USA
31 October 2010
248303BV00002B/2/P